THE SUPPRESSION OF S

JAMES J. LORENCE

The Suppression of
Salt of the Earth

HOW HOLLYWOOD, BIG LABOR, AND POLITICIANS

BLACKLISTED A MOVIE IN COLD WAR AMERICA

☩ ☩ ☩

The University of New Mexico Press Albuquerque

Library of Congress Cataloging-in-Publication Data

Lorence, James J.

The suppression of Salt of the Earth: how Hollywood, big labor, and politicians blacklisted a movie in cold war America / James J. Lorence. — 1st ed.

p. cm.

Includes bibliographical references and index.

ISBN 0-8263-2027-9 (CL : alk. paper)

ISBN 0-8263-2028-7 (PA : alk. paper)

1. Salt of the Earth (Motion picture) I. Title.

PN1997.S14 L67 1999

791.43'72 — dc21

98-58036

CIP

For the women and men of Local 890

Contents

Preface

Forty years ago, when I prepared for a career as a historian, a seasoned scholar of the old school proclaimed to an introductory methods class that "history is literature." Only a few years earlier, the men and women of International Union of Mine, Mill, and Smelter Workers Local 890 were making their own history in a dispute with the Empire Zinc Corporation that challenged the pattern of economic and social discrimination against Mexican-Americans in the Southwest. It was not until 1987 that I became aware of their struggle and its ramifications for the advancement of human equality and civil liberties in Cold War America. A cursory examination of the Herbert Biberman–Gale Sondergaard Papers at the State Historical Society of Wisconsin opened my eyes to a story with all the twists and turns of a classic detective novel. In the present study I assume the role of historian as storyteller. The production and suppression of *Salt of the Earth* involve a tale worth telling.

Acknowledgments

This book would not have been possible without the financial support of many institutions and foundations. Travel to distant manuscript repositories was underwritten by grants from the University of Wisconsin–Milwaukee Institute on Race and Ethnicity, University of Wisconsin-Marathon County Foundation, and the National Endowment for the Humanities. At a critical point in the project's early stages, a University of Wisconsin Colleges and University of Wisconsin-Madison research grant from the University of Wisconsin-Madison Graduate School enabled me to spend a summer at the University of Wisconsin Institute for Research in the Humanities, where a preliminary draft of the manuscript took shape. I am grateful to the Institute and the University of Wisconsin-Madison Department of History for the endorsement that brought me to Madison for this work. Finally, the University of Wisconsin Colleges provided a sabbatical leave, which was also supported by a generous fellowship from the National Endowment for the Humanities. Together, these grants afforded me the precious time for uninterrupted research and writing that resulted in the completion of the final draft of the manuscript.

Essential to my research was the assistance provided by knowledgeable archivists and librarians at many institutions. Especially helpful were Harry Miller at the State Historical Society of Wisconsin Archives and David M. Hays of the University of Colorado Archives, whose knowledge of the manuscript collections crucial to this project eased the research task. The acquisition of source material from distant repositories was efficiently handled by University of Wisconsin-Marathon County Librarian Todd Roll and University of Wisconsin–Stevens Point Archivist Bill Paul, whose interest in history made this investigation a collaborative undertaking. Special efforts to facilitate access to manuscript material were made by Thomas J. Rosko of the Seeley G. Mudd Manuscript Library at Princeton University, Debra Levine of the University of Chicago Library Special Collections, Susan Sherwood of San Francisco State University, Arel Lucas of Stanford University Library Special Collections, Melissa Howard of the Cornell University Martin P. Catherwood Library, Diane Kaplan of the Yale University Manuscripts and Archives Division, and Edward C. Weber of the Joseph Labadie Collection at the University of Michigan.

Others who provided vital assistance include: Debra Bernhardt and Peter Meyer Filardo of Tamiment Institute and Robert Wagner Labor Archives at New York University, Denise Conklin and Diana Shenk at the Pennsylvania State University Pattee Library, Octavio Olvera of the UCLA Special Collections, Brigitte J. Kueppers of the UCLA Arts Special Collections, Dennis Bitterlich of the UCLA Archives, David Koch of the Southern Illinois University Library Special Collections, Dwight Miller of the Herbert Hoover Presidential Library, Kathleen Ferris of the University of New Mexico Center for Southwest Research, University Librarian Sandy De Busk and Lucie M. Yassa at the Western New Mexico State University Library, José Villegas of the New Mexico Records Center and Archives, Cassandra Volpe of the University of Colorado Archives, Mike Smith of the Archives of Labor History and Urban Affairs at Wayne State University, John E. Haynes of the Library of Congress Manuscripts Division, Dana Sergent Nemeth of the American Museum of the Moving Image, Robert Marshall of the Urban Archives Center at California State University at Northridge, Peter Hoefer and Lee Sayrs of the George Meany Memorial Archives, Christy French of the Special Collections at California State University at Long Beach, Archie Motley of the Chicago Historical Society, Scott Curtis of the Margaret Herrick Library of the Academy of Motion Picture Arts and Sciences, Sarah Cooper of the Southern California Library for Social Studies and Research, Lottie Gordon of the Reference Center for Marxist Studies, Timothy Meagher of the Catholic University of America Archives, Peter Crim of the Silver City Public Library, and Ricardo Trujillo at KRWG-TV in Las Cruces, New Mexico.

Because the *Salt* story was so closely linked to the internal dynamics of the postwar American labor movement, union records were indispensable to the research task. Among the labor union officials and archivists who assisted me were: Gene Vrana of the International Longshoremen and Warehousemen's Union, Bernie Ricke of United Automobile Workers Local 600, Katherine Moore and Valerie Yaros of the Screen Actors Guild,

Karen Pedersen of the Writers Guild of America, Joel Dietch of the International Alliance of Theatrical Stage Employees Local 306, and Karen Pizzuto of the IATSE International office.

Special acknowledgment is due the Screen Actors Guild, whose national board and executives were important players in the *Salt* drama. SAG's Communications Department and archivist were generous with their time, expertise, and resources. The Guild has demonstrated a firm commitment to full disclosure of its role in sustaining the blacklist of the 1950s. By making its files available for research purposes, SAG provided me with valuable assistance in my effort to understand the origins of the public attack on *Salt of the Earth*. In the process, the organization has underscored its refusal to condone the actions of the Guild leadership during the blacklist years as well as a willingness to boldly confront the past. SAG's openness to scholarly analysis of its record has served the cause of history well.

Essential to the completion of my research were interviews with veterans of the American labor movement and other political activists of the 1950s. The key witnesses were Clinton Jencks, the late Paul Jarrico, and Virginia Chacón, whose recollections guided my interpretation of the events described and their long-term implications. I am especially indebted to Clinton Jencks for his interest in this project as well as the invaluable knowledge base he provided. Important insights were also provided by Arturo and Josefina Flores, Jenny Vincent, Dave Moore, Lorenzo Torrez, Steve D'Inzillo, and Lottie Gordon. I thank them for allowing me into their lives and for sharing experiences that aided me in understanding how the *Salt* story was linked to the search for the common good and the effort to build a more equitable society in a period of great stress. In addition, I am grateful to Rebecca Wilson and Rosanna Wilson-Farrow for authorizing access to the papers of their father, screenwriter Michael Wilson. Likewise, I thank Lia Benedetti Jarrico for her assistance in the search for photographic materials.

Some of the materials used in this book have appeared in previous publications. *Film History* graciously authorized me to reprint large portions of "The Suppression of *Salt of the Earth* in the Industrial Midwest: The Underside of Cold War Culture in Detroit and Chicago," 10 (1998): 346–58. Daniel Leab and Richard Kozarski assisted in securing permission to publish. I also thank Fitzroy Dearborn Publishers for allowing me to use material that appears in *Censorship: A World Encyclopedia* (London: Fitzroy Dearborn, 1999).

Many scholars were generous with their time and expertise. Most of all, I am grateful to Paul S. Boyer, director of the University of Wisconsin Institute for Research in the Humanities, who made me welcome as a summer fellow and shared his extensive knowledge of Cold War culture. His exhaustive and insightful critique of the manuscript helped me to avoid some of the pitfalls encountered in the writing of recent American history. I also thank Paul Buhle of Brown University for his helpful review of a later draft and his suggestions for its improvement. Stephen Meyer of the University of Wisconsin-Parkside, Colette Hyman of Winona State University, Clinton Jencks of San Diego State University, and independent scholar Stanley Mallach all read and critiqued portions of the manuscript at various stages of its development. Their advice has been useful in my effort to shape the final draft.

A special note of appreciation is due Stephen Vaughn of the University of Wisconsin-Madison, who helped me understand the internal operations of the motion picture industry and the politics of Hollywood. In addition to sharing his extensive knowledge of the movies, he made available primary source materials relevant to the suppression of *Salt of the Earth*. Likewise, Lary May of the University of Minnesota provided me with an important file from the Screen Actors Guild Archives, as well as other documents. And Ellen Schrecker of Yeshiva University, Ellen Baker of Columbia University, John Wiseman of Frostburg State University, and Douglas Monroy of Colorado College shared research materials with me. I also thank the following scholars for their many useful suggestions on sources: Steve Ross of the University of Southern California, Daryl Holter of UCLA, Elizabeth Jameson of the University of New Mexico, David Gutiérrez of the University of California at San Diego, Zaragosa Vargas of the University of California at Santa Barbara, Vernon Jensen of Cornell University, James M. Skinner of Brandon University, Mike Nielsen of Wesley College, Judith Stepan-Norris of the University of California at Irvine, David Myers of New Mexico State University, and Luis "Nacho" Quinoñes of Cobre High School in Silver City, New Mexico. Richard Candida Smith of the University of Michigan and screenwriter Tony Grutman assisted me in accessing a valuable privately held collection of taped interviews with the important figures in the production of *Salt of the Earth*. Their comments on the *Salt* story were also helpful.

I have also benefited immensely from the collective wisdom of the experienced staff at the University of New Mexico Press. Especially important has been the encouragement provided by editor Durwood Ball, whose enthusiasm for this project was essential to its completion and whose editorial guidance strengthened the final product.

Throughout the research and writing of this book, I have enjoyed the support and encouragement of Dean Dennis Massey of the University of

Wisconsin-Marathon County and of my department chair, David Huehner of the University of Wisconsin-Washington County. Charlene Schmidt handled the task of typing and manuscript preparation with efficiency and unfailing good cheer. My greatest debt, however, is due my partner, Donna Nyiri Lorence, who was a competent research assistant, wise counselor, and sympathetic friend. Her presence in my life gives meaning to my work.

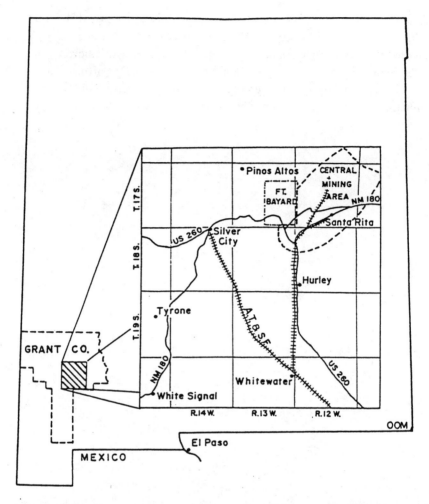

Central mining area, Grant County, N.M., in 1941. From Eugene C. Anderson, *The Metal Resources of New Mexico and Their Economic Features Through 1954* (Socorro, N.M.: State Bureau of Mines and Mineral Resources, 1957), 49.

ONE

Cold War America

The Great Fear Comes Home

Prologue

Grant County, New Mexico, is located in an area that was well beyond the mainstream of American political and social life in the tense early days of the Cold War. Tucked away in an isolated corner of the Southwest, it nevertheless became the locale for a series of dramatic events that mirrored the anticommunist hysteria experienced when wartime collaboration with the Soviet Union came to an end. By 1947 many Americans had developed deep suspicions of their former ally and given free rein to fears present in American culture since the Bolshevik Revolution had first altered the calculus of international relations. In 1950, when Bayard (New Mexico) Local 890 of the International Union of Mine, Mill, and Smelter Workers (IUMMSW, also referred to here as "Mine-Mill") challenged the Empire Zinc Corporation over wages and working conditions — and, beyond that, over the distribution of power in the postwar corporate state — it wrote the first page in a saga that was to test severely the freedom of expression guaranteed by the Bill of Rights.

The story of this strike, the motion picture that recorded its history, and the suppression of both the film and the labor union that gave it life provides a mirror of Cold War America that reflects not only the intense fear that gripped Americans in this period, but also the dark side of the corporatist settlement that locked business unionism and corporate power in a firm embrace in the 1950s. The remarkably contemporary film based on the Empire Zinc strike, *Salt of the Earth* (1954), stands as a revealing celluloid document, a record that chronicles a determined effort by socially committed men and women to question the accepted gender and racial relations of their time and to build better lives for themselves and their families through the medium of socially conscious unionism.

By examining the *Salt* episode in all its dimensions and ramifications, modern observers may glimpse the underside of a political culture that consigned ideological dissenters to the outer regions of the national economic, social, and intellectual community. The inspiration, production, distribution, and suppression of this work established a close link between the pariahs of a bureaucratized union movement and the blacklisted artists of Cold War Hollywood, both of whom resisted the forces of conformity and laid claim to personal and civil liberty. This study is an account of people and organizations who believed they saw an alternative to the fear and repression that marked Cold War America. The problems they confronted in the anxiety-ridden 1950s were rooted in the labor wars of the mid-1940s, which produced a new, militantly anticommunist power structure in the Hollywood union movement.

Cold War Hollywood: Militant Labor and the Rise of Anticommunism

As Cold War tension mounted between 1945 and 1947, the motion picture industry experienced its own version of combat in the form of a bitter labor struggle that had originated during the war when the upstart Conference of Studio Unions (CSU) attempted to establish the industry-wide unity already enjoyed by the sometimes corrupt International Alliance of Theatrical Stage Employees and Moving Picture Operators (IATSE). In 1945, when a CSU affiliate local walked out in an attempt to establish control of the set decorators, nearly all craft unions honored its picket lines, while IATSE worked to protect its own industry-wide position. For many years, Communism had been an important issue in Hollywood labor struggles, and in this instance, IATSE's international representative, Roy Brewer, determined to make left-wing influence in the reformist CSU the centerpiece of his effort to succeed in the jurisdictional struggle. This tactic enabled the aggressively anticommunist Brewer to establish ties with the conservative Motion Picture Alliance for the Preservation of American Ideals (MPA), which had long contended that Communist influence had tainted Hollywood unionism and threatened to undermine the entire motion picture industry. During the eight-month strike and a shorter CSU strike in 1946, violence racked the studio labor scene, creating a chaotic situation

Hollywood IATSE leader Roy Brewer at podium during CSU strike meeting, Dec. 19, 1946. Courtesy of Screen Actors Guild.

that led such leading industry figures as Jack L. Warner, Louis B. Mayer, and Walt Disney to align themselves in an emergent anticommunist front by 1947. In short, Communism had become a volatile issue in Hollywood even before the House Committee on Un-American Activities (HUAC) focused its attention on the motion picture industry in 1947.[1]

The significance of Brewer's decision to align IATSE with the MPA cannot be overestimated. By embracing the anticommunist cause in his attack on CSU and purging his own organization of critics, Brewer and IATSE became a part of the power structure that dominated the motion picture industry. Brewer's actions were entirely consistent with the stance taken by the International union and its president, Richard Walsh. Describing himself as "anticommunist for as long as [he could] remember," Walsh recalled with pride IATSE's victory over CSU in the studio strikes.[2] Their brand of business unionism was characteristic of the bureaucratized labor movement that was soon to join corporate America in a marriage consummated with the expulsion of eleven left-led unions from the CIO. Linkage with MPA meant that IATSE allied itself with the most anti-labor and anticommunist forces in Hollywood, including those who cared little for free expression among creative artists. The collaborative tactics employed in 1945 and 1946 foreshadowed the cooperation that resurfaced in the 1950s, when the production of *Salt of the Earth* challenged corporate America, the studio system, and Cold War orthodoxy. The die had been cast before the blacklist ever threatened free thought and free expression in a ·more direct way.

The studio strikes were part of a nationwide surge in labor militancy that by 1946 threatened to cripple the American economy as industrial workers staked their claim to a larger share of postwar prosperity. Against a background of labor unrest in both Hollywood and the nation, then, in October 1947 HUAC opened its investigation into alleged Communist infiltration of the motion picture industry. By the time the committee launched its inquiry, Brewer and IATSE had consolidated their position as the preeminent force on the Hollywood labor scene; in the process anticommunism had become the foundation of a new conservative business unionism in the movie capital, while left-wing unionism had been substantially undercut.[3]

So it was that Hollywood's defenses against Red-baiting were fatally weakened by the time the HUAC hearings got under way. With the Left in retreat, the MPA and its allies dominated the public spectacle in Washington. Despite resistance from the Hollywood Left, including some anticommunist liberals, diehard Popular Fronters, and the Communists, the forces of conformity overwhelmed the remnants of a shattered progressive coalition, thus isolating the industry's vulnerable radical minority. The story of their persecution and public abuse has been told well in other places and need not be repeated here.[4] More significant for this study is the insidious blacklist that was the product of the 1947 hearings. For with the emergence of this subtle system of thought control, the story of *Salt of the Earth* begins.

Response to HUAC: Hollywood's Collapse

In the wake of the disruptive HUAC hearings, Hollywood's resistance to external pressure weakened almost immediately. On previous occasions the motion picture industry had succeeded in deflecting the legislative and political assaults mounted by conservative critics. However, the new HUAC accusations were made within the context of postwar destabilization in

Europe, Soviet advances, and escalating fears of domestic subversion and foreign aggression. The Hollywood labor conflict of 1945–1947 exacerbated existing tensions and called attention to the strength of the Left in the motion picture industry, especially among the talent guilds. Anticommunist paranoia combined with the provocative behavior of the "unfriendly ten" to splinter progressive forces in both the Hollywood labor and political communities. After pledging to honor contracts and to resist any movement to curtail employment, studio management crumbled under the strain created by not only industry conservatives, but also by the American Legion, the Catholic Church, and hostile elements in the press. Under increasing pressure from Congressman J. Parnell Thomas, HUAC, and the MPA, Eric Johnston of the Producers' Association announced the industry's willingness to deny employment to any Communist or "member of any party or group which advocates the overthrow of the Government of the United States by force or by any illegal or unconstitutional method." With this statement, formulated in November 1947 at a meeting of the Producers' Association at the Waldorf-Astoria Hotel in New York, management acceded to the demands of the industry's anticommunist critics and laid the groundwork for a sweeping purge of Communists and other dissenters whose views and political associations might expose Hollywood to further scrutiny and attack.[5] The structure for a program of repression was in place.

Putting up a bold front, the producers insisted that they did not intend to be "swayed by any hysteria or intimidation from any source." However, no rhetoric could alter the reality of the studios' capitulation to the demand for conformity. More prescient was their acknowledgment of the potential risks in the new policy: "There is the danger of hurting innocent people, there is the risk of creating an atmosphere of fear. Creative work at its best cannot be carried on in an atmosphere of fear."[6] This warning foreshadowed the bitter experience of a generation of Hollywood artists, including the Hollywood Ten and those who were to create *Salt of the Earth*, not to mention the hundreds of creative talents whose professional lives were destroyed by the blacklist enforced in the 1950s.

The damage to the industry was nothing short of disastrous, whether calculated in terms of its leaders' moral failure or the tainted product of their collapse. While many factors affected film quality, the thought control imposed by the enforcers solidified the industry's reluctance to take chances and its tendency to avoid films that grappled with politically sensitive ideas. When movies did become engaged politically, the result was a spate of formulaic anticommunist pictures shot through with contempt for liberals, bitter anti-intellectualism, warped sexuality, and exaggerated violence.[7]

These puerile attacks on Communism were to be expected, in view of the industry's moral bankruptcy and economic fears. Conscious of Hollywood's enormous influence on audiences in the United States and the world, an all-industry conference in 1949 adopted a statement of principle reaffirming "faith in and responsibility to the American people." Promising to "entertain and instruct," the moguls deplored "any effort to forbid it [the industry] or the American people freedom of choice on the screens of this nation" and agreed to "cooperate with all men who believe in human decency." The producers pledged to guard well the screen, which belonged to the "free peoples of the world." Conscious of a Soviet effort to "render the American film harmless," the Motion Picture Industry Council was certain of the "effectiveness of American films in democracy's cause."[8]

To ensure the salutary impact of American films, in 1950 screenwriter/ novelist Ayn Rand penned an advisory pamphlet containing specific guidelines for producers, directors, and screenwriters seeking to "protect [their] pictures from being used for communistic purposes." Denying any interest in "forced restriction," Rand (and the MPA, which distributed the screen guide) offered suggestions for the "voluntary action of every honest man in the motion picture industry." She advised readers to take politics seriously and keep their films "clean of subversive propaganda." More to her point, filmmakers were to avoid attacks on business, free enterprise, the profit motive, wealth, and success. Conversely, the guideline discouraged the deification of the common man and glorification of "the collective." Political themes were acceptable but only if pictures "presented the political ideas of Americanism strongly and honestly." The pamphlet closed with a warning against hiring Communists to write, direct, or produce such films. Widely reprinted and blessed with the MPA imprimatur, *Screen Guide for Americans* influenced the political and economic content of 1950s feature films, as well as HUAC's definition of appropriate film messages.[9]

More significant was the pamphlet's sweeping rationale for blacklisting, which, when adopted, resulted in incalculable personal and creative losses. Loss of income, sullied reputations, livelihoods destroyed, and even lives cut short; all testified to the debilitating impact of the internal divisions that racked the industry for fifteen years. The cannibalistic behavior of an industry at war with itself left scars that have not yet healed. This lingering acrimony stands as the living legacy of the blacklist and the divisive domestic Cold War from which it grew.

Labor's Civil War: Cold War Residue

The blacklist imposed following the Washington hearings of 1947 was not, in fact, the first purge to affect the motion picture industry. As Mike Nielsen and Gene Mailes have convincingly demonstrated, Roy Brewer and IATSE had implemented "Hollywood's other blacklist" in response to the labor wars of 1945–1946. Nielsen argues that "the biggest blacklist ever created in Hollywood was not the one for 'subversive' talent guild members but rather the one that was drawn up by Brewer to rid the studios of anyone who would dare to question the authority of the International office of the IA."[10]

The "sanitizing" of the Hollywood unions and destruction of the CSU were part and parcel of the larger process through which organized labor accommodated itself to the demands of the Cold War and made its peace with the corporate state. By 1950, the CIO was to purge its radical elements and expel the left-led unions as it struggled to gain respectability in the new order of postwar unionism. After having secured its position, the once-militant industrial unionists would quietly accept merger with, if not absorption by, the AFL and adopt the tenets of business unionism that the Federation represented. The rightward drift of the CIO and its decision to spurn highly democratic unions — most important for this inquiry, Mine-Mill — formed a significant and important part of the backdrop for the project that became *Salt of the Earth*. In effect, blacklisted artists and blacklisted workers eventually joined to produce an eloquent cinematic statement of resistance to the predominant social, economic, and intellectual themes of Cold War America. Their story documents a clear strain of independence in an age of consensus and probes some of the social tensions and fault lines of this period of emerging corporate hegemony.

Close analysis of this film, its production, and the distribution of the finished product therefore provides a window into labor's internal battles during the formative years of the Cold War. The deep involvement of Mine-Mill in both the creative process and the marketing of *Salt* reveals a remarkably democratic union's determined struggle for self-preservation, as well as the political freedom of its leftist leadership in the face of government harassment and competitive unionism. While Mine-Mill was ultimately (1967) absorbed into the massive United Steelworkers of America (USWA), the spirit of radical unionism continued to infuse some of its most committed members and leaders, including the fiercely independent Mexican-Americans who toiled in the copper mines of the Southwest. The *Salt of the Earth* story is their story, one of courage and hope for a better future; its outlines mark a deviation from the anticommunist consensus documented in many studies of American cultural life in the 1950s. Most of all, it is an account of people making their own history.

The Disinherited: The Mexican-American Left and the Struggle for Worker Dignity

The central theme in *Salt of the Earth* involves the Chicano/Chicana fight for dignity against long odds as workers struggled to improve their lives in a brutal contest between capital and labor. The record of the Empire Zinc Company strike from 1950 to 1952, which will be fully documented in chapter 2, highlights an important and sometimes neglected dimension of the Mexican-American experience, the involvement of militant workers in union organizing to improve working and living conditions within the framework of industrial capitalism. Although Mexican-Americans had not played a major role in earlier unionization efforts in the Southwest, from the 1930s on they joined other industrial workers in the effort to create unions to address the most basic human needs.

For Mexican-Americans, unionization was the key to advancement on bread-and-butter issues; but it also became a tool through which they demanded social and political equality. Spurned by the craft-oriented AFL, they naturally turned to the CIO, which stood for a more sweeping economic and racial equality than that contemplated by the business unions of the 1930s and the 1940s. By 1945, IUMMSW represented 75 percent of all copper-industry workers in the Southwest, most of them Mexican-Americans. Perhaps 20 percent of the estimated 100,000 Mine-Mill members enrolled nationwide in 1950 were drawn from minority groups; of these an estimated 10 percent were Mexican-American. However, in Arizona and New Mexico, approximately 85 percent of the membership was Hispanic and another 2 percent Native American. And while Mexican-Americans constituted only 47 percent of New Mexico's population, nearly 90 percent of the Empire Zinc strikers were Hispanos. Mexican-American mineworkers consistently preferred the Mine, Mill, and Smelter Workers to the United Mine Workers, in large measure because Mine-Mill was viewed by many Chicano workers as not just a union but also a platform from which the drive for racial equality could be mounted. Even more outspoken in their endorsement of full racial equality were the Communists sometimes found within the leadership and ranks of CIO unions. As Douglas Monroy and Mario T. Garcia have demonstrated, Mexican-Americans inherited a radical tradition that reflected their "outsider" status as either deposed landholders or vulnerable immigrants in the American Southwest. This new militancy was rooted in an intense awareness of racial prejudice that was the product of the military conquest of Mexico's northern provinces in the 1840s and the economic displacement that followed American annexation. David Gutiérrez has shown that the pressures exerted on the Mexican-Americans of the Southwest led to a sharpened ethnic consciousness by the early twentieth century. Racial bias, social discrimination, and economic subjugation intensified Mexican-Americans' tendency to think of themselves as an "ethnic collectivity." By 1950, this heightened awareness had led the majority of Mexican-American miners in New Mexico and the Southwest to affiliate with Mine-Mill, which stressed racial equality and clung to the idea of coexistence with the Soviet Union.[11] Through the union, a small but militant Mexican-American left challenged the predominant assumptions of most American unionists in the early Cold War era.

Although Mine-Mill and militant unionism provided the primary outlet for the expression of southwestern Mexican-American radicalism in the 1930s and 1940s, it was not the only institution through which the Left spoke. The spirit of the Popular Front also survived in the work of a militant organization that grew out of Mine-Mill support for *Amigos de Wallace* in 1948. From this Progressive Party activity came a new self-conscious analysis of the Mexican-American problem as rooted in the issue of class. The clearest organizational expression of heightened militancy was the Denver-based *Asociación Nacional México—Americana* (ANMA), formed in 1949 to maintain coordination among chapters of *Amigos de Wallace*. The organization committed itself to the defense of Mexican-American people and all aspects of Mexican culture. Composed of two thousand members drawn primarily from the ranks of the CIO, ANMA viewed the Mexican-American population of the United States as solidly working class and acted upon that analysis to move its people toward class action. As a result, it embraced the civil rights movement in the United States and demanded economic equality for oppressed peoples at home and abroad. In addition, ANMA launched a national attack on discrimination in employment, education, and the media. Symbolic of its roots in the union movement was the leadership provided by Alfredo Montoya, a Mine-Mill activist who in 1949 became ANMA president. It was ANMA's misfortune that it became politically assertive at the precise historical moment when the American public was becoming more conservative and anticommunist.[12]

A weakened Communist Party also established its presence within the Mexican-American community, particularly inside the labor movement. As

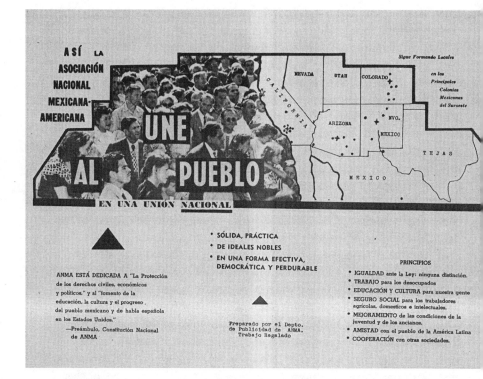

ANMA Promotional Brochure, ca. 1950. Archives, University of Colorado at Boulder Libraries, Western Federation of Miners and International Union of Mine, Mill and Smelter Workers Collection.

many as five hundred Mexican-Americans may have been party members by the 1950s, many of them CIO activists in left-wing unions, especially Mine-Mill. And although ANMA leaders Alfredo Montoya and Mauricio Terrazas would later deny Communist Party membership and influence in the organization, both recognized that the party was a staunch ally in the struggle for Mexican-American equality. The Communist Party worked to foster unity among ANMA, IUMMSW, and other leftist organizations in order to promote the class interests of the Mexican-American community. This commitment was evident in the national party's 1948 resolution promising a struggle within all trade unions to integrate Mexican-Americans into leadership positions and to fight discrimination in hiring and upgrading. In 1953, party activists cited Mine-Mill as an example of outstanding leadership in the drive for economic equality for the Chicanos who, they claimed, constituted more than 15 percent of the union's total national membership.[13]

Despite CP pronouncements, however, the 1950s were not hospitable times for progressive activists of any stripe, and Mexican-American radicalism faded in response to the blistering attacks from HUAC, McCarthyites, and conservatives within the mainstream union movement. In the late 1940s and early 1950s, a period labeled by historian Rodolfo Acuña as the "decade of defense," many Mexican-Americans tended toward accommodation as a matter of self-preservation. While radicalism was submerged, however, militancy did not disappear, as is evidenced by the birth and growth of ANMA and the stubborn assertiveness of Mine-Mill, even after its expulsion from the CIO. What was the impact of the radicals' last-ditch efforts to sharpen Mexican-American awareness of class inequities? At a time when many Mexicans moved toward assimilation, radical unions "provided an important means for the structural integration of Mexicans into the United States," while acting on the "radical notion of equality." By exposing them to working-class consciousness through working-class organizations, Douglas Monroy has argued, the Mexican-American Left supplied the "ideological complement of the structural proletarianization that capitalism brought."[14] It was this consciousness of class, together with an intense pride in culture, that found expression in the *Salt* project; and the film remains a tribute to Mexican-American determination to build a community that not only respected human dignity but also preserved cultural identity.

The Other Radicals: Chicana Activism

Among the key themes dealt with in *Salt of the Earth*, none is more significant than the intense struggle for human dignity waged by the film's central character, Esperanza. Beneath the surface of a male-centered Hispanic culture lay the simmering tension occasioned by long-standing differences concerning women's roles and responsibilities, some of which went deep into the heart of Mexican-American cultural tradition and heritage. For many, women were especially important as the cohesive agents that preserved family, community, and culture through guardianship of the home and fulfillment of a nurturing function. While women sometimes worked and fought side by side with men, they were typically found near hearth and home. Furthermore, these values were strongly reinforced by the teachings of the Catholic Church, which wielded heavy influence among Mexican-Americans. As a corollary to traditional family values, a double standard of sexual morality ensured males greater freedom in sexual relationships and confined women within a rigid code of personal behavior. Although many Chicanas had in fact become heads of families by the early twentieth century, it was not until the explosive 1930s that the rise of labor unionism brought a new female participation in labor conflicts and in the unemployed movement that radicalized many Mexican-American workers in the Southwest. Within Mine-Mill, women's auxiliary organizations were established in the 1940s, though they were assigned responsibility for the advancement of trade union principles through concentration on the traditional areas of health, education, and child welfare. Even more dramatic was ANMA's support for new and influential leadership roles for Chicanas. Moving beyond the assumption of auxiliary functions, the organization moved to integrate women at all levels of responsibility with the aid of an influential women's committee. An action program adopted by ANMA's New Mexico organization in 1949 pledged to "help our women to grow and learn and to work for themselves through organization." During ANMA's short life, women made up a significant minority of the membership and provided visible leadership at both state and national levels.[15] Viewed against the background of IUMMSW and ANMA practices, the decisive role played by women in the Empire Zinc strike, while not unopposed, was generally consistent with the thinking of activists within the Mexican-American Left.

Given these trends, it is not surprising that *Salt of the Earth* assigns a critical role to the women who turned the tide in the Empire Zinc strike; nor is the film's emphasis on the rise in feminist consciousness evident in Esperanza's experience, as portrayed in the film. Indeed, the documentary record indicates that the militance of Chicana women in New Mexico actually preceded the long strike of 1950–1952. For example, in 1949 the Bayard Local 209 Ladies Auxiliary submitted a "Resolution on Equality and Fraternity of Mexican-American Women," which was subsequently adopted by ANMA. Long-held ideas were tested during the strike, which enhanced women's prestige and advanced their roles in union activity. Although the changes instituted in 1951 and 1952 were not permanent, the women and men of Local 890 explored new territory in gender relations under the pressure exerted by their economic adversaries. While the steps taken were modest, they did mark a break with the patriarchal past. Recalling male resistance to women's picketing, Virginia Chacón (upon whom Esperanza's character is based) and Angela Sanchez (president of the women's auxiliary) later recounted the effort to "talk a little bit of sense into them." With the cooperation of "some of our brothers who were in our favor," the women and men "were able to make a better decision" that enabled them to "help [their union] brothers." Not only was Chacón proud of the role she played in advancing the strike's economic goals, but years later she would clearly remember a "change in the men." Sanchez agreed that the men had undergone a conversion that left them "not so much against women helping them."[16] While the principal participants were persuaded that the pivotal role played by women in the Empire Zinc strike resulted in real gains, objective analysis will qualify that assertion significantly.

The Community as Backdrop for Social Conflict: The People, Their Culture, and the Union Family

By most accounts, Grant County was not a likely venue for radical agitation, union activism, racial unrest, or challenges to the social assumptions and family values of Cold War America. Far removed from the centers of national public life and political power in 1950, its residents lived out social and economic relationships that were the product of centuries of exploitation and inequality. Beneath these tensions lay an insatiable demand for the "red gold" that made Grant County New Mexico's "copper capital." In 1954 the county's mines accounted for 1,965,189 of the 2,100,000 tons produced in the entire state, an output that established its "metal supremacy" in the eyes of business observers. Copper's economic dominance also made the mines Grant County's largest employer, accounting for two thousand jobs in 1950.[17] Overshadowing the communities and the people who inhabited this area was the specter of big copper: corporate control of the resource that sustained the economy and sometimes crushed the people who brought it to the surface and transformed it into real wealth. Over the years the Spanish had enslaved the Native Americans to work the mines, only to be displaced by entrepreneurial Anglos who later drove out the Mexicans, appropriated their lands, and employed wage labor as a means by which the red earth might be converted into profits. Lost in the exchange were the Mexican-Americans, who assumed the new role of exploited labor in a land once controlled by their ancestors. The original proprietors had been forced to make a hard trade.

Not only had mineworkers been ruthlessly exploited by corporate giants and thereby impoverished, but they also found themselves outside the mainstream of political and social advancement. By the late 1940s a demographic shift was under way as Anglos began to pour into New Mexico. The number of Hispano state legislators was in decline, a trend which reinforced ethnic tensions and produced fears that Mexican-Americans were losing ground. In 1950, 47 percent of the Grant County population was Mexican-American, yet Chicanos cast only 33 percent of the votes in local elections while a minuscule 8.7 percent of names on local jury lists represented their ethnic community. Educational disparities, reflected in the statistics documenting median school years completed (5.7 years for Mexican-Americans compared to 8.9 years for the population as a whole), reinforced political inequality.[18] Political, social, and economic disparities had created a fertile field for union organization, an opportunity seized by an aggressive Mine-Mill union in the post–New Deal era.

Unionism had not always fared well in remote Grant County. Alone among the West's major mining districts, it had escaped the violence that had accompanied the rise of militant labor in the late nineteenth and early twentieth centuries. While the Western Federation of Miners had organized locals by 1910, little evidence of their activity survives. Noting this "puzzling anomaly," historian Jack Cargill concludes that faced with strong management resistance, the predominantly Mexican-American workers of the area "labored in anonymity" until the 1930s.[19] Paradoxically, it was the descendants of these isolated and divided mineworkers who were destined to shake the western corporate and labor establishments of the 1950s with a strike that broke with precedent in terms of both gender and racial relationships.

Their target, the Empire Zinc Corporation, was not the largest mining interest in Grant County. While Kennecott Corporation dominated copper mining, Empire, a subsidiary of New Jersey Zinc Corporation, employed 128 men in a small-scale zinc mining operation. A low-cost producer, Empire insisted that it could not match the wage-benefit package that Mine-Mill had been able to negotiate with the giant Kennecott firm. Its argument was disingenuous because although it did not compare in size or stature with Kennecott, Empire's parent company, New Jersey Zinc, was the largest zinc producer in the United States. Moreover, Empire's Hanover mine in Grant County, while miniscule in comparison to Kennecott's massive Chino mine, ranked fifteenth in the nation in 1949 zinc production. Its low costs gave it a competitive advantage over zinc mines in the district. In 1949, Empire's balance sheet showed a handsome profit of five million dollars, which was to double one year later under the stimulus of the Korean War. In short, Empire was not a struggling marginal enterprise.

Although Grant County communities were not all company towns, corporate influence was exerted in a variety of ways. Grant County contained a mixture of company towns and semi-independent communities. Yet without absolute control of the entire mining district, management did exert substantial control over those communities in which they operated. For example, Kennecott dominated its company village at Hurley, as well as the town of Santa Rita adjacent to the giant Chino pit, through control of the area's major economic, religious, and social institutions. These communities were part of a larger complex of small towns that comprised the Grant County central mining district. Confronted by this system of external social control, Mine-Mill organizers focused not only on corporate employers, but also the entire structure of political, economic, and social subordination that held workers in industrial peonage.[20]

Management resistance to unionization took many forms, but none was more damaging than the concerted effort to promote disunity between Mexican-Americans and Anglos in the labor force. Wage and employment discrimination against Mexican and Mexican-American workers in Grant County may be traced back to the 1870s. Not only were the best semi-technical and skilled positions reserved for Anglos, but Hispanos labored at approximately half the wages paid their white coworkers. Moreover, segregated payroll lines, toilet facilities, washrooms, and company housing ensured that the color line was clearly drawn. Further damage was inflicted on Arizona and New Mexico mineworkers by regional wage differentials that placed them at a clear disadvantage in comparison with laborers in other areas of the West. The racial distinctions maintained at Empire Zinc were reinforced by housing discrimination based on both ethnicity and class. It is clear that corporate policy encouraged divisions in Empire's labor force by maintaining segregation and discrimination. Management's intent seemed clear to Local 890 president Juan Chacón, who later recalled that "the companies around here have always been afraid of Anglo-Mexican unity . . . [and] for a hundred years our employers have played up the big lie that Mexicans are 'naturally inferior' and 'different,' in order to justify paying us less and separating us from our brothers."[21] Emboldened by Mine-Mill's vision of economic and social justice, the workers of Grant County rose above the ethnic divide to confront and overcome the falsehood that had separated them for generations.

Despite the handicap imposed on the labor force by a long history of discrimination, the Empire Zinc strike led in the direction of a new class solidarity. The overwhelming numbers of Mexican-American workers facilitated the achievement of unity. By closing ranks across ethnic lines, the men and women of Local 890 anticipated the fervor of the civil rights movement, which was soon to transform race relations in the American South. A living symbol of interracial cooperation, Mine-Mill helped bring an end to the discrimination that had prevailed in southwestern mining communities. By the 1950s the union had become a counterweight to the massive corporate power that had left an indelible mark on both the people and the land.

To some union leaders, the price of industrial progress had been too steep. Mine-Mill International Representative Clinton Jencks, an extraordinary Anglo organizer in the Bayard–Hanover area who figured prominently in the *Salt* story, deplored the human and environmental costs of uncontrolled economic development, which he measured in terms of flesh and blood. Contemplating the ugliness of the open pits, he saw a symbol of capitalist exploitation that consumed the people whose lives were spent at labor there: the great pit at Santa Rita "gobbled up rock," and "gobbled up people," while supplying copper "through the labors of the people that have worked there. But at a cost that we cannot afford." Still militant years after Mine-Mill had passed into memory, the unreconstructed leftist harbored resentment against the economic forces that took the wealth created by workers without returning a fair share to those who produced it. And the mines extracted more than mineral wealth. The natural environment also changed forever with the development of the huge smelters, which spewed forth foul-smelling clouds that enshrouded mining towns like Hurley and even Silver City. For Jencks, the rocks had produced contamination, as well as great wealth: "I don't just see copper on those rocks. There's too much blood there. Blood of workers that have slaved away, and produced billions, and ended up with broken limbs, or tombstones of solid rock inside their lungs."[22] For the people of Grant County, employment opportunity had produced dangerous by-products; but the offensive odor was the smell of money, and it covered the land.

The Larger Picture: Postwar Corporatism and the Suppression of *Salt of the Earth*

The foregoing observations suggest a framework within which the suppression of a pathbreaking film seemed rational to dedicated Cold warriors and ill-informed local patriots who saw in it only provocation. Some of the key figures in its production, including Clinton Jencks and producer Paul Jarrico, have emphasized the wider contexts within which this act of blatant censorship may best be understood. For both, the overwhelming pressures created by the escalation of the Cold War and the domestic reaction to those tensions, including the blacklist, lie at the root of the campaign against *Salt*. "The effort to stop *Salt* was a logical result of the blacklist,"

Jarrico argued, which was itself a "logical result of the Cold War." In this sense, the campaign against the film was a predictable by-product of the early Cold War social and political environment, which was sufficiently repressive to deny the *Salt* group both "economic opportunity" and "freedom to express [their] ideas through film."[23] More comprehensive in his analysis was Clinton Jencks, who located the sources of controversy over the film not only in Cold War hysteria (which he readily acknowledged), but also within the wider context of a concerted effort to reverse the gains made by the American labor movement in the 1930s and 1940s. Major advances, including "grudging" acceptance of the 1935 Wagner Act, wage increases, union recognition, and orderly grievance procedures, had been tolerated due to the wartime national emergency, but with peace came a management counterattack against labor, which was intended to void the social contract of the New Deal era. In Jencks's view, management used the Cold War and the anticommunist hysteria that accompanied it to "restore corporate hegemony in the American labor relations system." This analysis is consistent with the findings of labor historian Elizabeth Fones-Wolf, who forcefully argues that American businessmen and industrialists worked to "recast the political economy of postwar America" by reshaping the "ideas, images, and attitudes through which Americans understood their world." To corporate leaders, the new capitalism would solve the nation's social problems through economic growth rather than income redistribution. The assault on both liberalism and organized labor played an important role in the rise of domestic anticommunism and the limitation of the social welfare state. Within this framework, Jencks's own activities within Mine-Mill, a democratic union with a sweeping social commitment, made both he and his organization prime targets for the political and economic power brokers who worked to strengthen corporate dominance in postwar America.[24]

Because the union's social vision was central to the Empire strike, which became the basis for *Salt*, this study begins with a more detailed analysis of Mine-Mill's history, as well as that of the labor wars of the late 1940s, which were crucial in shaping the future of IUMMSW and the other left-led unions of the CIO. A full review of these important social and economic developments will provide the historical context in which the attack on the film must be understood. Against the background of a sharp contest for social control in postwar America, the *Salt* story unfolds.

TWO

Cold War Unionism

The Isolation of Mine-Mill and the Empire Zinc Strike

In 1949 and 1950, the CIO responded to the pressures of the Cold War by methodically expelling eleven of its left-led unions after a long and divisive controversy over the influence of Communists within their leadership ranks. With the simple assertion, "That is that," President Philip Murray pronounced the pariah organizations dead, certainly irrelevant to a bureaucratizing union movement. Subsequent years were to demonstrate that vigorous efforts would be required to ensure their demise. A case in point involved the International Union of Mine, Mill, and Smelter Workers, which for years retained its vigor, as well as the loyalty of its Mexican-American membership in the Southwest. Ignoring the obstacles the union faced as well as the Red-baiting that escalated with the Cold War, the majority of Hispanos adhered to an organization that had served them well and brought them at least a modicum of the dignity so long denied them by both corporate overlords and the Anglo establishment.[1] The genesis of *Salt of the Earth* is best understood against the background of labor's internal warfare, which in turn explains the severe difficulties faced by Mine-Mill as it fought not only the giants of the CIO and AFL, but also the proponents of militant anticommunism in the 1950s. Out of this crossfire came the Empire Zinc strike and the remarkable events that transpired in its wake — developments far removed from the mainstream of American life and well beyond the consciousness of most Americans. Local 890's anonymity was soon to end.

The Party and the Purge: The CIO's Family Quarrel

When the CIO moved to purge its ranks of Communist influence in 1950, as many as one million industrial workers found themselves outside the official union family. Perhaps 20 percent of the CIO's members were unceremoniously dumped as CIO officials acted to remove the taint of radicalism from an organization that in the 1930s had possessed the potential for mobilizing workers in a class-based mass movement. Drawn primarily from the labor force outside basic industry, the expelled unions had organized the previously unorganized, the "outsiders" of the American working class. Mainline union leaders and even some leftists tended to discount the importance of these organizations. Viewed from the modern perspective of the working class as a comprehensive and inclusive formation, however, the expelled unions were the embodiment of labor-force diversity in 1950s America, gender-integrated and multiracial.[2]

The left-led unions were sufficiently catholic in scope to incorporate a significant number of Communists in their ranks, especially at the leadership level. Not only had party members been active in the formative organizational drives of the 1930s, but by the mid-1940s they had come to play a central role in union affairs. Equally important were the larger numbers of independent leftists who worked with the CP element because cooperation served the interest of the membership without contravening CIO labor policies. Thus, while actual party membership was modest, CP influence in the expelled unions was substantial, whether defined in terms of speeches, left-leaning publications, or success in promoting the acceptance of the party line in the formulation of union policy.

The implementation of the party line was often easily accomplished because of the similarity of CP and CIO positions. Yet on other occasions, disagreement led to independent action by some left-led unions. For example, party cadre within the CIO accepted the CP decision to support Wallace in 1948, but could not always swing their organizations behind the Progressive Party campaign. Support for Wallace varied from union to union and tended to mirror opinion within the organizations themselves. In short, the Communists did not exercise lockstep control of the expelled unions.

Because of the contentious contemporary debate over Communist influence in the left-wing unions, rational evaluation and historical generalization has often been difficult. In a judicious summary of the party's impact on the expelled organizations, historian Steve Rosswurm contends that CP influence was a logical result of the party's strong political leadership in union affairs. Moreover, Rosswurm correctly concludes that whatever influence Communists wielded was earned democratically inside unions — at least as democratically as in mainstream CIO unions. While the CP used the same tactics as other pressure groups, it often demonstrated subordination to the interests of the Soviet Union in its labor policies. Despite this fact, most CIO Communists were also good trade unionists who helped secure important benefits for their union brothers and sisters. But the leftist activists were even more significant for the social vision they brought to the democratic unions in which they worked.[3]

In fact, the CIO's family feud damaged American trade unionism far more than was recognized in 1950. By accepting the Cold War assumptions of both conservatives and anticommunist liberals, mainstream unionists undercut legitimate criticism of American foreign policy and tacitly endorsed the arguments of HUAC, Joseph McCarthy, and other repressive right-wing forces in American life. With this capitulation to fear, big labor assumed its position as junior partner in the American national security state.

As labor grew more conservative, its commitment to an emerging civil rights movement flagged. The potential for working-class activism in the cause of racial equality thus declined with the shift to business unionism. No longer was the CIO a beacon of hope for African-Americans, Mexican-Americans, women, and other underrepresented minorities, whose consciousness had been raised by the militant left-led unions that had unionized labor's untouchables. Indeed, it may plausibly be argued that the militance of socially conscious unionism had been defused by a decline in aggressive organizational activity. With the decline in democratic unionism came labor's acceptance of capitalism and the AFL-CIO's emphasis on controlling labor's share of the bounty. The incipient class awareness evident in the organizing drives of the 1930s had evaporated by the late 1940s as labor gained its place at the table. As part of this process, the expulsions contributed to the postwar capital–labor accord — what Rosswurm terms the "negotiated class struggle."[4] The price of accommodation was the waning of the historic CIO commitment to union democracy, social equality, gender equity, and racial justice.

Democratic Unionism and Social Justice: Mine-Mill and the Promise of Equality

Of the expelled unions, none was more committed to the goals of equality and democratic control than IUMMSW — the modern inheritor of the

Maurice Travis, International secretary-treasurer, IUMMSW, 1953. Archives, University of Colorado at Boulder Libraries, Western Federation of Miners and International Union of Mine, Mill and Smelter Workers Collection.

militance once identified with the aggressive Western Federation of Miners (WFM). The primary union of miners in the non-ferrous metals industry, it had a long history of organizing the unorganized without regard to race or job classification. The WFM, which had grown out of the struggles of Rocky Mountain miners in the 1890s, was in its early years an important component of the Industrial Workers of the World. In 1916, it formally became the IUMMSW, which despite its radical heritage made it an AFL affiliate. During the New Deal upheaval, Mine-Mill joined the industrial union exodus into the CIO, where its advanced views on women's roles and race relations made it a pioneer labor organization. As a class-conscious industrial union with a tradition of rank-and-file control, Mine-Mill was the embodiment of democratic unionism. But it had also chosen leftist leaders whose work histories had led them to assume radical political positions. Few scholars have doubted that IUMMSW leaders were left-of-center and few union veterans denied the presence of Communists in the leadership ranks. Yet many observers have noted the negligible political influence of the officers on the membership.

Former Mine-Mill legal counsel Nathan Witt, for example, asserted that IUMMSW "probably" had "the most radical history of any labor union in America." Similarly, former vice president Orville Larson was certain that "the Communist Party was interested in non-ferrous metal, just as the Communist Party was probably interested in other industries." And it is clear that President Reid Robinson and Secretary-Treasurer Maurice Travis were Communist Party members, as were some other Mine-Mill leaders in the 1940s.[5]

More debatable is the impact of Communist leadership on union policy and on rank-and-file workers. Larson discounted the idea of "parallelism," by which he meant the idea that "simply because the Communist Party was interested in it [the union], that meant automatically — so our enemies said — that the Communist Party controlled the Mine, Mill, and Smelter Workers." Similarly, Mine-Mill organizer Irving Dichter disingenuously insisted that "down below . . . the CP was a very negligible force" whose influence was "minor." Speaking of the rank and file, Larson summarized the perspective of many former Mine-Mill leaders, who believed that

these people and their families, their wives and their children, weren't making these sacrifices in all these strikes (and we've had many of them in the nonferrous industry) to support Communism, as has been charged. These people made these sacrifices . . . because they felt they needed the union and the union was doing the job to bring them some of the benefits in these mining camps that the other workers in American industry have. And this, I think, is a real tribute to the union.[6]

Among the most committed unionists to follow the Mine-Mill banner were the Mexican-Americans of the Southwest, many of whom embraced the union because of its civil rights posture and record of promoting racial equality in the workplace. To these hardcore unionists, the "Communist issue didn't matter a hoot." Nathan Witt agreed with the assertion that ideology took a back seat to racial equality with Mexican-American unionists who might not have known "whether they're Reds or not," but "certainly know how they respond to black Americans." Reflecting with pride on Mine-Mill's success in removing discrimination, Orville Larson maintained that its record in race relations was one of the union's greatest achievements. Even more significant was the organization's success in building solidarity between Anglos and Chicanos:

Most of the Anglos were from the non-union country—Oklahoma, Texas, and Arkansas. But they wanted a union. And they were perfectly willing to go along with the battle against discrimination with the Chicanos because they knew that they too were being discriminated against. They had enough sense to realize that.[7]

New Mexico was one of the key IUMMSW strongholds, an area in which the new solidarity bore fruit. Witt later recalled that "in New Mexico we had weight." These successes were all the more remarkable because in many areas of the state "they were still fighting the Battle of the Alamo" and "the company was able to play this to the hilt." Grant County communities maintained de facto racial segregation and the dual wage rate was a fixture, just as was Empire Zinc's policy of hiring only Mexican-Americans for underground work. Yet some Anglo workers were able to grasp the concept of class interest. Even among Anglo workers, Mine-Mill organizer Vern Curtis later recalled, "it didn't take a man working in the mine or a mill or a smelter long to find out that his problems were the same as the Mexican-Americans, and vice-versa. We had to fight the company, not each other."[8] Despite racial antagonisms, company policy, and the vulnerability of the Mexican-American majority in the workforce, the union had come to dwell in Grant County.

But by the late 1940s fallout from the domestic Cold War threatened the precarious foothold gained by Mine-Mill in the southwestern mines. By 1949 Mine-Mill had gone on record with convention resolutions urging that the Truman Doctrine and the Marshall Plan be terminated, positions parallel to those of the Communist Party. Moreover, the International executive board's decision not to sign noncommunist affidavits in compliance with the Taft-Hartley Act (1947) raised the stakes. Finally, from 1950 through 1953, the union's stubborn opposition to the Korean War was to confirm Mine-Mill's pro-Communist status for many observers of the union scene. In retrospect, it seems clear that IUMMSW's wide-ranging critique of the Cold War and domestic anticommunism exacerbated the union's already difficult situation. National CIO leaders, apprehensive over the union's controversial stands on these issues, concluded that their own interests and those of the mainstream unions were endangered by the preference for ideological coexistence expressed by the left-led organizations. The rising tensions boiled over when the punitive Taft-Hartley law forced the CIO and Mine-Mill to make a choice on the noncommunist affidavit issue. As for Mine-Mill, its decision in 1948 to endorse the Wallace presidential campaign set the stage for future persecution by underscoring the union's leftist image. Using this image, together with Mine-Mill's increased isolation within the union movement, as justification, management often refused to bargain unless union leaders signed Taft-Hartley disclaimers. Moreover, Mine-Mill's expulsion from the CIO in 1950 brought a wave of raids on its membership after the CIO assigned jurisdiction in nonferrous metals to the steelworkers. To further complicate matters, a secessionist movement in 1948 had already deprived Mine-Mill of a significant portion of its membership. By 1950, then, IUMMSW was awash in a sea of controversy that threatened to destroy the union as an independent organization; before long, the reverberations were to reach Grant County, where Mine-Mill prepared to seek a new contract with the Empire Zinc Corporation. Defiant in the face of escalating external pressures, Clinton Jencks dismissed Mine-Mill's expulsion from the house of labor with the assertion that his union had been "going for years, with and without the CIO," and would "stand alone, if necessary."[9] But the calculus of labor — management relations was soon to change, as the anonymity of New Mexico mineworkers came to an abrupt end.

The Empire Zinc Strike: Testing the Waters

Beset by numerous national problems, Mine-Mill Local 890 of Bayard, New Mexico, opened discussions with Empire Zinc management in July 1950. The International union's well-publicized national political difficulties placed its negotiators in an awkward position, which was further complicated by the economic reality of depression in the metals industry. When contract talks began, half of Grant County's two thousand mine employees were unemployed. At the outset, therefore, Mine-Mill found itself in a weakened position. And not surprisingly, the opposing parties were soon hopelessly deadlocked on a range of issues.

For the union, the key questions at the Hanover mine included management resistance to collar-to-collar (portal-to-portal) pay, discriminatory wage levels, and substandard working conditions, all of which adversely affected Mexican-American workers. On the issue of wages, Mine-Mill charged that Empire was determined to maintain wage differentials in order to promote ethnic tensions in the labor force and thereby keep the working class disunited. In short, from the union perspective, the basic issue was the demand for economic equality. However, pensions and benefits also became important issues as negotiations unfolded. Contrary to the film's argument, mine safety and underground conditions were not major points of dispute.[10]

Both company and union remained firm in their positions, including sharp disagreement on responsibility for the impasse reached by October 1950. While each blamed the other, the evidence indicates that Empire was determined not to budge, particularly on the pay issue. The breakdown in negotiations also reflected the militancy of Local 890 leaders like Juan Chacón and Ernesto Velásquez, as well as International representative Clinton Jencks. Chacón, who later played the lead in *Salt of the Earth*, was reputed to be a hard bargainer. The son of a Mexican immigrant miner, he had entered the mines himself at the age of eighteen. After serving in the World War II merchant marine and working as a civil servant and welder, he returned to the mines in 1946. Rising from shop steward to the position of Local 890 vice president, he was elected president in 1953, one year after the Empire strike. Alex Lopez of the United Steelworkers of America later remarked that Chacón's attitude toward management was "I'm Chicano and you're a gringo and you're fucking the Mexican." A rank-and-file recruit, he was a dedicated Mine-Mill man who was deeply impressed by the union's commitment to racial equality and nondiscriminatory policies. Chacón's strong sense of ethnic identity was matched by an unshakable conviction that class solidarity was essential to the achievement of racial equality.

Clinton Jencks, fired by a comparable belief in racial equality and the absolute need for class unity, was equally militant. A native of Colorado Springs, he had earned a B.A. at the University of Colorado in 1939. While at Boulder, the deeply religious Jencks embarked on a career of political activism as cofounder and first president of the campus chapter of the left-leaning American Student Union. After college, he participated in the St. Louis Inter-Faith Youth Council and the American Youth Congress, where he met his future wife, Virginia. An air force volunteer during World War II, Jencks was awarded the Distinguished Flying Cross for bravery in combat. Upon return, he became active in veterans organizing in Denver, where in 1946 he served as chairman of the city's chapter of the American Veterans Committee. In the same year, he took a position at the Globe Smelter division of the American Smelter and Refining Company and joined IUMMSW.

Recognizing his organizational talents, Mine-Mill offered him a position as International representative in 1947, which brought him to Grant County. The presence of Clinton Jencks and his activist wife, Virginia, on

Virginia and Clinton Jencks on *Salt of the Earth* set, 1953. Collections of the Wisconsin Center for Film and Theater Research.

the Grant County scene infused Mine-Mill supporters with a new spirit of organizational enthusiasm. To union leader Arturo Flores, the Jenckses' decision to live in the Grant County mining community and actively encourage Mexican-Americans to assume leadership roles underscored their deep commitment to the union cause and set them off from their predecessors. The very presence of Virginia Jencks, who worked almost full time as an organizer, was a tremendous bonus for Grant County workers, who, according to her husband, got "two organizers for the price of one." Their efforts bore fruit when five union locals agreed to form a single amalgamated unit, Local 890. Amalgamation marked an important transition in the history of Grant County unionism, as leadership was transferred from more conservative Anglo officers to militant Mexican-American unionists. Behind the new regime were returning World War II veterans imbued with a new sensitivity to ethnic discrimination and an assumption of entitlement. Their rising activism coincided with the emergence of a small but significant Communist Party group within the Grant County union movement. It is clear that the key activist in this organizational work was Clinton Jencks. The result was the development of a "vibrant, left-wing leadership that connected workplace with community issues."[11] Juan Chacón also credited Jencks with helping to "develop leadership among the workers, the Mexican-American workers." To Chacón, Jencks's commitment to equality explains why he was so harshly Red-baited: "they knew . . . that if he [Jencks] continued to develop the leadership . . . they [the Mexican-Americans] were going to be able to defend themselves and fight." Jencks had concluded immediately that the battle in Grant County "was not just a simple union struggle," but, rather, "the struggle of a whole people," in which his task was to work himself out of a job by persuading workers that they possessed the "power to make better conditions for themselves." And eventually he succeeded in "convincing the Mexican-American people that they didn't need a white Anglo intervening between them and the company."[12] The volatile combination of militant Mexican-American union leaders and the aggressive Clinton and Virginia Jencks meant that Local 890 would stand firm in its demands.

But Empire Zinc, a militantly antiunion company, drove a hard bargain, which ended in a union walkout after management refused to resume negotiations in October 1950. The strike was on, and the parties mobilized for battle. The union local drew support from the International and began an extensive public information program, while Empire dug in. New Jersey Zinc, determined to maintain the competitive edge it enjoyed as a result of its wage policies, instructed Empire to employ tactics designed to break the union and solidify its market position. The fundamental issues in the strike, then, were whether the company would hold firm on management prerogatives and whether it could minimize the union's impact on production costs. To achieve these goals, Empire was willing to invest more than a million dollars during the strike, expending financial resources well beyond Mine-Mill's capacity to match.[13]

The great strength of Local 890 lay in its human resources, organizational capacities, and effective use of external contacts. A democratic organization, it conducted the strike through an impressive committee system that divided responsibilities along functional lines. Strike benefits were drawn from the International, regional Mine-Mill locals, and Local 890's own strike fund, but regular appeals to other national unions produced only modest returns. More sympathetic were Asociación Nacional México— Americana leaders who responded to Local 890's appeals with concrete aid. In December 1951, its national committee made support for the Hanover strikers one of its "principal, immediate activities." ANMA president Alfredo Montoya maintained that the Empire Zinc strike was being watched closely by Mexican people everywhere because it raised the question of wage parity for all workers. Montoya pointedly asserted that Empire's attempt to break the union was especially significant because Mine-Mill had compiled an "outstanding record of organizing Mexican workers and fighting for equal job rights." Although it was strapped for funds, the radical organization endorsed and publicized the strike, while its Denver local gave financial assistance and sent donations of clothes to the families of the Bayard strikers.[14] But as the strike wore on, resources grew thin.

As early as March 1951 the company's stalemate strategy had begun to influence the International's leaders, who became concerned about negative publicity and the increasing evidence that the struggle seemed hopelessly deadlocked. After eighteen weeks out, the local still held firm. At this point, the International executive board assumed control of the strike in a move that alarmed some members of Local 890, who were determined to control their own destiny. By May, defections began to occur and a back-to-work movement, encouraged by management, seemed imminent.[15]

Finally, in June 1951, Empire made a bid to end the strike with an announcement that the Hanover mine would reopen, presumably with nonunion labor. When the union stepped up picketing, the company renewed its determination to use strikebreakers to reopen the facilities. Simultaneously, the police intensified their efforts to maintain order, which resulted in a dozen arrests on the picket line. The escalation of tensions led Federal District Judge Archibald W. Marshall on June 12, 1951, to issue a temporary restraining order prohibiting union members from picketing. Refusing to be intimidated, union members maintained their line, for the first time with the support of women and children. While the union seemed determined to persevere, grave doubts plagued its members as they gathered to discuss the implications of Marshall's injunction.[16] What followed transformed the strike and determined the outcome.

Up to this point, Jencks later noted, this strike was "like a thousand other struggles"; but the mining community's solution to the injunction problem "made it something new and special and unheard of." First, a vote was taken to authorize women to participate in the determination of strike policy. The crucial issue, however, was the proposal that women assume picketing responsibility, which was perfectly legal despite the restraining order. As Jack Cargill has noted, both Jencks and International representative Robert Hollowwa argued that this action would enable the strikers to avoid punitive fines and maintain the strike, all within the law, since only union members were prohibited from picketing. After extensive debate, several votes were taken and the men and women present decided that the women of Ladies Auxiliary chapter 209 would assume responsibility for picketing. It was this action that Jencks thought remarkable:

> One, it was an all-male industry. None of these women were working actually on the job . . . their whole lives were involved, but who thinks about the women that are in the home. They're only struggling to stretch the paycheck. They're only doing, you know. *Only* . . . and that's the way we've been used to thinking . . . number two. Against the background of a culture in which male dominance is exalted by the dominant religion, the Catholic Church. Machismo, you know. Holds the woman down, that whole thing . . . So when this explosion comes . . . the women taking over is the thing that excited the imagination of people all over.[17]

Women's participation in the strike, including support functions, letter writing, and public information activities, had actually been evolving over the previous eight months. While Auxiliary Local 209 had performed the ancillary functions typically associated with such organizations, its members had gradually moved toward more active involvement in union affairs. The institution of monthly family meetings, the construction of a larger union hall, and the assertion of the Communist Party's feminist ideology were all factors in the growth of women's activism within Local 890. Equally significant was the aggressive organizational work of the militant Virginia Jencks and Virginia Chacón, who, like Clinton Jencks, were convinced that women's participation in union activities was essential to the achievement of class and community goals. In fact, many women wanted to move beyond a supporting role to achieve the full respect owed them as union activists. Among the most militant auxiliary members were Angelia Becerra, Braulea Velásquez, and Mariana Ramírez, as well as Chacón and Jencks. Forced to become active participants in the struggle, they brought to the union a new vitality and gave the strike a needed boost. Even Juan Chacón, an early critic, eventually concluded that "the women could play a leading role."[18]

While women had always been crucial actors in the creation of a workers'

Mine-Mill Women on the picket line, Empire Zinc strike, 1951. At left, picket captain Henrietta Williams; foreground, Anita Torrez; at left dancing, Dolores Jimenez. Archives, University of Colorado at Boulder Libraries, Western Federation of Miners and International Union of Mine, Mill and Smelter Workers Collection.

community in Grant County as elsewhere, the strike now enabled them to assume a central position in the union family's resistance to management and unsympathetic local officials. Conscious of the precedent they were setting, picketer Elvira Molano defiantly noted that the court order "does not restrain us" and welcomed the support of "women from all over the country" who had joined the ranks to ensure that "the picket line [remained] solid." When Sheriff Leslie Gofourth began mass arrests for alleged violent behavior (some were charged with assault and battery), new pickets immediately appeared to replenish the line. Undeterred by tear gas and the threat of incarceration, the women and the crowd of male onlookers successfully prevented any disruption by strikebreakers. The outcome underscored the gender solidarity that marked the Empire strike and reminded management that it faced a united worker community.[19]

The novelty of the situation was also evident in the crisis confronted by

Scab workers attempt to provoke picketing women, Empire Zinc strike, 1951. Archives, University of Colorado at Boulder Libraries, Western Federation of Miners and International Union of Mine, Mill and Smelter Workers Collection.

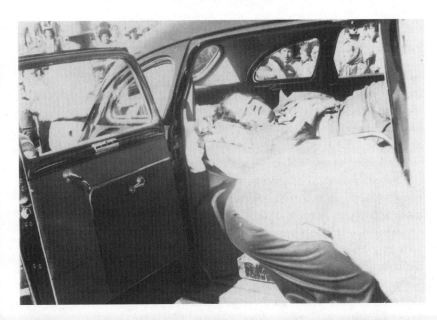

Empire Zinc strike picketer Consuelo Martinez, en route to hospital after being struck by scab-driven automobile, Aug. 23, 1951. Archives, University of Colorado at Boulder Libraries, Western Federation of Miners and International Union of Mine, Mill and Smelter Workers Collection.

the sheriff at the county jail, where he faced a horde of screaming, singing, chanting women and children whose voices reverberated throughout the courthouse. The mass arrests resulted in the imprisonment of sixty-two women and children, including a one-month-old baby. The film accurately portrays the militancy of their response. The *Silver City Daily Press* reported the prisoners to be in good spirits as they prepared for an extended struggle. In the words of one woman, "We're having fun — and we're going to stay on the picket line, too." When asked to sign pledges not to return to the line as the price for their liberation on bail, the women refused. In solidarity, they promised to remain until all were freed. Virginia Chacón recalls their reaction:

We said, "We'll all go together or not at all."
He [the district attorney] came about 6 o'clock and said, 'Well, I'm going to take you girls home.' And so we all shouted 'We're going straight to the picket line.' And they hired a bus, a chartered bus. And

they left us off at the picket line. Our husbands were there waiting for us . . . a lot of them got angry [because of the jailing].[20]

At least one observer maintained that the women's militancy was calculated to influence their men. Sonja Dahl Biberman, in Silver City to assess film locations, concluded that they "knew exactly what they were doing" as they fought to persuade their husbands that they "could not make progress unless they did it together."[21] Despite the tensions created by the role reversal that had taken place, union solidarity held firm.

The establishment of links with other worker groups was more complicated, in part because of Mine-Mill's pariah status within the union movement and in part because of the ethnic differences that separated hardrock miners from other laborers, certainly in Grant County. Several appeals for assistance appear in the records of the United Mine Workers union, particularly after the conflict had escalated in the summer of 1951. On July 13 Mine-Mill reported violence against women and children on the line at Hanover. Denouncing Empire's "reign of terror and bloodshed" against Local 890 members, their wives, and children, the Mine-Mill executive board appealed directly to John L. Lewis for his sympathetic intervention. Three weeks later, UMW received a supplementary press release detailing Empire's use of force against women and children.[22] No response came from Lewis.

Within Mine-Mill and among Mexican-Americans, the reaction was more enthusiastic. From the Chicano Left came warm endorsement. ANMA president Alfredo Montoya insisted that "the importance of the Bayard strike to three and a half million Mexican-Americans cannot be overemphasized." Similarly, California ANMA leader Bert Corona recalled that the strike "captured the attention" of both the "progressive labor movement" and the "Mexican community." Corona attributed this reaction to the widespread recognition that the Empire Zinc strikers were challenging the "whole pattern of job and wage discrimination against Mexican workers in the Southwest." To ANMA activists, this pathbreaking attack on the "southwestern differential" made the fight a "very inspiring one."[23]

Because of the Empire Zinc strike's historic significance, Local 890 received concrete assistance from Mine-Mill unionists and Mexican-American groups well beyond Grant County. For example, the mineworkers of the Phelps-Dodge properties in nearby Morenci, Arizona, identified with the cause of Local 890, since they, too, were forced to confront the issue of wage and workplace discrimination. When the Local 890 relief committee appealed for Christmas donations of cash, food, and clothing, the result

was a flood of contributions from throughout the International union—
Sudbury, Ontario; Pulaski, Tennessee; Pacific Grove, California, and elsewhere. Sometimes overlooked, but also significant, was the support provided by many Bayard business people, help in the form of credit extensions.
But without a doubt, the united support of the Grant County Mexican-
American community and Mine-Mill unionists was the crucial factor in
sustaining the strike. While one hundred strikers were out, nearly 100
percent of the larger amalgamated union members remained on the job and
were therefore able to pay dues to Local 890, thus providing help, both
"financially and morally."[24] Although they were shunned by both UMW
and the rival steelworkers' union, the Local 890 militants were not entirely
without friends.

Outside the union, however, local support was shallow for a variety of
reasons. The central problem was the residual ethnic friction between Anglos and Hispanics. While Mexican-Americans adhered to their union because it had stood publicly and forcefully against discrimination in the
community and the workplace, many Grant County Anglos, most of whom
were not union members, believed Mexican-Americans had no reason for
complaint in view of the job opportunity provided by the mining industry.
Beyond the problem of equality, the other divisive issue in Grant County
was clearly Mine-Mill's leftist image and the way Red-baiting dovetailed
with fears concerning foreign policy and national security during the Korean War. Mine-Mill's radical image combined with its open opposition to
the deadlocked Korean conflict to delegitimize the organization (in the
minds of many observers) as the rightful voice of the labor force in Grant
County and elsewhere. Ironically, ideology was not an issue for most Local
890 members, who consistently identified with Mine-Mill's democratic
practices and commitment to Mexican-American economic and political
rights.[25]

While the strike dragged on, in July 1951 the drama shifted to the courtroom, where a complex series of legal struggles unfolded. The heavy costs
thus incurred stretched the International's financial resources to the limit.
Local judges consistently ruled against the union and its leaders. Although
Judge Marshall's initial injunction became permanent, the women's picketing continued. Fearing further violence, Republican governor Edwin
Mecham now placed state police officers on the line and in late July offered
personal mediation, a proposal promptly accepted by the union but rejected by Empire Zinc. And the strike went on. Management's strategy was
to absorb the negative publicity generated by the women's picketing and
outlast the union in a battle of financial resources.[26]

By this time the union was sustaining heavy costs, though the company's expenses had also escalated significantly. Among the union's losses were counted an estimated 113,360 dollars in fines, as well as over 1,100 person-days in jail. The union leader most despised locally was undoubtedly Clinton Jencks, who to many Grant County observers was tainted with the Communist brush. Worse yet, Jencks had committed the unforgivable sin for an Anglo: he was regarded as a "Mexican lover." In rhetoric reminiscent of the racist response to the southern civil rights movement, Jencks was denounced as the quintessential "outside agitator" and was held responsible for stirring up the local Mexican-American population. His crucial role in the strike, however, is deemphasized in the film, for reasons which will become apparent. In contrast to the film's Anglo organizer, Frank Barnes, Mine-Mill legal counsel Nathan Witt remembered Jencks as "very active in that strike" — an activist who was "very combative." Similarly, Virginia Jencks was "very aggressive." Because the strike "had racial overtones," local Anglos despised the Jenckses, who were "constantly engaged in debates" with the Anglos on "racial questions." In contrast, they were admired by the community they served; loved for the enemies they made. An often-repeated sentiment was summarized in the words of Arturo Flores: "if Clint [was] a Communist, the Communists must be very good people." Witt maintained that Clinton Jencks's later indictment on a Taft-Hartley violation was "mainly an outcome of that strike" and the fact that he and Virginia were outspoken radicals. In Witt's view, they were not "open Communists" but were "open left-wingers" so they "stood out."[27] There is no definitive evidence that Jencks belonged to the party at this time and he has never acknowledged membership. More significant is the fact that he moved easily among leftists, some of whom were Communist Party members, and that his personal economic, social, and political beliefs were consistent with CP positions. Moreover, as a committed union leader and social democrat, he was often willing to work with those political forces that shared his dedication to economic justice and racial equality. In short, the Jenckses were part of a vibrant radical movement culture. None of which necessarily made Clinton Jencks a Communist, but much of which exposed the Jenckses to bitter conservative criticism. And like Mine-Mill, they paid a terrible price for their outspoken adherence to "progressive" ideas.

Faced with negative public reaction and unacceptable financial burdens, both union and company looked for a strike settlement in the fall of 1951, but not before further violence had flared on the picket line. On one occasion, a contingent of strikebreakers and sheriff's deputies injured three women when a truck attempted unsuccessfully to force its way through the

Local 890 activists with strong women's contingent at IUMMSW international meeting, ca. 1953. Top row, left to right: Robert Kirker, Juan Chacón, Virginia Jencks, Germán de Luna, Virginia Chacón, Clorinda Alderette, Frank Alderette. Bottom row, left to right, Nick Castillo, Arturo Flores, Ernesto Velásquez, Clinton Jencks, Clinton Michael Jencks. Archives, University of Colorado at Boulder Libraries, Western Federation of Miners and International Union of Mine, Mill and Smelter Workers Collection.

lines. By late August 1951 the violence had produced a crisis, which abated only after state police were stationed on the strike scene. Empire worked to emphasize the image of mob action with a prominent newspaper advertisement, while the press focused on union responsibility for the breakdown in order. The *Silver City Daily Press* reported that because they had been "hurt too much," nonunion workers had chosen to retaliate.[28]

At this time, the strike merged with the International's plan for a national walkout designed to promote an industry-wide bargaining structure. However, when Mine-Mill president John Clark urged Local 890 workers to return to work pending receipt of a new proposal from Kennecott, the Bayard amalgamated local chose to remain out in support of the Hanover strikers. Meanwhile, other Grant County unions honored the Mine-Mill picket line, including the railroad unions servicing the mines. Beyond the community, however, support was not forthcoming, as AFL locals separated themselves from the Empire controversy and from the leftist image projected by Mine-Mill. For example, strike committee representative Vicente Becerra was unwelcome at several union meetings in Albuquerque; despite the rebuff, however, the AFL metals trade council did cooperate with Mine-Mill.[29]

Although Mine-Mill enjoyed wide public endorsement from many regional and local labor organizations, its ongoing competitive struggle with the steelworkers union soon led to conflict. A Silver City vigilante committee, which had harassed and beaten Jencks during the violence of late August, now turned to the USWA-CIO with an offer to help them gain control of workers in Mine-Mill's jurisdiction. Accepting the invitation, the CIO steelworkers union sent in organizers, billed as the Grant County Organization for the Defeat of Communism. By so doing, they established a pattern later repeated in many subsequent raids on the IUMMSW jurisdiction. Steelworkers publicity attacked Mine-Mill for keeping the Local 890 workforce out of work and stressed the issue of Communism in its appeal to Grant County mineworkers. In response, Mine-Mill reminded mineworkers that USWA-CIO organizers were present in Grant County at the call of a vigilance committee instigated by a few local businessmen who "resent[ed]" Local 890 because it had "brought our people dignity and self-respect." Attacking steelworkers sympathizers as perpetrators of violence in Hanover, Local 890 blistered their leader, Bayard garage owner Charlie Smith, for encouraging surrender to Empire Zinc and promised to send the steelworkers "crawling into the holes they came from."[30]

When the steelworkers' drive flopped, the disappointed anticommunist committee attacked the CIO union for its unwillingness to open its purse to defeat the Communists (that is, Mine-Mill). In an outraged response to the local patriots, USWA district representative Charles J. Smith denied the charges and reminded the Silver City committee that the steelworkers union had long since "cleansed itself of the communist element." The steelworkers' official scolded the Grant County anticommunists and asserted that "from the nature of [their] letter" he could "readily understand how the Communists obtained a foothold in [the] area." Both the steelworkers and their local allies had in fact missed the major point about union organizing in New Mexico, which was the reality that unionism among hardrock miners was a social movement rooted in the drive for full equality. In Grant County, where the steelworkers union stressed the Red menace in the raid on Local 890, the Mine-Mill International shrewdly imported its African-American regional director, Asbury Howard, from Alabama to describe USWA violence and discrimination against black workers in the South. Howard's assignment was to show how the steelworkers had hampered Mine-Mill's effort to "build unity and organization" among southern laborers "regardless of the color of their skin." As Robert S. Keitel has correctly noted, the steelworkers' early campaigns were ineffective because of their "failure to understand the social psychology of the western miners." Stressing the Communist threat (a low priority for local workers) and ignoring the racial issue (a high priority), USWA made little headway in 1951 and 1952 in its bid to compete with Mine-Mill.[31]

While the Steelworkers failed to make significant inroads into Mine-Mill's ranks, Local 890 was beset by its own difficulties. In late August 1951, the International terminated International representative Robert Hollowwa, an aggressive leader who had gained the women's confidence. A sharp internal debate over this dismissal coincided with a decline in numbers on the picket line. At the same time, new charges by Wisconsin senator Joseph McCarthy against IUMMSW executive secretary Maurice Travis breathed new life into the issue of Communist influence in Mine-Mill's leadership. Faced with Empire's intensified efforts to place imported strikebreakers in the Hanover mine, Local 890 in December 1951 urged the Federal Mediation and Conciliation Service to again call for negotiations. More surprising was Empire's decision to enter into discussions. Some evidence suggests that Empire, like other mining firms, actually preferred negotiations with a weakened Mine-Mill to the prospect of dealing with a healthy giant like USWA; indeed, New Jersey Zinc's employee relations manager for the Empire Zinc division, Richard Berresford, later maintained that the firm was "not trying to destroy this union," but rather wanted to "give it proper leadership."[32]

Outcomes: Paths Not Taken

Finally, in January 1952 the International and the company agreed to end the fifteen-month walkout with a settlement that left many of the local's concerns unresolved. Workers did gain modest wage increases, seniority protection for strikers, some important fringe benefits, and a uniform contract-renewal agreement that appeared to align Local 890 with other area locals. While sanitation issues were not a part of the formal agreement, the strike settlement and the subsequent installation of hot running water in company housing do appear to be linked. Despite these gains, the union was saddled with payment of thirty-eight thousand dollars in fines, to be turned over to Empire Zinc. Moreover, charges against strike leaders were not dropped, and six, including Jencks, served prison time. Moreover, portal-to-portal and holiday pay were not part of the agreement, though wage increases were intended to substitute for this concession; and while the settlement succeeded in breaking the "Mexican scale," Empire wages still lagged behind many other companies.[33]

More complicated is an assessment of the intangibles, and there were several. If Empire's real target had been, as Sidney Lens has suggested, the "militancy and strivings of labor itself," management fell short of its goal. An integrated union, which included a large contingent of determined Mexican-American workers, had established its independence and the self-respect of its members in the face of great odds. For the brothers and sisters of Local 890, dignity had been a central issue, and the outcome certainly preserved the sense of worth that had been so important from the outset.

Similarly, the women of the Grant County worker community had experienced an important change. Though for many the gains proved transitory, for others the return to what the film's Esperanza calls "the old way" was not complete. Clinton Jencks, interviewed in 1996, remained firm in his conviction that a new level in human equality was achieved as a result of the strike and that the women "expressed a new sense of unity, especially after the mass jailing, which brought them together." Some participants saw meaningful change in personal relationships. Henrietta Williams, for example, sensed a new respect from men like her husband. She experienced a stronger bond with her husband as they became closer "because we understood each other more." To be sure, not all the women's advances were permanent. For many union families, household relations eventually lapsed into the "old way." By the 1970s, Juan Chacón later noted, the women's auxiliary had become much less active than it had been in the days of crisis. More direct was Jencks, who acknowledged the pull of the past in the form of the impulse to "retain male dominance in the union." As Jack Cargill has noted, the strike-induced change in women's roles did not necessarily end in a "general critique of their subordinate status." Women were brought into fuller participation in union affairs, but the evidence suggests that most men and women understood the strike situation as an unusual and temporary shift in gender roles.[34]

So it was that not long after the settlement, Local 890 was expressing concern over a decline in auxiliary membership. To Virginia Jencks, the strike was *lost* primarily due to pressure from the International for an agreement. She lamented the dropoff in attendance at women's meetings, which had "reached a low that [was] heart-breaking." Jencks told *Salt* screenwriter Michael Wilson and his wife Zelma of her disappointment over the dismissal of women's issues by the union, asking: "Is it enough for a union where the women saved a strike for seven months?" Her anxiety spilled over into outrage when, in February 1952, the International union sent a representative to provide workers' education for a Local 890 women's class. The speaker

> said nothing to us as women, or for us, and although there were sixteen women there, they were not involved in the discussion in any way. I'm still sore about it and sore about the way this progressive guy never spoke about women in his discussions . . . I'm losing objectivity. Clint tells me I'm a man-hater. Lately, I'm damned sure he's right.[35]

Her anger escalated in June 1952, when Mine-Mill proposed that the Jenckses move to a new position in either Arizona or Utah. The union's initiative precipitated a personal "crisis" for a woman whose work had come to be "regarded organizationally." The anxiety deepened when her husband tried to persuade her that her presence "as a wife" would aid him in the new assignment. While she understood his argument, she found the union's relegation of her activities to subordinate status "unpalatable."[36]

Virginia Jencks's sour reaction to Mine-Mill's disappointingly conventional perspective on women's union activities suggests that the strike had failed to alter long-standing assumptions concerning gender relations. But when Michael Wilson, a gifted playwright, crafted the screenplay that was to become *Salt of the Earth*, a more inspirational outcome became possible. Through his skillful creation of a composite character in Esperanza and a blend of fiction and reality in his story, Wilson moved to redeem the strike's vision through an upbeat interpretation of the events described. The reality both within Local 890 and the International was much more complex, as later experience would confirm.

The International union's traditional side surfaced at the annual convention in September 1952, when a Canadian local proposed that "as a mark of special recognition to the women of Bayard" and the "valiant fight they put up in support of Local 890," all women delegates representing the auxiliaries be seated with all rights, including the vote. Fearing the loss of the auxiliaries' support services, the delegates summarily rejected the resolution. One year later, however, delegates to the 1953 convention, having concluded that "women are people," voted to support a publicity campaign

Virginia Jencks, as Ruth Barnes in *Salt of the Earth*, ca. 1953. Courtesy of Jenny Vincent.

to promote the distribution of *Salt*. More will be said of this later, but it is important to acknowledge at the outset the vision expressed by Mine-Mill when it endorsed (at least in principle) a sweeping program of gender equality, including a new women's organizing campaign side by side with a strengthened auxiliary program. Yet while Mine-Mill took a strong stand on full women's participation in union life, it failed to follow up with concrete action and adequate financial resources to give life to these proposals.[37] In the final analysis, ambivalence on women's issues prevailed, even within a radical union far more advanced than most in its commitment to racial and sexual equality.

Mine-Mill's tentative steps toward an advanced program on women's issues testifies to the difficulties experienced when traditional values undergo revision. For committed leftists like Virginia and Clinton Jencks, the failure to sustain the consciousness level achieved during the strike was a bitter pill to swallow. A sense of frustration fills Virginia's March 1952 letter to the Wilsons, which captures her regrets over paths not followed. Describing a recent visit to Hanover, she recalled a sense of nostalgia, a

longing that came over me for the same manifestation of solidarity we had in those days. Even the bitter was exhilarating [*sic*], and the wonder is that so many people are expressing the same longing . . . it is almost a lost, lonely feeling, particularly among the women, who are now separated and apart. The men are still fighting together, daily on the job. But the women who showed courage and determination seem almost like by-products of the strike now that it is over. Some of us women discussed it this morning, and everyone asked what we could do so that the pickets and defendants would get recognition and a feeling of accomplishment and personal pride. In socialist countries there are many ways of showing how a person is a public hero, but here we have let this historical strike and these historic people fade away.[38]

For others, the unity so highly valued by Virginia Jencks represented unwanted revolutionary solidarity. Empire spokesman Richard Berresford later insisted that the key question raised by the strike involved Communist activity in the labor movement. In Berresford's view, "no strike involving so few men and over their particular issues" could have lasted so long unless it had "become endowed with a higher strategy." He further argued that Mine-Mill's collaboration in the effort to film *Salt* demonstrated that those radical influences persisted. His analysis was faulty, correct only to the extent that a Communist steering committee within Mine-Mill brought issues to the union's "Progressive Caucus" and promoted those programs.[39]

While sectarian influence was clearly a factor in the International, the internal dynamics of Local 890 were the product of local conditions and the aspirations of the membership. The CPUSA presence within the local was real. Party activist Lorenzo Torres later recalled that a "good core" of Grant County union leaders were party members, and Virginia Chacón readily acknowledged that she and her husband were among them. Nonetheless, the union's spirit and actions were related more to the WFM radical tradition than to the influence of Communist agitators. Moreover, they were rooted in the aspirations of the area's Mexican-American community and its burning desire for an end to discrimination. One Local 890 unionist flatly asserted the conviction of most Hispanos that "the issue in the Empire Zinc strike was equality." The problem of racial discrimination and unequal wages transcended the influence of imported union organizers like Clint Jencks. "The issues were there, and would have been there even if El Palomino [Jencks] had never been born." While Communists may have lent dedication, leadership, energy, and spirit to Local 890's cause,[40] few rank-and-file unionists were party members and the local's activism was not primarily an expression of Marxist ideology; rather, worker militancy in Grant County was the extension of Mexican-American culture and community solidarity.

For Clinton Jencks, the Empire strike was the beginning of a long nightmare. The beatings, vitriol, and incarcerations were one thing; part of the standard fare for any aggressive union organization. More damaging, however, was the bitter political attack mounted against him once the strike had ended. Jencks was one of the first labor activists indicted under the Taft-Hartley Act's provisions for falsifying a noncommunist affidavit. More will be said of his fate, including the considerable energy and treasure expended by Mine-Mill and his friends in the union movement who worked to defend him against the reckless charges spawned by the anticommunist excesses of the Cold War era.

But before his persecution began, Jencks, the union, and another group of political outsiders had launched an ambitious project intended to test the limits of free expression at the height of the domestic Cold War. When the paths of Mine-Mill's outsiders and Hollywood's blacklistees crossed, the result was the birth of an idea that preserved the story of Local 890's struggle for future generations. The product of this new collaboration, *Salt of the Earth* (1954), stands as an enduring reminder of both the Mexican-American struggle for equality in the Southwest and the corrosive influence of the Hollywood blacklist that stifled the creative impulses of many motion picture artists in the 1950s. The remainder of this study examines the conception, production, and (limited) distribution of a film that told the story of exploited labor and the Mexican-American community within a feminist framework strikingly contemporary in its themes. In addition, this account of *Salt*'s suppression records the limits imposed on creative freedom by the most powerful economic and political institutions of the 1950s, whose leaders were determined to serve the anticommunist state by restricting viewer access to a politically inspired yet morally engaged work of art. By so doing, ironically, they ensured the film's place as a document of the domestic Cold War and a vivid reminder of damage inflicted upon a fragile Constitution by fearful men and women in a time of moral crisis.

THREE

A Chance Meeting and the Birth of an Idea

Origins of Salt of the Earth

From the beginning, *Salt of the Earth* was the product of an extraordinary collaboration among men and women drawn from both the artistic community and the world of labor. Before exploring the origins of the film, it is important to examine the backgrounds of the key figures in the conception and production of the film, for its content cannot be understood without reference to the experiences and assumptions of its creators. Just as knowledge of the Mexican-American workers' struggle in Grant County is essential to an analysis of *Salt*, so the ideas of the key personnel in the project — Herbert Biberman, Paul Jarrico, and Michael Wilson — must be considered if the impact of the blacklist and of the ideological struggle in Hollywood on the film's development is to be evaluated.

Partners in Progress: The Formation of a Radical Circle

The intellectual strand that united *Salt*'s director, writer, and producer was certainly their common engagement in Hollywood politics and active involvement in the Communist Party in the 1940s. Jarrico, Biberman, and Wilson had, in fact, become respected party figures by the early 1950s. The senior partner, Herbert Biberman, had long admired Soviet Communism and worked since the mid-1930s within the Hollywood CP. All were interested in the incorporation of social content in feature films and in the uses of art as a political weapon. Their work also shared a focus on racism, the shortcomings of capitalism, and the search for a more egalitarian community.[1] The three were clearly united in a commitment to the production of engaged art that would grapple with important ideas as part of the advance toward a better society. Each was an active and principled radical.

Perhaps the most resolute with regard to the *Salt* project was Biberman, the strongest organizational talent among them. A native of Philadelphia and son of a Jewish clothing manufacturer, he had studied theater at the Yale School of Drama, where he earned the Master's degree in 1927. During a subsequent European tour, he became interested in both the Soviet theater and social system. After returning to the United States, Biberman worked as stage manager and director of several New York repertory companies in the late 1920s. When serving as stage manager for the Theater Guild, he met the gifted actress Gail Sondergaard, whom he married in 1930. She was to become one of the most influential forces in his professional life.

When not engaged in directing and stage-managing, Biberman also spent time with the American Laboratory Theater. Here he met many aspiring actors and actresses, including the young Julius Garfinkle (later John Garfield). Garfield's biographer maintains that Biberman worked (unsuccessfully) to convert the actor to Communism because he believed that "the theater existed as an agent for social revolution [and he] evangelized his convictions."[2] Before he left New York, then, Biberman had embraced social realism in his work and dedicated himself to a life of political activism that was to end in his HUAC appearance and subsequent blacklisting.

By the 1930s it had become clear that Biberman's main professional contribution was to be made as a stage manager/director rather than as a playwright. Moreover, he began to tire of the Broadway theater and in 1934 moved to the West Coast, where he hoped to make a mark in the motion picture industry. In the same year, he also joined the Communist Party, and from that time on radical politics shaped his personal and professional lives. Although his screen credits were few, he continued to write feverishly in a variety of forms. Much of this work was never published or produced, and from 1935 to 1947 Biberman labored in the demimonde of low-budget filmmaking, a result that led film scholar Bernard Dick to conclude that he was a "classic case of the dilettante, well-educated and widely read, who can neither find nor choose an outlet for his gifts."[3] While Dick argues that Biberman's obsession with radical politics doomed him to mediocrity, it is equally true that he was to make an important and enduring artistic contribution with *Salt of the Earth,* and that his role in the effort to challenge the blacklist ensures that his work will remain historically significant as part of the domestic history of the Cold War.

Prior to his involvement in the *Salt* project, Biberman had been active

Members of the Hollywood Ten and their supporters, ca. 1950. Herbert Biberman at right. Collections of the Wisconsin Center for Film and Theater Research.

in Hollywood's political life as a cofounder of the Hollywood Anti-Nazi League and supporter of Russian War Relief and other radical causes. After modest professional successes in the 1930s, he became absorbed in Popular Front politics, but less active in the motion picture industry, at least until the war created an opportunity to direct for RKO. The result was two wartime propaganda films, *Action in Arabia* (1944) and *The Master Race* (1944). After working on two more unexceptional films in the postwar era, Biberman became embroiled in the HUAC controversy of 1947, testifying before the committee along with others of the "unfriendly ten." Arguing that the inquiry was an attempt to intimidate the motion picture industry and prevent the production of socially relevant films, he insisted that his political views were not HUAC's business and that cooperation would legitimize an unconstitutional invasion of personal privacy. Eventually, Biberman served a six-months prison term for his adherence to that conviction.[4]

Equally committed to a belief in personal liberty and the importance of radical self-expression was screenwriter Paul Jarrico, who eventually became Biberman's partner as producer of the ill-fated *Salt of the Earth*. The product of a radical family, Jarrico's early political development reflected the example set by his parents, particularly his father, a socialist-Zionist Russian immigrant. A socialist by inheritance, the younger Jarrico looked for an even more militant expression of radical action, a quest that led him into the Communist camp by 1934. As a confirmed Marxist "deeply interested in social science and thought," Jarrico believed that Marx "had a lot to contribute to an understanding of society and history." His radical political consciousness therefore preceded his activism as a screenwriter; only after politicization did he become a "cultural worker." By 1937, Paul and his wife Sylvia, herself the daughter of Russian Jewish immigrants, had become active leftists, and members of a group of left-wing screenwriters that included Budd Schulberg, Richard Collins, and Ring Lardner, Jr., among others. And in 1939, the Jarricos formally joined the Hollywood Communist Party.[5]

For these politicized screenwriters, World War II presented a golden opportunity to employ art as a social weapon by affecting film content. For Jarrico, *Song of Russia* (1944) was the most important result. The extent to which such efforts could be successful became a point of contention among the screenwriters circle. Whereas Jarrico's group thought it possible to "influence content" with radical political results, others like John Howard Lawson were more pessimistic about the possibility of radicalizing the standard Hollywood fare. An early illustration of Jarrico's belief in the film's potential for the expression of radical views was his work on *Tom, Dick and Harry* (1941), which earned him an Academy Award nomination. *Tom, Dick and Harry* told the story of a woman who fantasized about marrying wealth, only to fall in love with a man who didn't believe in success or the pursuit of money. Although Jarrico originally thought of his screenplay as an attack on the success myth, he later concluded that the film had relatively little political relevance. In retrospect, Jarrico recognized the film as successful romantic comedy, but certainly not as a vehicle for the communication of a radical perspective to the mass audience.[6]

Among the issues of deepest concern to the young radicals was the "woman question." Jarrico later recalled that the group believed it possible "to have a fairer picture of women and of their capabilities, of their value, and not just treat women as sexual objects." Similarly, CP writers thought

Paul Jarrico, producer of *Salt of the Earth*, ca. 1980. Courtesy of Lia Benedetti Jarrico.

that "minorities could be represented with greater dignity." That vision was later to be realized in *Salt*, which reflected a consciousness of gender discrimination among Hollywood leftists, an awareness which existed "long before it became a mainstream issue." Jarrico's ideas coincided with those of the party subculture described by Deborah Silverton Rosenfelt as opposed to the evils of "white chauvinism" and serious about the "woman question." Both traditional and modern Marxist theorists emphasized the relationship

Screenwriter Michael Wilson with Rosaura Revueltas being interviewed by Mexican journalists, ca. 1953. Courtesy of Becca Wilson and Rosanna Wilson-Farrow.

between gender and class, a link that was assumed to be rooted in the concept of women as property subject to domination. And between 1948 and 1953 the CPUSA challenged male chauvinism, as well as white chauvinism.[7] These views found expression when the *Salt* group set out to tell the story of Grant County's mineworkers and their families.

When Jarrico received his subpoena from HUAC in 1951, he remained defiant. He told reporters that though he was uncertain about his position before the committee, "if I have to choose between crawling in the mud with Larry Parks or going to jail like my courageous friends of the Hollywood Ten, I shall certainly choose the latter." Fired by RKO the same day, Jarrico later pled the Fifth Amendment. For twenty years thereafter, he did not work in Hollywood.[8]

Like Paul Jarrico, his brother-in-law, screenwriter Michael Wilson had enjoyed substantial success before the blacklist narrowed his professional opportunities in 1952. The product of a traditional middle-class background, born in Oklahoma, Wilson was drawn into left-wing politics first as an undergraduate and later a graduate student at Berkeley, where he began to associate with a group of committed radicals, some of whom were women. In 1938 two of these radical graduate students recruited him into the Communist Party. At Berkeley, he also met Zelma and Sylvia Gussin, children of immigrant radical working-class parents, both women who took their own radicalism very seriously.[9]

According to Zelma, whom he later married, Wilson's views on women's issues were "very advanced compared to most [males]," though he still had a chauvinist side. He had an equally strong interest in racial questions, which early in his career he tried to develop in a novella dealing with the question of Mexican-American "wetback" labor in the Southwest. He never completed the project, in part because, by his own admission, he was "out of [his] depth." However, Wilson's early exposure to women's issues and the problems of Mexican-Americans served him well when he wrote the screenplay for *Salt*.[10]

In prewar Hollywood, Wilson devoted most of his attention to Hopalong Cassidy westerns. Unlike many older leftist screenwriters, who when war broke out immersed themselves in propaganda efforts at home, the younger Wilson entered the marines. Returning to Hollywood after the war, he resumed his prewar political activities, especially within the Screenwriters Guild, where he aligned himself with Paul Jarrico. Wilson remained convinced that the writer bore a special responsibility to "preserve human values in his work" despite the front-office control of film content that was unavoidable in a capitalist society. Even after the HUAC hearings he was professionally successful, sharing an Academy Award for the screenplay for *A Place in the Sun* (1951) and earning a nomination for his own work on *Five Fingers* (1952). By 1952, when he became unemployable after being named by HUAC as an "unfriendly" witness, Wilson had established a reputation as one of the most talented of the blacklisted screenwriters.

At this time, Wilson was a member of a close-knit group of leftist "cultural workers" who found themselves essentially cut off from the industry that had afforded them employment and an opportunity to advance their ideological goals through an important mass medium. Their activities within the Hollywood CP had coincided with substantial recognition for their professional contributions. Since the late 1930s, the "*Salt* circle" identified by Deborah Rosenfelt had been part of a common intellectual, political, and social subculture that for many participants reflected working-class Jewish backgrounds.[11] While their ethnocultural origins were not unusual for Hollywood, this radical group displayed an especially keen sensitivity to issues of race, class, and gender. Committed to advanced (for their time) views on women's issues and to racial equality, these activists also shared a conviction that class struggle was the paramount concern. Fired by both radical political consciousness and creative energy, the outsiders looked for a new channel through which the blacklist might be challenged. Without access to the studio system, they turned to the concept of independent production. *Salt of the Earth* was the ultimate result.

A Strategy Takes Shape:
The Independent Productions Corporation

Unable to find work in Cold War Hollywood, Biberman, Jarrico, and black-listed producer Adrian Scott (another of the Hollywood Ten) banded to-gether with other blacklisted artists in September 1951 to form the Inde-pendent Productions Corporation (IPC), a business organization intended to circumvent the 1947 Waldorf Statement and turn a profit in the process. Biberman later asserted that the organizers "were neither starry-eyed nor defeatist," but rather realized that "a climate of fear had been set up which was meant to ostracize us." The company understood that it would receive no facilities or services from the industry because the "shotgun marriage" between Hollywood and HUAC "had been too recently consummated," which meant that the "reluctant bride was too closely under the eye of her assaulter-husband for her to take any chances publicly." Undeterred, they launched their business venture fully anticipating commercial success, as well as a political victory, since the blacklist "would have collapsed of its own absurdity — and of the inability of an industry to effectuate a blacklist in a free market."[12] For IPC the day of the independent producer seemed close at hand.

But no artistic project could be contemplated without sound financial backing. Fortunately for IPC organizers, a Biberman business associate, Los Angeles theater owner Simon M. Lazarus, shared their outrage at the blacklist and also saw a solid financial proposition in their plans. A practical man with a history of interest in the idea of independent pro-duction, as well as deep pockets, Lazarus agreed to become the corporat-ion's president, confident that an opportunity to turn a handsome profit was at hand. His record of support for left-wing causes also drew the attention of Hollywood anticommunists and other Red-hunters. When, in 1953, HUAC suggested that Communists might have been funding the project, he angrily responded that IPC was a "business venture" and "for a business venture you don't go to the Communist Party or any other party to get money." To Biberman, his greatest value to the corporation "was based on his position in the community" and his "very great partisanship for us." Because of his willingness to associate with blacklistees, Lazarus could "give the community the sense that the industry's barring of [them] was about to be exposed for the cowardly and improvident action that it was."[13]

Lazarus was actually more than an interested investor. He had drawn fire because of his own insistence on the protection of artistic freedom. As a theater operator he exhibited political films, which "brought him into disrepute." Steadfast in his refusal to name names for HUAC, he forcefully exercised his Fifth Amendment privilege before the committee. As a result of his defiance, as well as his financial involvement with IPC, Lazarus, like other members of the corporation, was soon to be monitored by the FBI's watchful security team,[14] for whom the progress of *Salt of the Earth* became an obsession.

Despite his commitment to the project, Lazarus was slow to accept a commensurate share of the potential profits to be realized, preferring to see the blacklistees benefit financially from the enterprise. At Biberman's and Jarrico's insistence, however, Lazarus accepted two shares of the corporation. Biberman later recalled the debate over IPC's demand that both Lazarus and attorney Charles Katz take more as the "fiercest discussion we ever had." At the time, Biberman was convinced that Lazarus "was the man whose position and enthusiasm got this company sold to business men" in Hollywood and that "without him . . . we never could have gotten off the ground." There is some truth to Biberman's assertion, since he had been struggling since 1948 to enter independent production through another company, Film Associates, Inc., which never succeeded. In Jarrico's words, "it wasn't until 1951, when we were good and dead professionally, that we could get involved with movies that packed a real social and political wallop."[15] IPC was the vehicle for that advance.

Originally, the corporation had several scripts under consideration. Among the films planned was a movie based on the career of concert artist Paul Robeson, a documentary on Frederick Douglass, a film on labor unions, and a feature film on the trial of an African-American woman. From the outset IPC "searched for films that would reflect the true status of union men and women." Similarly, minority peoples and women's issues provided fresh material for independent artists intent on creating films that might explore social realism and human struggle. At first, top priority went to a script by another blacklisted writer, Dalton Trumbo (himself one of the "un-friendly ten"), exploring the experiences of an African-American woman who lost her children in the course of a divorce in which she was accused of harboring Communist sympathies. However, in late 1951, the IPC circle encountered a story that presented a wonderful opportunity to give life to the group's interest in issues of race, class, and gender. The Empire Zinc strike "seemed the best embodiment of the elements for which [the com-pany] had been striving."[16] The result was *Salt of the Earth*, a film that successfully combined the political, social, and economic goals that IPC pursued in its challenge to the film industry's establishment.

A Fortuitous Meeting: San Cristóbal and the First Step

As of late summer 1951, after four months of evaluating scripts, IPC had not yet launched its first project. It was fortuitous, therefore, that Paul Jarrico chose this moment to spend vacation time at San Cristóbal, north of Taos, New Mexico, where Jenny Wells Vincent and her husband operated a ranch frequented by left-wingers of many stripes. In the exaggerated words of one cynic, proprietor Craig S. Vincent operated a "guest ranch for Com-munists." The Vincents were, in fact, owners of a vacation ranch that advertised in the liberal journal *PM* and attracted a leftist clientele, whose political views were generally compatible with their own. Vincent was a left-wing Democrat and seasoned New Dealer, while his wife had gained substantial notoriety as a folksinger and supporter of left political causes, including that of the beleaguered Mine, Mill, and Smelter Workers Union. Both were well-known political figures throughout New Mexico and Colo-rado. At the Vincent ranch, Jarrico and his wife, Sylvia, met Clinton and Virginia Jencks, who were themselves on leave from union duties at the Hanover, New Mexico site of the Empire Zinc strike.[17]

Physically exhausted by the rigors of the strike, Jencks was recuperating at San Cristóbal, where he became intrigued by Jarrico's search for mean-ingful stories to be used by IPC. To Jencks, the company offered a potential vehicle for reaching a national audience with the Local 890 story at a moment when the union's members were "desperate for equality." Seizing the opportunity to aid the Mine-Mill cause in Grant County, he invited Paul and Sylvia Jarrico to "come down . . . and meet the people." For his part, Jarrico was sufficiently intrigued by the Empire Zinc strike that he decided to stop in Grant County on his way back to California. At Hanover,

The key figures in the Independent Productions Corporation on location during filming of *Salt of the Earth*, 1953. At extreme left, Paul Jarrico; in center in front of rooftop camera, Herbert Biberman; at lower right, Michael Wilson. Collections of the Wisconsin Center for Film and Theater Research.

the Jarricos visited the strikers and became even more interested in the events unfolding before their eyes. Sylvia Jarrico, who joined the women's picket line, remembers her own reaction as an intense response:

> I was attracted by everything, everything about it. Well, it's a strike, it was a strike for equality of Mexican-American miners. I mean, as fundamental and irresistible, and intransigent an issue as you can find. It was obvious. The minute you know what the issue is, you know that people will never give up. And sure enough, they were acting like people who would never give up . . . nothing stopped them. That was the wonderfulness of the story . . . it was absolutely irresistible motion picture material.[18]

As a committed feminist, Sylvia Jarrico embraced the story with enthusiasm, but no more so than her husband, Paul, who was deeply impressed with the parallels between the Empire/Mine-Mill story and the blacklisted artists' own political and economic predicament. Whereas Mine-Mill had been expelled from the CIO for alleged Communist influence, the blacklistees had been "kicked out of Hollywood . . . for the same reason." Convinced that this was the material IPC had been looking for, he told Biberman and Scott that "this is a story that's got everything. It's got labor's rights, women's rights, minority rights, all in a dynamic package."[19]

Biberman concurred in this judgment, which led the filmmakers to commit what Jarrico called a "crime to fit the punishment" already meted out to the victims of the blacklist. To Jarrico, the "crime" was the effort to depict the "dignity of women, labor and a racial minority." Shortly thereafter, they persuaded Wilson to visit Grant County so that he could form his own impression and begin research for a preliminary treatment. Wilson agreed to the plan, and in October 1951 proceeded to Bayard to learn more of the events he was to interpret. At first, the screenwriter's presence on the strike scene was a puzzle to the strikers, some of whom thought he was a scab and therefore watched him closely. Once the picketers realized he was not a company man, however, a closer relationship developed as Wilson explored the aspirations and fears of the worker community. Jencks later described Wilson as a "beautiful human sponge" who refused to "impose his own will" on the people whose lives were affected by the strike. To Jencks, his willingness to listen and to observe events taking place before his eyes helps to explain *Salt*'s honesty: when Wilson eventually returned in 1952 with a draft treatment, "that story was true."[20]

But to ensure the prospective film's truthfulness, extraordinary steps were taken to consult the men and women of the Bayard mining community; indeed, Wilson insisted on approval of film content from the people of Local 890. Virginia Chacón later recalled that from their earliest meeting, the union community regarded Michael Wilson as a "friend" and a "fighter" for social justice. Nonetheless, they cautioned him that if a movie was to be made, they did not want "Hollywood shenanigans." To ensure accuracy and community approbation, Wilson returned to Bayard in the spring of 1952 to hold an open meeting at the union hall, at which time union members offered vigorous criticism of the draft treatment. While generally supportive of the draft, miners and their families called for a number of revisions. As a result of these discussions, including input from the International, Wilson concluded that "the enemy (absentee bosses) had to be dramatized as they had not yet been . . . not so much as persons but as a force." By emphasizing management responsibility for bitterness and a lack of self-confidence among Mexican-Americans and differences between men and women, the intensity of the struggle could be dramatized. Moreover, some scenes seemed unreal and were removed or altered; stereotypical portrayals of Mexicans as sexually promiscuous or prone to chronic alcoholism disappeared. Yet the essential integrity of Wilson's treatment, including his decision to focus on women's issues through the interaction between Esperanza and Ramón, remained intact. Biberman summarized the projected outcome as a film that would be "neither a story of the strike nor a story of male chauvinism," but rather an account of women's "emergence" and their "decisive contribution" to "victory in struggle for the group — the class."[21]

Wilson's determination to make Esperanza's personal experience the central feature in the film's structure raises the question of possible Communist influence in the crafting of the *Salt* screenplay. While *Salt* was attacked in 1954 as Communist propaganda, the fact is that the party's primary emphasis in the postwar era had been placed on class and the failure of capitalism, while the feminist ideas associated with the well-known "woman question" constituted a minor theme. Yet Wilson chose to make Esperanza's growth the central dramatic feature of his work. Biberman and Wilson agreed that the story should not be a "condemnation of male chauvinism among Mexican-Americans." Instead, they projected a "paen [*sic*] of praise for these women united with their men." And although the film's miners, Mexican-Americans, and women all engage in their own struggles for equality,[22] it is Esperanza's quest for dignity that clearly dominates in *Salt*. Here Wilson's and Biberman's priorities superseded any external influences.

Nonetheless, it is true that party organizer Frances Williams of Los Angeles did successfully urge revisions in Wilson's initial emphasis on the role of the film's white union organizer (Barnes). These changes were needed, according to one union member, to undercut the screenplay's portrayal of an Anglo organizer "saving the Mexican masses." Not only did the party consider this revision politically wise, but the shift was also consistent with the views of Clinton Jencks, upon whom the Barnes character is modeled. Concerned about the Anglo organizer's character, Wilson was determined to avoid portraying him as "the St. Paul of the working class, bringing the union gospel into 'backward areas.'" To assist him in the task, Jencks instructed the screenwriter on the typical mistakes made by Anglo organizers among Mexican-American workers.[23] If anything, as previously noted, the resulting screenplay understated the actual role played by Barnes (Jencks) in strike leadership.

The product of the consultative process was a film that, regardless of where the major emphasis lay, took a strikingly advanced position in its treatment of class, racial, and women's issues. By the time Wilson had written and revised the screenplay, it had been subjected to a collaborative review unique in film history. By one estimate nearly four hundred people had read the script before production eventually got under way. It was an approach that Wilson would have detested if imposed upon him, but which, in this instance, he welcomed as a means of learning more about his characters and the film's subject so that he could better represent them. As Rosenfelt has noted, the key distinction lay in the "consent and mutual respect" evident in the *Salt* process. The end result in Biberman's words, was a script that "found deep approbation among all."[24]

In later years, the motion picture would draw substantial criticism. Historian Juan Gómez-Quiñones, for example, has argued that the film failed to capture the "complexity of the strike, its context, and its aftermath." However, his assertion that Wilson, Biberman, and Jarrico were "unaware of the full political and historical context of the union and its participants" probably exaggerates their naivete. Jack Cargill agrees that the IPC team created the *myth* that the strike had produced a *new realization* that "equality and respect must be given to be received" and that "human actualization is fundamentally a process of cooperative and interdependent relationships." Other scholars have faulted the filmmakers for one-dimensional reductionism. Bernard Dick, for example, notes that Wilson's script and Biberman's direction oversimplified a complex problem by stressing "the indivisibility of equality" and the centrality of Esperanza's "vision," her quest for dignity. Similarly, Michael Neves sees *Salt* as a "timeless fable," a "morality play" that expressed oversimplified but "correct" attitudes.[25]

Without a doubt, the screenplay that survived the collective criticism left much to be desired, especially as a documentary record of historical events. But filmmaking and screenwriting are intensely personal creative processes; and it was never IPC's intention to produce a documentary film. Hence, Wilson's decisions may best be understood as the choices of a creative artist determined to interpret the entire experience of the Mexican-American community depicted. The synthetic quality of his script, including the composite aspects of his characters (most notably Esperanza), reflected the license granted the craftsman to shape a vision of historical and contemporary reality. It was this perception of the Empire Zinc story that Wilson, Biberman, and Jarrico shared with their audience.

Despite their failings, including romanticism, naivete, and an incomplete grasp of Chicano/Chicana history, most observers have acknowledged the significance of the final product. Reservations aside, for example, Gómez-Quiñones views *Salt* as an "enduring artistic classic testimonial that evokes the travails of struggle and communicates its lessons." In agreement, Cordelia Candelaria concludes that in terms of cinematography, content, and equity, its "achievement" was "of genuine classic proportions." Film scholar Allen L. Woll, in an analysis of Hollywood's treatment of Mexican-Americans, regards the film as the "most realistic treatment of Mexican-Americans during the 1950s," one that avoided stereotypes, used Chicanos and Chicanas as actors and actresses, and displayed a "sensitive attitude" toward the people whose lives it portrayed. With all its faults, Brian Neve concludes, *Salt of the Earth* was a "rare effort to beat the system," which has worn well over time, surviving until "the way in which it was ahead of its time, especially in its treatment of feminist issues, could be recognized."[26] Most important, however, is *Salt*'s significance as both a celluloid document of the resistance to Cold War repression and a record of a people striving to make their own history.

The strength of the collaborative process lay in part in its energizing impact on the Grant County participants. Clinton Jencks later described the spirit of spontaneity that prevailed at the Bayard union hall when the script was read:

And the first part everybody sat and listened. And pretty soon they forgot they were listening to somebody read . . . people began to interrupt. They'd say "No, no, it wasn't like that at all." Or they'd say, "No, you can't do that. That gives the wrong impression about our people. About the way we are . . . " there were some things that were more Los Angeles than they were New Mexico. And those were the things that were rooted out. But the beautiful thing about it, is that, it's the kind of person Michael was, that he didn't have to defend this as a child . . . he was big enough.[27]

The collective reading process impressed Jencks as a dynamic free-for-all, which empowered the people whose story was being told, and simultaneously empowered Wilson to tell it more honestly and accurately. It was this integrity that later attracted the interest of award-winning Mexican actress Rosaura Revueltas, who was to play the role of Esperanza. While the *Salt* group's ideological background was compatible with Revueltas's own left politics, she was especially drawn to the project because it promised to portray the dignity of the Mexican-Americans with whom she identified. To Revueltas, the daughter of a Mexican miner who had once known poverty, the screenplay created a role she had long hoped to play, one that "would honor [her] people." She found truth in Wilson's depiction of miners who "were *my people*, even though they lived across the border." Her belief in the film was matched by the enthusiasm of the workers who had participated in the consultations that had strengthened the film's portrayal of their struggle. The eventual outcome, in Biberman's estimation, was a screenplay that was "the expression of a *community*, largely Mexican-American numbering some seven thousand people." To underscore the consensus support for the final version, Local 890 gave its unanimous approval at a formal union meeting. Few members of the worker community would have disputed Juan Chacón's later conclusion that the final product of their efforts, *Salt of the Earth*, was at least from a union organizer's perspective, a "tremendous film."[28]

Symptoms of Resistance: The Opposition Appears

Even before the collective review process had been completed, ominous developments signaled the emergence of opposition to IPC's initiative. While Wilson honed the screenplay, Biberman, Jarrico, Lazarus, and Scott worked to raise the money needed to produce the film and began preparations for casting and shooting. An important preliminary detail involved the recruitment of a crew through normal industry channels, which led to exploratory discussions of the company's needs with Roy Brewer, the International Alliance of Theatrical Stage Employees' international representative in Los Angeles.

While determined to assemble a union crew, IPC had no illusions about IATSE cooperation. Even before *Salt* became the company's first priority, Brewer had rebuffed Lazarus's bid for a studio crew to produce a film based on Trumbo's script. Then, in May 1952, IPC sent Lazarus to Brewer as a "scout" to see if studio space and a crew would be available for the *Salt* project. Brewer threatened to "destroy" Lazarus upon learning of his association with Biberman and Jarrico. He told Lazarus that "their idea of what was a good labor picture" was definitely not his and that as Communists "they would only be interested in using labor for their own ends." Berating the IPC organizers as a "very disturbing influence" in Hollywood and as enemies of IATSE, Brewer warned Lazarus against any involvement with them. When informed of Wilson's work on the *Salt* script, Brewer angrily told Lazarus that "over his dead body" would the picture be made. According to Lazarus, a red-faced Brewer pounded the table and vowed that even if they made the picture "someplace else" it would "never be shown in the United States."[29]

Even the experienced Simon Lazarus was stunned by the ferocity of Brewer's attack on his associates. Puzzled by the "animosity expressed," he told Brewer that since they were still living in the United States, he assumed that American citizens had the "right to work and make a living." In response, the anticommunist union leader warned Lazarus that any investment in IPC would be "absolutely wasted." Brewer concluded his diatribe with a promise to "see [Lazarus] in hell before [he made] any pictures." When Lazarus reported the results of the meeting to Biberman, he asserted that he had "just seen Hitler."[30]

With Brewer's cards on the table, IPC approached the project with a new realism. Familiar with Brewer's staunchly anticommunist labor record reaching back to the studio strikes, the company's promoters now knew that production with Hollywood support was impossible. More significantly, they understood that Brewer spoke for a constituency much wider than his own union: his threat also represented the studios "more directly," since from Biberman's perspective "he had become their boss—not they his." Brewer's opposition constituted a serious challenge to the IPC plan, since in addition to his IATSE position he chaired the AFL Film Council and was active in the conservative Motion Picture Alliance for the Preservation of American Ideals. Representing these organizational bases, he had also become a key figure in the Motion Picture Industry Council (MPIC), which spoke for all Hollywood unions and the major industry organizations. By 1952 a vociferous anticommunist and prominent force on the Hollywood political scene, Roy Brewer represented a clear obstacle to IPC's independent production program. His denial of an IATSE crew, which ensured that Hollywood unionists were prohibited from working on one of the most pro-union films ever made,[31] was but the first step in a broad attack that was to result in disaster for the *Salt* project.

By mid-1952 the battle lines had been drawn in the struggle for the right to be heard. Biberman later asserted that every effort to "splinter the Brewer-studio axis" failed, and under the aegis of MPIC, the great "industry-wide . . . conspiracy was total."[32] What Biberman and his associates underestimated at the time was the breadth of Brewer's reach. Still defiant, they prepared to begin production. Because Hollywood production was not feasible, Biberman was forced to consider an even more innovative organizational scheme to facilitate financing and managing a film shot on location in New Mexico. Once implemented, his proposal further solidified the relationship between outcasts, as IPC and Mine-Mill drew closer in an attempt to circumvent the obstacles created by anticommunists in both Hollywood and the remote Southwest. In the end, Local 890's story and the Mexican-American struggle for equality were to become a part of film history. In one more way, the union would make a difference.

FOUR

Making History on Film

Production Problems and Conservative Reaction

By spring 1952 IPC had made great strides. On March 22, Biberman told the corporate board that he had laid the basis for film production in Mexico, arranged studio facilities in Hollywood, and commissioned several scripts-in-progress. The Trumbo script had gone into a second rewrite and John Howard Lawson had agreed to collaborate with African-American writer Carlton Moss on the Frederick Douglass project. But Biberman saved his most positive words for the *Salt* project. Recounting with pride the collective review process Michael Wilson was soon to initiate, he promised a screenplay "born out of deepest respect for the people about whom it is written, reflecting their reality, their truth, their ambitions, their beauty, and their human interest."[1] To all concerned, the company's future seemed full of promise.

Forging a New Link: The Mine-Mill Connection

Biberman's optimism was in part the product of his own visit to Silver City early in 1952, at which time he had formed a solid working relationship with the men and women of Local 890. Always a romantic, he wrote that his visit was "most rewarding" and that he felt "wedded to the people there after two days." He had come to understand Wilson's choice of the "salt of the earth" image as a reference to the Chicano culture: "it is their quality." Still filled with emotion (and a touch of condescension), he later told his family that he could not wash Silver City out of his "memory and being" because of the "intense normal experience among hard pressed people who

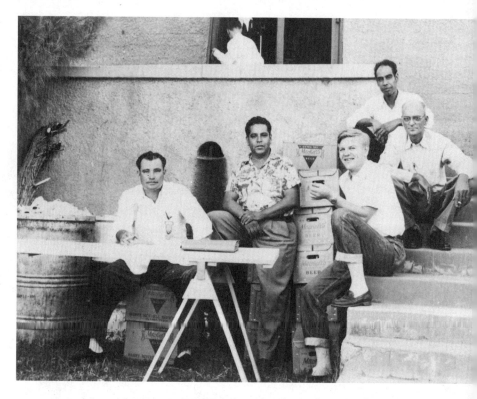

Clinton Jencks and E. S. Conerly with Clifton-Morenci union activists at time of IUMMSW convention in Nogales, Ariz., September 1951. Archives, University of Colorado at Boulder Libraries, Clinton Jencks Collection.

make so much out of so little — whose culture is so real and stout and such a saving grace — and such a militant, proud thing."[2]

While Biberman waxed enthusiastic, it had become clear that Local 890 was reluctant to proceed without the blessing of the International union. The idea of formal collaboration was not entirely new to Mine-Mill leaders. As early as September 1951, Virginia Chacón recalled, Harry Bridges, left-leaning president of the International Longshoremen and Warehousemen's Union, had encouraged the Chacóns and other Mine-Mill activists to consider participation in a film scheme. In 1951, when Bridges joined IUMMSW leaders as keynote speaker at the union's annual convention in Nogales, Arizona, he informally recommended that Mine-Mill consider cooperation in such a project, should it develop. Not long thereafter, when International president John Clark and his wife visited the Hanover picket lines, Mrs. Clark told her husband that Bridges had been right and pressed him to establish contact with the moviemakers.[3]

At the same time, Biberman's January visit to Grant County enabled him to discuss plans for the film with Clinton and Virginia Jencks. Virginia, not easily impressed, informed Michael and Zelma Wilson that Biberman had been "enchanting" and that "everyone loved him." Expressing great interest in *Salt*'s progress, she promised help and encouraged IPC to "talk to Mine-Mill big shots" about the film. Fearful that the strike's "lesson" was "in danger of being lost and forgotten," she urged that it be taken to a larger audience.

Both Virginia and Clint saw the movie as an instrument to "tell America about the Mexican-Americans living it . . . about them as workers, and about the miracle of the women." Virginia expressed special concern about the International's view of the Empire struggle, which, she argued, was "not the kind of strike desired by the International." Angered by Mine-Mill leaders who "resented the women on the lines, and fought-fought-fought all the time against them," she looked to the film project as a way of commemorating the great sacrifices made by all members of the worker community.[4]

What she did not know was that Biberman had begun to develop another scheme to keep the film alive by shooting on location with unprecedented cooperation from IUMMSW. His idea was to arrange union sponsorship of the film in order to "give prestige to the picture" among working-class audiences. To that end, Biberman suggested a "formal arrangement with the International to act as producer" so that Mine-Mill could hire IPC and IATSE workers and secure the mine's permission for shooting on location. In June 1952, IPC proposed collaboration "with the real intervention of the International" to produce a picture that would be "something never before approached in our country." After preliminary discussions with Mine-Mill vice president Orville Larson, Biberman offered Secretary-Treasurer Maurice Travis the company's talent and financial resources in return for the International's imprimatur as producer. Effusive in his praise for Mine-Mill as an exemplar of "militant and progressive unionism," Biberman concluded that the venture was a "M, M and S kind of job . . . requiring an M, M and S kind of initiative."[5]

When Travis took the proposal to the International executive board, he stressed the company's commitment to "produce progressive films" and cited Biberman's argument that the picture could be "something terribly important to [Mine-Mill's] welfare." He also noted that the union's obligations would be substantial, though no financial responsibilities would be incurred. As he saw the arrangement, IPC wanted the Mine-Mill name and

some short-term personnel assistance, for which the union was to be com-
pensated. Moreover, IPC promised 5 percent of net profits in the form of
a contribution to Local 890's strike fund. Although he made no formal
recommendation, Travis warmly endorsed the proposal, confident that it
could have "terrific educational value in our own ranks" while "serving the
working class generally throughout the world."[6] If questions of union legal
liability could be answered, he was ready to move on the plan.

Satisfied that the union's financial and legal obligations would be limited,
the board pledged its full support to the project. By giving its blessing, the
International freed the local to cooperate fully in the production process
and, as "co-producer," became the conduit through which IPC funds would
be expended. By working through IUMMSW, Biberman and Jarrico hoped
that IATSE resistance to supplying union labor might be circumvented.
While the International bore little financial responsibility, the important
preproduction arrangements could be made.[7] As of October 1952, the path
to production seemed open.

Once the Mine-Mill executive board had sanctioned the project, IPC
moved quickly to implement its plans. While Wilson shared his script with
Travis, Biberman gave the story outline to Mine-Mill's Los Angeles International representative James L. Daugherty. Meanwhile, Biberman consulted with Travis in Denver and prepared to scout locations and evaluate
local talent in Bayard. While great progress was made, one serious obstacle
remained—the problem of securing a competent, union film crew in the
face of Brewer's obstructionism. Indeed, to the IPC leftists, the very idea of
a nonunion crew was "wormwood in [their] mouths."[8] Confronted by this
roadblock, the company searched for a solution.

Biberman thought he had found an answer in a New York CIO documentary film union. When he approached the organization, it became
clear that the union feared "association with either IPC or Mine-Mill."
More significant, however, was the political reality that the CIO group was
then in the midst of negotiations for a merger with IATSE, and that it
thought Brewer or Walsh "might blacklist *them.*" When IPC leaders appealed to the Communist Party to intervene with communists in the union,
party "higher-ups" refused to help. The CP, Jarrico later recalled, concluded that the IATSE ties superseded *Salt* in importance and therefore
refused to assist IPC "when they could have helped." Despite its reservations, the CIO crew agreed to service the film (though many of them would
subsequently back out);[9] but for the moment a thorny issue appeared to
have been resolved.

By the end of the year, Jarrico and Biberman had assembled a team that included several blacklistees, as well as three African-Americans, whose employment broke with Hollywood's standing Jim Crow hiring practices. With fifty thousand dollars in IPC funds safely deposited in a Silver City bank, the union stood ready to assume its coproducers' function. Finally, the arrival of Biberman, Jarrico, and associate producer Sonja Dahl Biberman in December 1952 marked the final stage in preproduction work, including the difficult task of making the remaining casting decisions.[10]

Since the previous summer, casting had become Biberman's most urgent problem. Because IPC organizers had resolved to rely on the people of Local 890 and other nonprofessionals for most of the cast, recruitment was an early concern. Determined to avoid the errors made by other filmmakers in their depictions of Hispanic characters, Biberman and Wilson prepared to break with the past. Although Wilson had originally designed the character of Esperanza with Sondergaard in mind, Biberman balked at the idea of Anglos in the lead roles: "we couldn't entrust Mexican-Americans with the important Mexican-American roles. The Hollywood tradition!"[11]

Struck by the hypocrisy of this idea (and pressured by the mining families), Biberman set about the search for Hispanic actors for the roles of Esperanza and Ramón. After Mexican-born Hollywood actor Rodolfo Acosta withdrew from the cast under studio pressure, Biberman eventually warmed to the idea of relying upon nonprofessional Grant County workers. Sensing the importance of the casting issue, Sondergaard graciously stepped aside in favor of the accomplished Mexican actress Rosaura Revueltas. Revueltas, whose film career in Mexico had only begun to develop, had already won awards for two previous films made in her own country. A member of a family prominent in the Mexican arts community, she had ties of friendship with Mexico's intelligentsia, including Diego Rivera, David Alfaro Siquieros, and her brother José, a writer in his own right. Her selection was the result of an exhaustive screening process. Even more difficult was Biberman's long and often frustrating search for the "right" male lead. He first approached a Chicago Mine-Mill leader, Rodolfo Lozoya, whom he had met at the 1952 union convention in El Paso. Effusive in his endorsement of Lozoya, Biberman described the union leader as a "human being of such inner power, such majestic proletarian purity and strength" that he (Biberman) quivered at the impact of his presence. When this plan failed to materialize, Biberman traveled to Mexico to audition prospects, some of them friends of Revueltas; but at the end of the search, no Mexican actor seemed right for the part.[12]

It is possible to find in Biberman's agonizing over the lead actor and actress an element of Anglo condescension. Concerned about one Mexican

Rosaura Revueltas as Esperanza Quintero in *Salt of the Earth*, ca. 1953. Courtesy of Jenny Vincent.

candidate's "authority" and "stature," the troubled director worried that "the choice is so limited here — so very limited." Still another actor was a "problem" because he was not "himself a fully-formed being." Biberman doubted that the prospect could "give himself fully to something so special." Even Rosaura Revueltas, whose professional credentials were strong, presented problems for a brief time. Although Biberman finally concluded that she "may be very good," his approbation, tinged with unconscious racism, came only after she had "cast off the Spanish sentimentality."[13] Even the dedicated Marxist, it seems, was capable of borderline racist thoughts.

While the Revueltas decision was made in September, the male lead remained a headache until January 1953, when the issue was settled with the selection of Juan Chacón, Local 890's newly elected president. The decision for Chacón was not taken without substantial debate. While Biberman harbored serious doubts, Revueltas and Sonja Dahl Biberman lobbied hard

Herbert Biberman gives direction to Rosaura Revueltas, on *Salt of the Earth* set, 1953. Collections of the Wisconsin Center for Film and Theater Research.

for him. Sonja Biberman saw Chacón as a man who "exuded a certain amount of posture" and "commanded respect." Both she and Revueltas agreed that he could play the role "with great simplicity, but with real understanding of the character." The two women "pushed and pushed" until Biberman reluctantly accepted their advice. For his part, Chacón warmed to the task. He later recalled that after a halting start, it was not difficult for him to become Ramón.[14] Chacón's self-confidence became evident in the finished product, in which both lead actors communicate a striking quality of simplicity and dignity, which remain the hallmarks of *Salt of the Earth*.

While the lead roles presented the major challenge, the IPC determina-

Juan Chacón studying *Salt of the Earth* script, 1953. Collections of the Wisconsin Center for Film and Theater Research.

tion to use local people themselves in other roles meant hard work to identify prospects. As early as July 1952 Biberman had enlisted Clinton and Virginia Jencks as talent scouts for the company. He asked them to encourage the people of Local 890 to study the motion pictures as "a medium in which they will soon be involved" and he recommended that a list of candidates for speaking roles be compiled. Biberman also urged that the Ladies Auxiliary prepare for their roles, which would take courage "of a sensitive, fearless, cultural kind" if they were to "fulfill the goal toward which we are moving together." Jencks worked to recruit the supporting cast, but encountered resistance when union members objected to playing the parts of company men and deputies. Finally, after much persuasion and several community meetings, the task was accomplished; and by January most of the cast had been assembled.[15]

To coordinate the activities of IPC and Local 890, a production committee was established, composed of film company personnel and union members, including four IPC representatives and eight union and auxiliary members. This democratic procedure ensured full community participation in the production process; the committee "took up everything," including both matters of detail and "artistic decisions." The committee had "policy-making" duties and was responsible for "seeing that [the] picture ran true to life from start to finish." This active community and union participation in management decisions fostered the development of collective consciousness as the project progressed. In short, the union spirit was contagious, and it produced a strong sense of group ownership. At the December 22 meeting, Local 890 member Louis Lopez summarized the rank and file endorsement of the film in simple terms: "I think this is a great opportunity and we should grab it."[16] And once the community embraced the project, its support was firm.

The Production Process: The Union Community Makes a Film

At first, the relationship among Hollywood Anglos and Mexican-American unionists was somewhat formal, as might be expected in view of the social and cultural gap separating the collaborators. Clinton Jencks described a "feeling of awe" experienced by members of the mineworkers community when the Los Angeles sophisticates descended upon Silver City. In Paul Jarrico's words, "we arrived as men from Mars." Yet, before long, the differences receded in importance as the participants' mutual investment in the project became clearer. To Jencks, the transformation was nothing short of "amazing," as the mining community forgot that it was "supposed to be in awe of these people because of their professional status." The Hollywood "upper class types" worked with Chicana women on *all* sorts of tasks, including baby-sitting and diaper-changing. Gale Sondergaard and Sonja Biberman "showed in what they did every day how enthusiastic they were about the project." In response, the union families embraced the film and the outsiders who dwelt among them. Before long, Jarrico recalled, "we were on wonderful terms with the people whose story we were trying to tell." Local 890 union leaders were taken off the job to work full time on film production and new leaders rose to fill their shoes, leadership that was ten deep. Unionists worked "with absolute certainty" on the project, secure in the belief that the cause was important to them and to the entire union movement. It was, in the words of Mine-Mill organizer Arturo Flores, a wonderful opportunity to "tell their story of struggle against the corporation." In agreement, Jencks later described the relationship as "enthusiastic, close and intimate," one in which differences "were debated within a common vision and objective."[17]

For the women of the union community, the production process was another opportunity for growth in stature within the organization. The Ladies Auxiliary assumed major responsibility for a variety of tasks essential to the project's completion, including not only child care and food management, but also publicity, communication, and transportation. And with many women needed as actresses and extras, child care became a significant problem. Recalling the "beautiful things" that happened, Clint Jencks emphasized male insensitivity to the women's problems, at least until Sonja Biberman helped the men to see their "responsibility to provide child care," which, in turn, was important in "making the film possible." Jencks argued that the experience gained on the Empire picket line gave the Local 890 women the "confidence that they [had] a right to demand this."[18]

The child-care issue constituted an important link between two stages of women's experience in Grant County, the period of militance by necessity and that of assertiveness by right. The support of outsiders such as Sylvia Jarrico, Sonja Biberman, Gale Sondergaard, Virginia Jencks, and Frances Williams may have encouraged the Ladies Auxiliary to assert themselves more aggressively, but there was also another, more significant evolutionary process under way. Sonja Biberman later claimed that the filmmaking process facilitated a reaffirmation of prerogatives already gained during the Empire strike, in which union men and women had stepped forward to "win the struggle together." The *Salt* project, she observed, created a renewed opportunity.

> It was one of the most exciting things, and those women . . . learned not only through the strike, but even in the making of the picture; I think they re-lived, and re-affirmed their own convictions, that they had already, you know, the principles that they had set. And sort of re-enacted again, made them doubly proud of their standard. Very extraordinary women to work with there. The men, too.[19]

Not long after production began in January 1953, the enormity of the challenge to the men and women of the IPC–Mine-Mill collaborative became clearer. In January the New York CIO technician's union informed Jarrico that because of its struggle with IATSE, its crew would be unable to work on the film as originally promised. As we have seen, the CIO local feared identification with both Mine-Mill and the Hollywood blacklistees. Without a union crew, Biberman and Jarrico were forced to fall back on a nonunion Hollywood crew, which presented a "union label" problem. Clint Jencks and Local 890 president Ernesto Velásquez proposed giving the backup crew temporary IUMMSW union cards, a solution eventually adopted. While the problem had been managed, IATSE's Hollywood international representative, Roy Brewer, had shown his hand; and it was a strong one. IPC now understood that a new obstacle to its program had been introduced, the "fear of association" with the company due to the "danger of reprisal in the form of loss of work opportunity."[20] The "guilt by association" so characteristic of domestic anticommunism in Cold War America had begun to influence the *Salt* project.

Despite the momentary setback, Biberman and Jarrico remained optimistic. Much to his surprise, Biberman found the amateurs drawn from the community to be "fascinatingly and incredibly talented people" who responded to his directorial guidance "with a rapidity that belongs only to the long suppressed." The greatest shock came when Juan Chacón proved to be "just incredible," as "sensitive as a human being can be." Perhaps exaggerating, Biberman told his family that he had "never, never seen such a miracle." When the nonprofessionals were complimented on their work, some asserted that as minority workers who had often experienced punishment for open expression of their true thoughts, they had learned to act before Herbert Biberman ever entered their lives. Whatever the explanation, their honesty and authenticity was to fill the screen. By using actual participants in a dramatic re-creation of their own life experiences, Biberman worked to mold a "new synthesis of life and art."[21]

Although the work of Chacón and the local performers encouraged Biberman, he was less certain about the initial performance of the experienced Rosaura Revueltas. Carried away by Chacón's success, he thought it possible that he would "steal the show" unless Rosaura "settles down to real work." As Biberman saw his task, he had to "get her simple enough for the part." There is some evidence of tension on the set, which took the form of a "blow-off" by Revueltas. After one "big tiff," director and actress came together "on a much higher plane." As a result, Biberman came to see her "becoming more Mexican-American each day," which convinced him that "there is a chance she may rise to her proper and imposing place among them all." The conflict was a symptom of struggle for control of the set and

Herbert Biberman confers with Clinton Jencks, Juan Chacón, and other Local 890
actors on *Salt of the Earth* set, 1953. Archives, University of Colorado at Boulder
Libraries, Western Federation of Miners and International Union of Mine, Mill and
Smelter Workers Collection.

the action. Unaccustomed to the collective criticism inherent in his own
experiment, Biberman was troubled by its implications:

> For the first time in my life, I lost my authority on the set in the first
> week of shooting . . . with some of my colleagues not understanding
> what was happening and siding with others against me .`.` . . and in a
> moment when I had no assistance and was literally almost frantic. But I
> stuck it out and have now reached the kind of relationship in which my
> authority is set and in which I can add the contributions of many
> others in proper relation to my own.[22]

All things considered, the collective approach went well, and despite the unavoidable personality clashes, the community established among union families and Hollywood professionals held up under rising pressure from external sources. Two weeks into shooting, Biberman was convinced that his cast was equal to the task: "these people will come off . . . some of them brilliantly. . . . The picture will make its point." Moreover, as director, he drew great pleasure from working with the people of Grant County. In a letter to his family, Biberman expressed his view of the project, in which the self-affirming aspect of the enterprise was clear:

> The fantastic aspect of this work is that it makes so real what we have believed for so long . . . that the talents hidden in the vast majority of the world's people is monumental beyond estimation and that as it is exploded into life we will have a world beyond all the calculations of men and women. This is the inspiriting aspect of this work. This is the great reward. Surely when this picture has been completed . . . it will be they more than all others put together who will have endowed this work with its impact. That they have been helped, even, is of less importance. It is they who inherit the stored energy and spirit of countless generations . . . and who now, in a small moment of opportunity, almost unknowingly ooze out of themselves the beginning of the vast and unmeasured power and dignity of the working multitudes of this earth.[23]

When Biberman addressed Local 890 on January 21, 1953, he spoke primarily of the unity created by the film project. He later recalled that at this point, businesspeople, bankers, and tradespeople "remained cooperative and friendly." As late as February 9, according to Paul Jarrico's chronology of the film's progress, "relations with Mine-Mill brothers and sisters as well as the general community [were] excellent." The picture was on schedule and "doing fine" when "the stuff hit the fan."[24]

Obstacles: The Resistance Mounts

The first "stuff" to impede progress took the form of critical press accounts on February 9, 10, and 12, in which "Hollywood Reds" were reported to be shooting an "anti-American racial issue propaganda movie" in the New Mexico desert. The *Hollywood Reporter* noted that in response to a tipoff from a New Mexico teacher, Screen Actors Guild president Walter Pidgeon had informed HUAC, the FBI, CIO, and State Department of a grave threat to national security. One day later, *Reporter* columnist Mike Connally asserted that the "commies" film had been "ordered by John Howard Lawson, who gets his orders from the Kremlin." More detailed was the report by labor columnist Victor Riesel, which emphasized the geographic proximity of this Communist enterprise (led by "commissar" Clinton Jencks and "Tovarisch" Paul Jarrico) to the Los Alamos proving ground.

Behind the press attack was an unsolicited letter to Pidgeon from a New Mexico schoolteacher, June Kuhlman of Hurley, who expressed concern over the film because of the "supervision" of Local 890. Kuhlman also appealed to Eric Johnston, president of the Motion Picture Association of America. Certain that the result of the film project could not possibly be "good American propaganda," she declared her "love" for "these people" and refusal to "see a minority group so used." Kuhlman closed by asking the Screen Actors Guild and MPAA to advise her on "how to do [her] American duty." While the Johnston office seemed unconcerned, the Actors Guild moved quickly to exploit the situation. Her plea soon reached the desk of SAG public relations director E. T. "Buck" Harris, who after securing more information, passed the story on to Riesel, Roy Brewer, and HUAC investigator William Wheeler. Harris, who immediately saw the publicity value of an anticommunist stance, told Riesel that Hollywood leaders were "going to do what [they could] to expose this" (his first draft, later revised, had explicitly urged Riesel to "make it clear that Hollywood is fighting communism"). Thrilled with the inside information Harris had fed him, Riesel promised to break the story as soon as possible and asked for more.[25]

The result was Riesel's blistering attack on the film project, which dwelt upon the alleged threat of atomic spying, danger to the nation's vital zinc concentrate mines, and potential danger to the Korean War effort (in the person of Jencks). Speculating that the "pro-Soviet" Mine, Mill, and Smelter Workers had been "chosen" to "experiment in a new Russian-line maneuver," Riesel charged (incorrectly) that the union paid for the picture and employed the Hollywood blacklistees. Finally, he noted that the film propaganda would feature the "so-called abuse of the foreign-born in the U.S." and turn Americans into "ogres who exploit the peoples who are not all-Caucasian." Finally, Riesel obliged his Hollywood informant by nominating Pidgeon and SAG for a new kind of Oscar for their "support of democracy."[26]

One day later, Brewer weighed in with a warning from the AFL Film Council, suggesting that Mexican-Americans were being misled by Hollywood outcasts whose film was to stress police brutality against a Mexican child (a false charge). He asserted that "no motion picture made by communists can be good for America" and called on government agencies to "investigate carefully." MPIC added a vigorous denial of any connection between the legitimate movie industry and IPC or the picture, which, it insisted, had "nothing to do with Hollywood."[27]

The foregoing narrative clearly establishes the catalytic role of the Screen Actors Guild in the mobilization of *Salt*'s enemies. Close analysis reveals that from the outset, Harris seized the initiative by approaching prominent Silver City citizens to secure full details on the *Salt* project as background for an aggressive attack on the film. Among his "anti-commie contacts" were: Paul Wright and Harold Welsh (publisher and editor of the *Silver City Enterprise*), Bill Safford of the *Silver City Daily Press*, and Ward Balmer (public relations man for the Kennecott Copper Company). Harris described all his informants as "most cooperative," although Balmer demanded confidentiality because Kennecott had publicly adopted a "hands off policy" on the movie. Together, they provided extensive detail, which SAG was able to communicate to IATSE's Roy Brewer, HUAC's William Wheeler, and California congressman Donald Jackson. And in a significant observation recorded in his full memorandum on the project, Harris suggested that one "positive step" to be taken immediately would be to have the Immigration and Naturalization Service "check on" Rosaura Revueltas's citizenship status to determine if she could be charged with violation of her visitor's visa.[28]

SAG's vigorous response to events in New Mexico are best understood against the background of the escalating attack on Hollywood that had climaxed with the HUAC hearings of 1951. As a result, SAG president Ronald Reagan and executive secretary John Dales crafted a tough anticommunist stance and worked with MPIC to cleanse the movie industry's image in response to persistent allegations of Communist influence. Dales later asserted that SAG found a blacklist "unthinkable," but "reluctantly" understood why the studios could not risk employment of unrepentant ex-Communists. He remained confident that Reagan's "thinking" was "equated with the Guild's thinking." This view found expression in the SAG rank-and-file endorsement in 1953 of a bylaw barring communists from membership and requiring a non-Communist pledge from new members.[29] Within this context of close public scrutiny and MPIC's search for an industry-wide response to internal and external challenges, in February 1953 the *Salt* problem came before SAG officers and board members.

The ramifications of SAG's sensitivity on the issue of Communism and the negative publicity stemming from the press reaction to the *Salt* project

were serious—and immediate. Once Walter Pidgeon had asked for a federal investigation, IPC's technical support from Hollywood firms evaporated. Pathe Laboratories halted work on film developing and Studio
Sound refused to continue processing sound tape. The loss of technical
services created major problems, since no other labs were willing to take
work from IPC. And the local repercussions of these attacks complicated
community relations in Bayard and Silver City. On February 15, Jencks
reported to the International that work on *Salt* had proceeded well, with
local members "pitching in on a serious job" until "the witch-hunters broke
lose." The press had been uninterested "until they had something to attack." Local theaters, businesses, and financial institutions were no longer
willing to cooperate with the company, especially after the *Silver City Daily
Press* asserted that it was "time to choose sides." The sweeping attack on
IPC confirms Biberman's later assertion that the filmmakers "never had
one day of normality in the entire course of making the film."[30]

In the face of mounting community pressure, the men and women of
Local 890 closed ranks behind the film project. The "movie mobilization"
was an important topic at a February 18 union meeting. At that time, Joe T.
Morales took the floor to question the "Red-baiting of the picture," while
Angel Bustos used the occasion to attack the "reactionaries and the Taft
Hartley [bill]." After E. S. Conerly reminded the angry group of "the way
that this picture is working through people," Michael Wilson rose to thank
the union for its continued backing. To Jencks, the union community's
steadfast support was explainable in terms of the film's place in the Chicano
struggle and the women's new consciousness. He later maintained that *Salt*
was a "peak of struggle" that brought people together in a way that was
"beautiful." Similarly, Sonja Biberman remembered that once the IPC
group became a "menace," the Mexican-Americans they had worked with
"were just fantastic." It was they, she noted, who after IPC left Bayard,
"would still be in the midst of all this kind of confrontation"; this, she
concluded, was "where the Johnny Chacóns really show[ed] their mettle . . .
they [were] brave people."[31]

This inner strength was to be sorely tested in the coming months, during
which official harassment and informal pressures escalated. Most dramatic
was California Republican congressman Donald Jackson's frontal assault
against IPC on the floor of the House of Representatives, in which he
charged that a film being made "under Communist auspices" was part of an
attempt to undermine the American war effort in Korea. In a widely publicized speech on February 24, 1953, Jackson, an active HUAC member, repeated many of the false allegations about the film, including the assertion

May 1953 25c

THE VOICE OF THE NEW WEST

frontier

CONGRESSMAN DONALD L. JACKSON
He sniffed a plot.

SILVER CITY

Who Caused the Trouble?—By ELIZABETH KERBY

Frontier magazine explores California congressman Donald L. Jackson's charges of Communist influence in the filming of *Salt of the Earth,* May 1953. Collections of the Wisconsin Center for Film and Theater Research.

that it promoted race hatred and subverted national security. Moreover, he insisted that the picture included exaggerated portrayals of police violence against the worker community. Jackson promised to "do everything in [his] power to prevent the showing of this Communist-made film in the theaters of America."[32] Within the context of the overheated anticommunist fervor of the anxious 1950s, his threat was not to be taken lightly.

Jackson's words drew immediate and enthusiastic support from Buck Harris, who commended the congressman for an "excellent speech" and noted the "splendid coverage" it had received. Harris's reaction mirrored the views of the SAG board, which had encouraged Jackson to take a public stand on the issue. All in all, the Guild took pride in the results of its campaign to expose the Red menace in the New Mexico desert. On February 17, Harris informed Riesel that there had been a "most effective follow-up" to his column and that national news magazines would soon join in the exposé. At this point, SAG president Walter Pidgeon sent his personal thanks to schoolteacher Jane Kuhlmann in New Mexico, assuring her that her "alertness" had ensured that steps had been taken to "protect the interests of our nation."[33]

Not all observers shared SAG's opinion. In response to a contact from Biberman, the American Civil Liberties Union warned Jackson that his demand for a ban on the film's exhibition contained "the seeds of censorship," and was therefore "inconsistent with the democratic right of free speech." ACLU called on Jackson to clarify his statement to remove any suggestion that the government "act as censor." Prompted by IPC's Adrian Scott, who urged a "counterattack," Jarrico issued a public statement branding Jackson "an unmitigated liar" and challenging him to remove his "cloak of Congressional immunity and fight like a man." He also insisted that the film, which portrayed Mexican-Americans and Anglos working together, would "serve as a good ambassador for the United States."[34]

Challenged to defend his position, Jackson brushed off the ACLU complaint by insisting that his words were not to be construed as an endorsement of censorship. As evidence, he cited his statement in a constituent newsletter claiming that he was "not prejudging the content matter," but merely "labeling the supporters." HUAC, he told ACLU's Elmer Rice, should not "appear in the role of a censor."[35]

These assurances were in fact meaningless, since Jackson had already launched his own back-door assault on the film project. As a follow-up to his speech, Jackson urged the State, Commerce, and Justice departments to explore any means to ban the film's export, as well as the possibility of prosecutions under the alien agents registration law. New Mexico Democratic senator Clinton P. Anderson joined in this effort with an appeal to Assistant Secretary of State Thruston B. Morton for some legal maneuver to prevent overseas exhibition of a film containing such a "distorted and untrue picture of life in this country." Jackson also asked the AFL Film Council and the major studios for their suggestions for measures that might prevent the film's completion and distribution. In response, Brewer pledged to use union ties to prevent *Salt*'s exhibition in the United States, while Morton proposed further discussion of export control. Even more threatening was the reaction of film mogul Howard Hughes, who outlined in meticulous detail the steps that could be taken to kill the film during the postproduction process:

> If the picture industry was to prevent this motion picture from being completed and spread all over the world as a representative product of the United States, then the industry . . . need only do the following:
>
> Be alert to the situation. Investigate thoroughly each applicant for the use of services or equipment.
>
> Refuse to assist the Bibermans and Jarricos in the making of this picture.
>
> Be on guard against work submitted by dummy corporations or third parties.
>
> Appeal to the Congress and the State Department to act immediately to prevent the export of this film to Mexico or anywhere else.[36]

The carefully crafted Hughes letter was a blueprint for suppression. As Jarrico later noted, the struggling company encountered trouble at every step mentioned in the Hughes plan, which "spelled out the procedure" to prevent the film's completion and distribution.[37]

But before processing had even begun, the government moved to intervene. Not long after Jackson's first speech in Congress, two Immigration Service officers arrested lead actress Rosaura Revueltas on questionable charges of failure to have her passport stamped on entry (a government error). Revueltas concluded that she was seen as "dangerous" because she had played a role "that gave stature and dignity to the character of a Mexican-American woman." In fact, SAG's Buck Harris had suggested her detention as a means of halting production. Her incarceration prevented

her from completing the picture as planned, and when on-location shooting was finished, she remained in custody. After lawyer Ben Margolis filed a
writ of habeas corpus to secure her release, the courts in El Paso stalled for
time, valuable time in which Revueltas was prevented from completing her
work. To Margolis, "it was obvious that they were playing games with us."
While the case "was just a made-up case" with "no substance to it," the
government's legal ploy served its purpose by erecting one more barrier to
effective filmmaking. Once the company finished shooting, Revueltas accepted voluntary deportation, there being no reason for her to remain in
New Mexico. But she did not go quietly. At a press conference, Revueltas
vowed to complete the film and predicted that "this film is going to make
history."[38]

The actress's arrest further enflamed public opinion in the Silver City
area, where the press linked her predicament with Jackson's speech. The
congressman's attack on IPC, portions of which were repeatedly broadcast
on local radio, stimulated popular resistance to the film project. In this
"super-heated" atmosphere, a vigilante movement began to coalesce under
the leadership of the self-styled "Central Protective Committee," which
ended in several acts of violence and incendiarism against union property,
union people, and filmmakers. On March 3, encouraged by the local press,
the vigilante groups assaulted Jencks and union officer Floyd Bostick and
warned the IPC staff and crew to leave town "or be carried out in black
boxes." Three days later, Bostick's home and the union hall in Carlsbad
burned to the ground. Despite the escalating violence, the Justice Department's Civil Rights Division concluded that "no substantive or other civil
rights violation [had] occurred" that would "warrant prosecutive or inves-
tigative action." Local 890 fought back, asserting that negative press coverage of the film project was no surprise. Union leaders insisted that "the
movie will do a better job of telling the truth about us than they do of lying
about us." A union broadside issued a challenge to the hostile press: "Fire
Away. We Can Take It!" Despite the viciousness of the attacks prompted by
the *Salt* project, union members were proud of the result, which, in Jencks'
words, represented a "peak of struggle" on the road to the construction of a
"fully human kind of society, a socialist kind of society." Union members,
their families, and Hollywood's "cultural workers" had shared briefly in a
meaningful experiment in collective action. The result was the development of mutual respect and understanding among people of very different
backgrounds, who joined to create a work of art that all believed would
advance the cause of working people everywhere. Jencks later found mean-

ing in their group effort to "break out of . . . isolation" by trying to "link up with other people," which was the "main reason we wanted to make the film." The union community was "reaching out . . . and we found people that were willing to help us. . . . And that was beautiful."[39]

The escalating attack on the union's role in making the film stimulated a visible growth of Mexican-American assertiveness and pride. When local vigilantes held a meeting intended to force IPC out of the area, Local 890 countered with its own emergency meeting so unionists might defy the "Ku Klux Klan goons" and "bring this county back to sanity." At the union gathering, angry participants passed a resolution "to back up the union in its fight to produce this picture." Moreover, Amalgamated Local 890 threatened a larger walkout against Kennecott and other area companies to underscore widespread mineworker endorsement of the *Salt* project and Mine-Mill's right to support it. Yet one New Mexico FBI operative reported local concern because the union allegedly "played up" the "issue of racial dissension," which further agitated the "towns people."[40] While exacerbated by the *Salt* controversy, the racial conflict was in fact the product of historical patterns of tense race relations reinforced by political and economic inequality. Hence, union support for the *Salt* project reflected the rise of ethnic self-consciousness in Grant County—a development whose time had come.

While enthusiasm for *Salt of the Earth* ran deepest among the union families of Local 890, the International also expressed satisfaction at its completion. Understating the resistance in Bayard, *Mine-Mill Union* claimed that only a "tiny minority" had interfered with production, but nonetheless acknowledged that state police (sent after an appeal to Governor Edwin Mecham by Craig Vincent) had been needed to provide protection in the final days of shooting. Concerned about internal dissatisfaction, International secretary Maurice Travis assured all locals that "not one thin dime of our union's money is being used on this production" and defended Mine-Mill sponsorship as a way to offer needed intellectual content and variety to the nation's movie fare. More to the point, Travis explained the attack on the film in terms of management's reluctance to "have the world . . . know that their foremen and deputies do take out their sadistic hatred on the men, women, and kids, mostly of Mexican-American origin, who fight for their bread and butter." Similarly, Mine-Mill publicity man Morris Wright saw the film as evidence of "a new understanding of what it means to be a worker, what it means to have a union." IUMMSW also expressed pride in the film as a means of advancing a sense of solidarity that crossed racial lines; within Mine-Mill, "Mexican-American and Anglo brothers and sisters worked together and fought together" in the struggle against Empire Zinc, "one of the most viciously anti-labor companies in America."[41]

The links forged in this moment of crisis also promised to promote international awareness of the need for worker solidarity. Mexican-American laborers in the Southwest were incensed over the affront to Mexican national Rosaura Revueltas. Symptomatic of their attitude was a *Progreso* editorial in which ANMA cited the Revueltas case as the "most brazen and shameful in the annals of inter-American relations." Moreover, before her deportation, the Mexican National Association of Actors demanded her immediate release and appealed to the Hollywood Screen Actors Guild to intervene. Led by film idol Jorge Negrete, the Mexican guild expressed "deep indignation" over the entire incident and threatened to retaliate against American movie stars then working in Mexico. Similarly, Mexican film workers expressed concern over the issue and considered a strike to dramatize their concern. And upon return from an Inter-American Conference of Mining, Metal, and Machine Workers in Mexico City, ANMA's Alfredo Montoya reported to Travis on "indignation and resentment over the Revueltas case in all quarters and classes." Distressed over the "isolation of U.S. unions from Latin American Unions," Montoya suggested that ties could be strengthened through cooperation on "such a strongly felt issue as the Revueltas detention." Meanwhile, in the United States, Local 890 sent Joe T. Morales to Washington to appeal for her return to New Mexico, as well as better protection for the local. Morales lobbied New Mexico's congressmen, while the International appealed to NAACP and the state government in Santa Fe for help. All protests fell on deaf ears, however, and the deportation went forward.[42]

When the Mexican actors' union appeal reached the SAG board in Hollywood, no help was forthcoming. Indeed, Executive Secretary John Dales told the Mexican union that the case was a matter for their respective governments to resolve. Dales also adopted the official industry and IATSE position that IPC was a nonunion company, which provided justification for SAG inaction to aid a fellow actor. After a full report on the *Salt* project, the Guild board concluded that the film was "apparently completely un-American propaganda." When sanctions against participating actors were discussed, board member Ronald Reagan asserted that SAG had done more than any other American union to eliminate Communists and that, therefore, it should not "dignify the status of such people by taking punitive measures against them." While no further action was taken on *Salt* cast members, SAG did create an informal committee to investigate the "situa-

tion concerning members accused or suspected of subversive activities" and
to make recommendations to the Board on the question of discipline.[43]
Thus, the results of SAG's deliberations were no more promising for American actors than for the ill-fated Rosaura Revueltas.

Not long after the humiliation and deportation of Rosaura Revueltas,
official persecution of the *Salt* circle took another turn with a legislative
inquiry into the business enterprises and political opinions of IPC president
Simon M. Lazarus. From the earliest stages of the controversy, HUAC,
INS, and the State and Commerce departments had been keenly interested
in the financing of the film. Now HUAC, in response to a suggestion from
SAG's Buck Harris, turned up the heat by compelling Lazarus to testify in
Los Angeles on his involvement with the company. Acknowledging his role
in the *Salt* project, Lazarus proudly disclosed his association with the picture. Prior to his testimony, he issued a sizzling press release criticizing
HUAC for its attack on free enterprise through "Congressional investigation and censorship." While refusing to reveal his political affiliation to the
committee, he disclosed to the press his lifelong membership in the Democratic Party. Lazarus went on to lecture HUAC on the protections afforded
by the Constitution and the Bill of Rights:

> A motion picture is a most public document. It is meant for the public
> and the public has its constitutional rights and its human rights to
> receive it or reject it. To interfere with this honored American process
> is not merely unconstitutional but is an insult to the intelligence and
> patriotism of the people themselves. I will not join in any attack upon
> the competence and intelligence and the patriotism of the American
> people.[44]

HUAC's keen interest in Lazarus reflected government determination to
trace funding for *Salt* to external sources and the hope that foreign investment could be identified. In his testimony, he had refused to identify investors in the company and declined to indicate whether the Communist Party
had provided any financial backing for *Salt*. Similarly, he repeated the assertion that Mine-Mill had not funded film production. And despite all the
sound and fury, the committee found no evidence that foreign capital or
"Moscow gold" had supported IPC or *Salt*. A frustrated assistant attorney
general Warren Olney pointedly reminded J. Edgar Hoover that if foreign
funds could be identified, prosecution under the Foreign Agents Registration Act of 1938 would be possible. In view of that option, Olney encouraged the FBI watchdogs to "determine the source of funds being used by

the subject [IPC] and the union in the movie project" as well as the existence of any "arrangement or understanding" with a "foreign government, organization, or individual."[45] Try as they might, however, *Salt's* critics were unable to establish the hoped-for foreign linkages that would have enabled the government to move more aggressively against the film.

While the government was somewhat bound by legal restrictions, IATSE enjoyed more freedom to maneuver in opposition to the *Salt* project. Since the completion of shooting merely ended the first phase of film production, other avenues of resistance were open to Brewer, the IA, and the studio interests with whom he was increasingly identified. Brewer later argued that as a "labor man," he "didn't want the American working man and the labor movement associated with the movie's view of . . . racism against Mexican workers" because the film would "foment anti-American feelings in Latin America." In 1953, however, he also accepted anticommunist screenwriter Martin Berkeley's idea that the Communist Party had adopted a new party line calling for "the development of forms through which labor (meaning . Communists) can exert a unified class influence on the Democratic Party." At a major Hollywood AFL Film Council meeting in late February, chaired by Brewer, Berkeley told the assembled unionists that they must avoid alliances with "so-called progressive groups and caucuses." Labor had a responsibility to "purge itself of subversives" and watch for "innocent-seeming activity on behalf of minority groups."[46] The Spring issue of *IATSE Bulletin*, which appeared shortly after the disruptions in Silver City, prominently featured the Brewer-Berkeley warning.

Persuaded that *Salt* was "an effort by our enemy" to discredit the United States in Latin America by asserting that white workers were "treated differently than Mexican-American workers," Brewer mobilized IATSE's Hollywood affiliates for resistance. IATSE had "refused to participate in making the film," Brewer insisted, because experience had taught that "the kind of film they would make would not help the labor movement." Although Brewer later implied that the refusal to service the film in the processing stage was spontaneous, the written record confirms his active initiative in the effort to kill the film by disrupting production. For example, after a Mexican trip, Brewer informed the Film Council that Luis Sanchez-Tello, head of the Mexican film workers' unions, promised that the film "would not be serviced or processed below the border." And in the United States, a Brewer poll of the Hollywood business agents revealed that no work was being done on *Salt* in Hollywood, "nor by Hollywood persons except for those who have been involved in pro-Communist activities."[47]

Pressure tactics were only one part of the IA campaign against *Salt*. More subtle was Brewer's decision quietly to permit some AFL craft workers to work on the picture. In May 1953, IPC hired Barton (Bud) Hayes as chief editor, thereby adding a bona fide IATSE member to the team. What Biberman and Jarrico did not know was that Hayes was reporting regularly to Brewer and the FBI. With IA approval, Hayes worked on the film for two months in order to maintain a check on what Brewer termed "Red-tainted activities" relating to the film's production. As a result of his inside work, the FBI was able to closely monitor all phases of film processing during the months of May, June, and July 1953.[48]

On July 21, 1953, Brewer urged Hollywood guild and union members to refuse to work for or with any persons connected with *Salt of the Earth*. His statement also solicited corporate cooperation with the AFL Film Council in halting production on "one of the most anti-American documentaries ever attempted." Why did Brewer go public at this point? An important factor was the Film Council's awareness of color work then underway outside Hollywood, where the film and the controversy were less well known to laboratory operators. In response, Jarrico denounced the "illegal conspiracy" that had finally "come out in the open," vowing that Brewer would "live to regret his part in that conspiracy." IPC followed up, on July 28, with written requests for service to Los Angeles area laboratories, which produced either negative responses or silence. Pathe Laboratories, Consolidated Film Services, and Sound Services all refused to process the film at this time. Simultaneously, Jarrico demanded that Brewer issue a statement to AFL Film Council guilds and unions, Hollywood organizations, and corporations, assuring them that there would be no council reprisal, intimidation, or discrimination against firms supplying services to IPC.[49]

Despite IPC's strong response to Brewer's escalation of the struggle, the reaction was not encouraging. On legal advice, Brewer advised locals to ignore Jarrico's letter, which according to IATSE lawyer Michael Luddy, would prevent Jarrico from distorting a reply "in typical Communist fashion" for "propaganda purposes." The practical result was that Jarrico and Biberman confronted major obstacles in the finishing process because the laboratories continued to deny them crucial technical services. As a consequence, postproduction work on *Salt* that normally took three or four months was not complete for nearly a year. Not surprisingly, IATSE drew praise from its ally, Congressman Donald Jackson, who in August 1953 pronounced the American motion picture industry the "cleanest in the world." Speaking before the AFL Film Council, Jackson credited Brewer and other labor leaders with "playing a key role in the fight against the Red menace."[50]

Brewer's rapid ascent to power was capped by his installation in June 1953 as president of the aggressively anticommunist Motion Picture Alliance for the Preservation of American Ideals. At a "spiritedly patriotic meeting of film notables," he drew "repeated cheers" as he attacked Communism and emphasized MPA's "important and responsible position" in the crusade against the Red menace. Brewer believed that there was reason for great optimism in view of the progress already made. As early as March 1953 he had told IATSE president Richard Walsh that the "forces of Communism" had been "pretty well broken in [the movie] industry." In Brewer's view, it was "the strength of [IATSE] which . . . brought about this victory."[51]

Despite the plaudits, an internal squabble was developing within the IATSE power structure. Roy Brewer's new prominence came at an opportune moment in view of his plan to challenge incumbent Richard Walsh for the IATSE presidency in 1954. By the end of 1953 the dominant figure in Hollywood unionism and a leading force in motion picture industry circles, Brewer now began to assail Walsh for alleged softness on Communism, as well as his unwillingness to allow the Los Angeles locals sufficient autonomy. The International union's record of support for the AFL Film Council's stance on *Salt* was clear; but even though Walsh agreed that the film was subversive, Brewer asserted that he "wasn't strong enough" on the issue of Communism and made opposition to domestic Communism a key plank in his election campaign. And while Walsh would beat back the challenge in 1954, the additional pressure exerted by Brewer's charge shaped the IATSE response to *Salt*, especially during the abortive effort to ensure wide distribution after the film's release.[52] While the scope of the boycott to come could not have been imagined, the blueprint for suppression had been outlined by summer 1953, when the technicians' response to the escalating *Salt* controversy became clear. With the battle lines clearly drawn, the *Salt* group prepared for the final stage in the creative process.

FIVE

Preparing for Battle

Planning for Distribution

With shooting complete and processing under way, Wilson, Biberman, and Jarrico next turned to the task of converting raw material into finished product. It was at this final stage of the production process that the film's political content became an issue within Communist Party circles. Although the party was eventually to embrace *Salt of the Earth*, strong evidence suggests that CP influence did not determine the shape of the final product. Paul Jarrico later recalled that the IPC circle "did not have the full support of the Party in making the film." As previously noted, the CP chose to back a New York union's refusal to supply a crew for *Salt* because the party made the organization's merger with IATSE its first priority, a move which made Jarrico and Biberman "furious."[1]

More significant was the battle over content and interpretation that pitted Wilson and Jarrico against the Communist Party's Hollywood intellectual leader, John Howard Lawson. To Lawson, film was "ideology," a weapon in the "battle of ideas." Like Jarrico, Wilson, and Biberman, Lawson saw cinema, as well as other artistic and literary forms, as a tool for the promotion of social change. As the Hollywood party's ideological leader, he had exercised substantial influence over left-wing screenwriters in the years before his incarceration in 1950 as one of the Hollywood Ten. By most accounts, Lawson, while brilliant, tended to be egotistic and dogmatic in his insistence on reviewing the work of his party comrades. In screenwriter Albert Maltz's words, it was "expected that you would show your work to Jack." Maltz acknowledged Lawson's helpfulness, but expressed reservations about the way in which CP members accorded him a level of respect that "amounted almost to awe and subservience." To Maltz, this deference "worked itself into a most terrible kind of censorship."[2]

Although Lawson's influence within the Hollywood party had been somewhat diluted since his prison term, lingering respect for his intellectual powers and political instincts led Wilson, Jarrico, and Biberman to consult him during the filmmaking process. Lawson read and commented on, first, the script and, later, the rough-cut film. Although by his own admission, he was "not closely associated with the film," as the party's leading West Coast intellectual, Lawson was taken seriously by the film's creators. In fact, after his incarceration, party leadership "passed into other hands," as noted by Jarrico, who succeeded him as Hollywood section chairman. In the final analysis, Lawson's complaints, which were substantial, constituted what Jarrico termed "just another obstacle" to be surpassed.[3] Jarrico's comment fails to convey the serious consideration given to Lawson's criticisms before they were finally dismissed; it is clear that the filmmakers labored mightily to strengthen the film in response to his critique.

Lawson's analysis began with a disclaimer. He prefaced his remarks with an assurance that the picture was a "very positive, beautiful, and exciting achievement" certain to be "respected by progressive people here and abroad" and to make a "considerable impact" on the ongoing "struggle in [the] film field." Because of Salt's promise, its creators deserved "enormous credit" for not only their artistic accomplishment, but also their "tenacity" and "courage" in overcoming adversity. From Lawson's perspective, any criticism was to be understood within a "positive frame of reference."[4]

While Lawson admired the filmmakers' achievement, he decried "sectarianism" in their work. By focusing on the Mexican-American struggle, he argued, the basic "unity of all workers" and "solidarity of the whole labor movement" had been missed. To Lawson, there had been too little emphasis on the International union's role and the significance of the strike itself. While the film made a "major contribution to a people's culture in the United States," more attention to the relationship between the Anglo organizer, Frank Barnes, and Ramón was required. While the "woman question" and the class struggle were verbalized, the action and conflict failed to develop those issues. Finally, Esperanza's narration tended to reinforce a "sectarian feeling" rather than allow the audience to "participate in the events and grow in understanding with the people in the film."[5]

Beyond sectarianism, Lawson expressed concern over a second major problem, the scene depicting a quarrel between Ramón and Esperanza, followed by a scene in which Ramón goes hunting with his male coworkers. Together, he insisted, these scenes suggested that the couple had not "learned in struggle" from "what [had] occurred." While Esperanza expressed her "new sense of dignity" and the importance of the women's "essential role in the strike," Ramón's response was to threaten a slap and retreat to the hunt. Lawson maintained that these scenes reflected "white chauvinism" by suggesting that Mexican-Americans were "likely to treat women with physical brutality." This "obligatory scene" led directly to the Quintero family's eviction and community resistance to it, but as the movement was structured only the peoples' gathering to fight the company's action responds to Ramón's quarrel with Esperanza and desertion of the strike. The quarrel, Lawson went on,

> undermines their relationship, and leaves us with a feeling of distaste and unpleasantness. This is especially the case since audiences, even · working class audiences, have little understanding of woman's role, and will tend to regard the scene as puzzlingly bitter. To say that this scene adds considerably to the "sectarian" quality of the whole work may seem like a rather subtle interpretation; nonetheless, I feel that the quarrel seems like the author's commentary on the woman question, and that its juxtaposition with the hunt and the eviction seem like an attempt to force a 'message' which is not realized in emotional terms. It tends to break emotional contact with the audience, cutting their feeling of sympathy with the two people.[6]

Lawson sent this critique because, in his view, it was essential that Wilson and Jarrico "know something of the political and artistic questions around this work." He lauded the film's "pictorial beauty" and "wonderful"[7] characters, but made it clear that changes were in order.

Given an opportunity to respond to Lawson's criticisms, Wilson, Biberman, and Jarrico disputed the charge of sectarianism as a "sweeping and curious formulation." The strike, the Mexican-American struggle, and the woman question, all integrated into the picture, were "advanced stuff" characteristic of a "vanguard work." The filmmakers maintained that the "basic content and viewpoint" of their work could not be altered because they were "embedded in the script that was approved and shot." Changes could be made, but they insisted that it was "valid and necessary" to "deal with specific aspects of the class struggle involving special types of oppression and divisive maneuvers" so long as the "general struggle is helped to be clarified." This, they argued, their work achieved.[8]

While firm on the first criticism, the filmmakers saw some value in Lawson's suggestions with regard to the "obligatory scene." Recognizing the

Juan Chacón as Ramón Quintero threatens violence against Esperanza (Rosaura Revueltas). Publicity still, *Salt of the Earth*, ca. 1954. Collections of the Wisconsin Center for Film and Theater Research.

dramaturgic need for motivation behind Ramón's departure and return, they considered the possibility that there were "overtones of white chauvinism" in the film's structure. One solution was to have Ramón "visibly" change by "some marked thing that he says or does which might indicate that he has thought the thing through." Rejecting Lawson's proposed scene-switching solution, the filmmakers insisted that the scene as it stood brought "all the elements in conflict to one crucial point and catapults them into final action." Wilson, Jarrico, and Biberman thought the conflict and quarrel essential to an explication of the "disastrous effect of male supremacy" in the final scenes. Without it, nothing was "at stake in human terms." If all that remained in the conclusion was a victory over the enemy in the strike, the picture would "veer sharply toward agit-prop mechanistic drama." The filmmakers flatly rejected Lawson's overall view of the "obligatory scene":

> We do not find Esperanza's passionate outburst acrimonious or arbitrary, and the essential point is that she could not have said this at any earlier point in her development; as for Ramon, he is not only demoralized by an overestimation of the power of the enemy, but simultaneously disturbed by the shattering of his old concepts of family life and relationships. Her words strike home because they are there, but he cannot yet accept them. In his anguish, he can only run away. We do not think that our audiences will find this "puzzlingly bitter." We feel they will find this human frailty as real as their own experience, and their censure of him will be coupled with understanding and identification.[9]

The length of this rebuttal (seven pages) reflected a clear awareness of Lawson's standing as Communist Party ideologue in Hollywood, as well as the knowledge that the disagreement was to be aired in party circles. Its authors expressed a willingness to make modest revisions in the film, so long as the changes did not evade problems by making "structural revisions of a picture already filmed." Put more simply by Lawson, "my view of the film was strongly opposed by the director and his associates." Jarrico agreed that Lawson's "very critical" remarks were "finally just disregarded."[10]

Criticisms aside, Lawson later warmed to the film in its final form, which he wrote and spoke of "very highly." Even while urging revisions, he proposed that a major party publicity campaign be mounted to develop "mass support" for *Salt*. Alarmed by IPC's financial problems, Lawson recommended a nationwide effort to sell the recently published *California Quarterly* version of the script, with special emphasis on trade-union sales in the East. Not only would such a campaign raise funds for the beleaguered company, but it could also promote the wide distribution of the completed film. Anticipating resistance to its exhibition, Lawson proposed a campaign for the "right to distribute and exhibit the film" based less on the picture's merits than on the "right of people to judge for themselves." He called for an attack on McCarthyism that would remind Americans that "the drive to burn books is linked inevitably to the drive to burn film." In this way, political, cultural, and union leaders who might have questions about the film could rally around a "struggle for the right of its creators to produce it

Will Geer as sheriff. Publicity still, *Salt of the Earth*, ca. 1954. Courtesy of Jenny Vincent.

and the right of audiences to see and judge it for themselves."[11] Lawson's promotional ideas were not included in Wilson's copy of the critique, though they appear as a two-page addition to the draft in Lawson's personal files. It is clear that these recommendations were shared with a wider audience, very likely Hollywood CP leaders.

The outcome of this exchange was a reaffirmation of Wilson's screenplay, Biberman's judgment, and Jarrico's response to frustration. The final print retained a focus on Esperanza's personal struggle for dignity and her stormy yet ultimately rewarding relationship with Ramón. Moreover, the film's structure did not change significantly from that contained in the rough cut. Despite Lawson's carping criticism, the film succeeds in emphasizing human equality and worker unity within the context of class struggle. By listening patiently to Lawson's advice and making minor adjustments, the key filmmakers demonstrated their sensitivity to the party's concern for the primacy of class conflict and heroic struggle in political art; however, the

Local 890 children in jail scene. At left, Willie Andazola; at right, Gary Alderette. Publicity still, *Salt of the Earth*, ca. 1954. Collections of the Wisconsin Center for Film and Theater Research.

eventual decision to dismiss Lawson's central criticisms confirms their retention of artistic control of their own work. The *Salt* circle created a cinematic product that confirmed their mutual faith in art as a political weapon and marked a breakthrough in the motion picture industry's depiction of both the Mexican-American struggle for equality and women's quest for dignity and status. In 1977, Michael Wilson asserted that "We were all political — the film came out of our political beliefs." This does not mean that their work was party propaganda. Yet the film's success as politicized art was implicit in the reaction of the Soviet vice minister of culture, who, in 1959, told Jarrico that when people asked him "the meaning of socialist realism," his response was invariably: "See *Salt of the Earth*."[12]

Not all observers shared this enthusiasm. To others, the film was no more than a propagandistic replication of the Soviet party line. A commonly used analytic device was to establish "parallelism" between the Communist Party line and the film's dominant themes and to therefore conclude that Communist Party influence had shaped the final product. Typical of this approach was an FBI report, filed at Albuquerque in March 1953, which drew laborious and elaborate parallels between the film's themes and recent pronouncements in CP publications. The FBI analyst noted that IUMMSW public relations director Morris Wright had emphasized the film's attempt to deal with "the union's struggle for safety in the mines" and the "advance of the Mexican-American people toward equality," coupled with the "acceptance of women by their men as partners in personal and union struggle." Moreover, he added, Jencks and Jarrico had reported the remarkable discovery that "southeastern New Mexico has a large group of people who have been treated as second-class citizens and who have fought and are winning their battle for first-class citizenship." This observation, according to the FBI watchdog, resembled the Communist Party's view that "labor solidarity and unity must be fought for daily, not just on special occasions." This conviction, he insisted, represented the "very heart and soul of Communist and Progressive trade union work." Worse yet, communists argued that the Mexican people were oppressed by imperialism in a special way, "as both workers and as members of a racial minority." And finally, there was "a male supremacist wall" that female comrades "must break through before they can become a cadre." To the FBI analysts, this emphasis on the need for male cooperation with women and sensitivity to the special problems they faced confirmed linkage between party ideology and the themes explicated in *Salt*. In short, the FBI applied the same reasoning to *Salt* that CIO Red-baiters had used in evaluating the policies and practices of the left-led unions in 1949 and 1950.[13] The conclusion was no more valid in 1953 than it had been earlier, but by the mid-1950s the simplistic equation of policy similarities with response to external influence was not unusual, in view of the anticommunist consensus of the domestic Cold War.

But to Mexican-American unionists, the film had an alternative meaning. *Salt of the Earth* was for Local 890 a public declaration of independence. President Juan Chacón asserted that the union had as much right to make a film as did any producer. By sponsoring the film and making the picture, the union had "shown again that no attacks or falsehoods could break [their] union spirit." Chacón argued that mine management and the major Hollywood producers had a common interest in perpetuating "the big lie

Henrietta Williams as Teresa Vidal, addressing union meeting. Publicity still, *Salt of the Earth*, ca. 1954. Collections of the Wisconsin Center for Film and Theater Research.

about people." To Chacón, freedom of the screen for ordinary people to tell their stories in dramatic form would destroy the walls between people: "*Salt of the Earth* [was their] attempt to break through." In agreement with this analysis, Mine-Mill's Morris Wright reported that the Local 890 membership endorsed the film's truth-telling and refused to be silenced.[14]

Biberman's old friend, screenwriter Albert Maltz of the Hollywood Ten, applauded IPC's achievement as an act of perverse idealism. Biberman, he wrote, had made a film in "a damn town no one ever heard of, about people no one ever heard about," thus ignoring "the things that count" in safe, middle-class America. To Maltz, *Salt* was a "monumental achievement," which brought great pride to Biberman's colleagues on the Left. It was a

Esperanza's saint's day celebration. Publicity still, *Salt of the Earth*, ca. 1954. Archives, University of Colorado at Boulder Libraries, Western Federation of Miners
and International Union of Mine, Mill and Smelter Workers Collection.

motion picture "born from a concept of struggle, made in struggle, and to
be released only through struggle."[15]

Concerning the last point Maltz was on target. Like Lawson, he did not
underestimate the power of the movie industry establishment to control
the entertainment fare available to the American public. By summer, Hollywood's Left intellectuals were turning their attention to plans for a coun-
teroffensive against those who hoped to limit freedom of the screen. At the
heart of this campaign, as Lawson had counseled, was the mass distribution
of the summer issue of *California Quarterly*, which had been devoted to
commentary on the making of *Salt* as well as the reprinted script. *California
Quarterly*, a literary magazine edited by blacklisted screenwriter Philip Ste-
venson, was intended to provide a forum for radical artists whose work fell
victim to censorship in the mainstream media. Designed to reconstruct a
Popular Front coalition, the publication of the *Salt* script set off a lively

debate not only over the merits of the film, but also the viewing public's right to judge the work.[16]

California Quarterly understood the volatility of the controversy it had entered. The advance advertising cover used to promote the issue informed potential readers that they were "holding the cover of the hottest issue in the U.S.A. . . . the issue of free speech." Through *California Quarterly*, the script was widely disseminated in July and August 1953. Biberman hoped that, in this way, the film project itself would win the sympathies of "representative people" nationwide and "rally positive support for its exhibition." And, as Jarrico later noted, the distribution campaign did produce many favorable reactions. Among the magazine's most avid readers, however, were the Los Angeles FBI monitors, who compiled a full clippings file detailing the response to the mass distribution campaign.[17]

In their essay for the *California Quarterly*, Jarrico and Biberman acknowledged that the harassment would continue for the foreseeable future, which made it imperative that allies join them in the effort to "defeat the censors and saboteurs." To reach their supporters and the wider public, they appealed to those "morally concerned with free communication" for help in creating an atmosphere in which *Salt of the Earth* could be judged on its merits. *Hollywood Review*, voice of the leftist California chapter of the Council of Arts, Sciences, and Professions (ASP), urged readers to examine the script and decide whether the film was "dangerously un-American or profoundly democratic." The *Review* asked that serious questions be considered:

> Does a trade union have a right to make a movie telling its own story? Can a congressman tell his constituents and the general public what movies they may or may not see? Can a minority group, in this case Mexican-Americans, traditionally caricatured by Hollywood films, use motion pictures of their own making to present their own people with dignity and understanding? Can women be presented with dignity and respect without benefit of congressional permission? Can artists blacklisted by Hollywood seek their living by helping working people, as they did in this case, to tell the real stories of American life that Hollywood does not choose to tell?[18]

The responses varied. Longtime friend and ally Dalton Trumbo, firmly ensconced in his Mexican villa, was thrilled by the script, which he regarded as both "progressive" and a "brilliant example of screen craftsmanship." Because the screenplay honored oppressed peoples by "presenting them truly," official Hollywood was not likely to thank IPC for its contribution. Trumbo predicted resistance "straight down the line to prevent the release of [the] picture." But he also forecast eventual success because the evils of the blacklist "left you [the filmmakers] a clear monopoly of all that is decent in the American cinema." Equally enthusiastic were editorial responses from the Mexican press, which emphasized the script's exposure of discrimination. *El Universal* saw it as a "drama of the oppressed," while *Cine Mundial* endorsed *Salt* as "eminently on the side of North American democracy." Both discounted charges of Communist influence as a capitalist smoke screen that could not obscure the film's truthfulness. Less sanguine, the *Los Angeles Times* acknowledged the *California Quarterly* demarche as a "bold attempt to justify the production of the film," but realistically pointed out that theater owners, most of whom saw *Salt* as a "hot potato," simply "wouldn't want to touch it."[19]

Aware of the danger, the film's sponsors had already begun preparations for a fight. As early as March 26, not long after the violence in Silver City, Biberman had begun to solicit further cooperation from Mine-Mill as the project moved toward completion. Citing substantial support from the journalistic and religious communities, he told Maurice Travis that the picture was destined to "pull the rug out from under the labor-baiters and Red-baiting Congressional racketeers" by putting the decision on the film in the hands of the viewing audience. Acknowledging IPC's debt to Local 890's talented participants, Biberman emphasized the "beauty and artistic skill which resides in working people." While he recognized that there were still "many hurdles to vault," he saw no insurmountable obstacles to the picture's completion, probably by August 1953. Biberman closed his report with a restatement of the filmmakers' commitment to the project:

> We can't talk about the fight for a better America without engaging in it. And we can't make a better America without making friends on a vast scale. For that we have to have real evidence of our ability to offer our friends something better than what they now have. This picture will offer EQUALITY, MUTUAL SELF-ADVANCEMENT, and the DIGNITY AND FRATERNITY OF LABOR to our entire people. FROM OUR POINT OF VIEW THIS IS WORTH NOT MERELY TWO YEARS OF SACRIFICE, BUT A LIFETIME.[20]

Most important, in Biberman's view, was the precedent established through collaboration. The *Salt* project marked the first time in American history that "workers and artists" had "gone into the hay together on this scale."

Biberman concluded that the offspring of this relationship would be "a new breed of working class culture" that would start the American people on the "road to peace, sanity, and humane working conditions." To this end, the IUMMSW–IPC collaboration needed to be strengthened, perhaps through the formation of a labor committee of "national stature" to "act in behalf of the right of the film to be seen."[21]

The first step in this process was taken with the effort to promote the *California Quarterly* campaign within Mine-Mill and the union community. In June, Biberman again urged the International to assist the company by helping it assemble an inclusive trade-union committee to endorse and promote the film. Moreover, he asked that the *California Quarterly* script be sent to hundreds of union leaders throughout the United States, thus alerting American unionists to their stake in the success and wide dissemination of the film. Beyond Mine-Mill, left-wing independent unions such as the International Longshoremen and Warehousemen (ILWU) and United Electrical Workers (UE) were most responsive to this appeal. Alvah Bessie, formerly of the Hollywood Ten, worked within the ILWU to publicize the script while Carl Marzani committed the UE to the *Salt* project with a promise to schedule an early showing. Meanwhile, Mine-Mill's response was to promote script sales within the union by urging locals to purchase copies through the International, a curiously modest step by comparison with Biberman's vision of a promotional campaign. Citing the "tremendous amount of interest" in *Salt*, the International recommended that their members read the script as a first step in evaluating the adverse publicity already given the film.[22]

The pro forma character of the International's initial promotional letter masked simmering tension over the existing relationship between the "cultural workers" and organized labor. It was left to the reliable (and sometimes blunt) Clinton Jencks to spell out those differences in a frank personal letter to Mike Wilson, who always had a good instinct for capturing the attitudes and feelings of his union collaborators. Jencks began with a stark admission that the "proper kind of working relationship between the [International] union and the production company" had not been established. He recognized that Travis and the International officers had not taken the project seriously at first, though they had taken the "heat against the union" since the assault on the picture had begun. Jencks emphatically asserted that the film could be a "positive weapon" for the union, but only if the collaborative arrangement underwent a "sober re-evaluation." The problem, he thought, could be traced to mutual misunderstanding between the "cultural" and "manual trade union" workers, rooted in a faulty understanding on both sides of the need for "sharing mutual respect and responsibility for *all* aspects of the work itself." Jencks admitted that the union had been "superficial and cynical" because "cultural forms" had been historically controlled by management and "directed against the interests of the workers." Moreover, because the International officers had at first been in "awe" of the "cultural workers," there remained a "certain lack of confidence in them as class allies," which, in turn, inhibited the union leadership from offering constructive criticisms. For their part, IPC had underestimated the union's capacity for contributing "*creatively*" in the "*cultural, expressive area.*" Finally, Jencks accurately described the company's "romantic attitude toward the union" rather than a "sober, realistic, objective, and serious one" that might emphasize not just the creative side of the project, but also the film's use "as a weapon." Because both Travis and Orville Larson "doubted the objective value of the weapon we are trying to fashion," the *California Quarterly* plan and the advance work on film distribution had been undermined. Travis, in particular, felt that the International's value had been underestimated, and that successful nationwide exhibition "could only be reached through the active participation of the union."[23] Something was terribly wrong with the effort to promote unity of all workers.

Unmentioned in Jencks's account of the International's reservations was the fact that Wilson and Jarrico had permitted Clinton and Virginia Jencks to see an unfinished version of the film. Jarrico's editing notes make it very clear that he consulted with the Jenckses on film content and structure — and that the filmmakers took *their* criticisms seriously. Jarrico later recalled that this especially close relationship with the Jenckses contributed to the Mine-Mill leadership's coolness toward IPC while the film went through the later stages of production. The Jenckses' privileged position combined with an unavoidable "built in tension" between IPC and IUMMSW to produce strained relations among the collaborators as the project moved toward conclusion in the summer of 1953.[24] Jencks's letter to Wilson may well have been designed to defuse these underlying conflicts.

Having punctured IPC's vision of its successful collaboration with unionists in the class struggle, Jencks proposed solutions to the problem. First and foremost, he urged that the rough cut be shared with Travis and Larson, so that they could "evaluate, discuss, and contribute." Beyond this, the company needed a liaison person to stay in close touch with the union, while the International had to clarify the lines of responsibility in dealing with IPC. Only if the parties took one another seriously and valued true collaboration, Jencks argued, could the breakdown in communications be repaired.[25]

The Jencks letter jarred both company and union into a closer, more meaningful relationship. Within a few months IUMMSW was to assume a more prominent role in the frustrating battle to exhibit the film. In August 1953 the International acted on Jarrico's suggestion by purchasing five hundred copies of the *California Quarterly*'s special *Salt* issue for widespread union distribution. And not long thereafter, Mine-Mill assigned a union representative, William Gately, to the task of coordinating promotion and exhibition in cooperation with union public information officer Morris Wright. While as Jarrico later noted, IPC had not made major demands on the union,[26] Mine-Mill's initial reluctance to become actively engaged had led to an element of alienation among collaborators; the union's cooperative gestures, though welcome, did not completely relieve the tension. The International was again disappointed when, because of the constant harassment, the company was unable to complete the film before its September convention. In its own attempt to heal the wound, IPC sent Wilson to the IUMMSW convention in St. Louis to explain the delay and rally the troops. As a result, the spirit of cooperation was revived as the final battle over distribution loomed larger.

Even before the IUMMSW convention, Wilson acted to implement Jencks's advice on promoting closer relations with Mine-Mill. In a letter informing Travis and the International that the film was not finished, Wilson acknowledged a breakdown in "close and consistent liaison" between the "responsible film people" and the union officers. More remarkably, Wilson admitted that the IPC principals were largely responsible for the problem. While he mentioned that preoccupation with the completion of the film and the conspiracy to suppress it had damaged cooperative links with Mine-Mill, he assured Travis that the breakdown was not the result of any desire in Hollywood to "go it alone." Rather, he and his colleagues fully understood the "crucial role of the union in this project." Wilson told Travis that his letter was intended to "establish a closer working relationship that can see this project through to success . . . success for the trade union movement." Promising a film of which the union would be proud, he proposed that Travis and Larson come to Hollywood for a preview of the rough cut before the convention. Wilson saw the failure to complete the film as a "big blow" to IPC because the company knew that the "free exhibition" of *Salt* depended on "organized mass support, the nucleus of which is Mine-Mill," and that such enthusiasm could have been "best mobilized at the convention." He closed with a direct plea for the International's counsel and help.[27] The warning from Jencks had clearly been taken seriously in Hollywood.

As IUMMSW prepared for its annual convention, the International office worked to prepare delegates and members for discussion of the now-controversial film project. In a full-page spread, *Mine-Mill Union* cast the debate as a conflict between sanity and hysteria. The union organ reprinted an editorial from the Santa Fe *New Mexican* (August 6, 1953), which argued that based on the published script, the film was "no more subversive than 'documentaries' put out by corporations" to " 'sell' the corporations' economic or social point of view." The *New Mexican* asserted that the union had "every right to tell its side of the story," and that the film's suppression was unwarranted; indeed, it concluded, "the country is in no stronger position when it suppresses movies than when it burns books." *Mine-Mill Union* urged its members to ponder the editorial's endorsement of the right to make an independent judgment as well as the "union-busting purpose behind the Red-baiting hysteria."[28]

When Wilson addressed the convention in September 1953, he followed up on this theme by connecting the conspiracy against *Salt* with the "anti-labor forces" that for years had tried to "wreck the Mine-Mill Union." It was what Jarrico called "a solid speech." As Wilson told the story of the film's production and origins, he focused on union members' active participation in policy-making on the film's production board, as well as in acting roles. Attacking the bosses for their "union-busting attitude," he argued that management feared the concept of union-made films *"about* union men and women," which might encourage other labor unions to tell their own stories. Recounting the details of constant harassment, he explained why a final copy of the film had not been produced. He concluded by framing the basic issue in the debate as the "right of a trade union as well as a big corporation to use mass communication to tell its side of the story." Appealing to IUMMSW activists to become aggressive advocates for *Salt*, he urged them to embrace the film as "an instrument for Mine-Mill." Recalling Mine-Mill's history of militant trade unionism and precedent-setting action, Wilson suggested that the *Salt* project could be another union landmark, which he hoped would be "in some way worthy of the people, the Mine-Mill people who made it."[29]

After a successful convention speech, Wilson met with Mine-Mill's executive board to advance concrete suggestions for union action on behalf of the film. He began with an explanation of problems to be expected in the distribution process, which would be hampered by denial of access to the studio chains and those distributors who depended on the Hollywood product. The IPC marketing plan depended heavily on independent theaters whose interest was to be excited by a proposed long run following a

New York opening. Wilson promised that the company would handle the business promotion of the film, but recommended that Mine-Mill act to "build audience participation in advance of the opening." At this point, he turned to the still-pending question of a union organizer to handle the advance campaign. The board responded warmly to Wilson's appeal in the belief that in every IUMMSW district, theaters could be found to show the film. To guarantee *Salt*'s success, the board then approved a union promotional campaign and agreed to assign a union representative to manage the film's promotion.[30] With a rousing speech and an effective board presentation, Wilson had done much to repair the breech that had lingered through the summer doldrums.

Convention delegates acknowledged the struggle of Local 890 and IPC in two ways. It was this convention, as previously noted, that approved a sweeping program to integrate women and the Ladies Auxiliaries more closely into the full life of the union. And the resolution adopted pointedly stressed the importance of incorporating Mexican-American and African-American women into Mine-Mill, where they had a "tremendous contribution to make." The statement drew strong and eloquent support from Local 890's Angel Bustos, who argued that *Salt* would show what women could do to "help the workers in the struggle." More significant for IPC, of course, was the executive board's decision to launch a promotional campaign with union personnel before *Salt*'s premiere.[31] By October 1953, union labor and "cultural workers" had drawn closer in self-defense and hope for the future.

Within a month, Mine-Mill had begun its campaign. On October 17, a regional conference at Carlsbad, New Mexico, explored the fuller integration of women into union activities. Upon request from the El Paso local, Local 890 delegates explained how the women had controlled the picket lines in the Empire strike and had aided in the election of Senator Dennis Chavez. As a follow-up, organizer Chet Smotherman described the women's role in the production of *Salt* and outlined the International's plan to ensure the wide distribution of the film. Within a month interest was also building in Silver City, where another Rosaura Revueltas film played to full houses after an advertising campaign reminded local viewers of her work on *Salt*.[32]

At the national level, the promotional effort was well under way by November, by which time exploratory meetings had been held with union groups in Illinois, Michigan, Utah, Idaho, and Montana. The key figure in this campaign was Mine-Mill's designated advance man, William Gately, one of the union's International representatives who was reassigned to the *Salt* project. On November 30, Gately reported some commitments and several expressions of interest, pending release of the film. By mid-December, he had also made contacts in Philadelphia, Washington, New Haven, and Boston, though he reported no new commitments.[33]

Early promotional strategy focused on the use of script readings as a stimulus to viewer interest in the immediate prerelease period. In late October, Wilson urged Travis and the board to help fund a national tour by blacklisted actress Anne Revere, whose readings would not only create audience interest in *Salt*, but also could provide an organizing event to facilitate the formation of sponsoring committees in key communities. Revere, a gifted character actress, had appeared in a number of successful films, including *National Velvet* (1945), *Gentleman's Agreement* (1947), and *A Place in the Sun* (1951). After her name appeared in *Red Channels* in 1950, probably owing to her public protests against HUAC, she was called to testify before the committee in 1951. Once she invoked the First and Fifth Amendments, she became unemployable.[34] Her animus toward the Communist hunters led her to present a series of readings to promote *Salt*, which held the potential for breaking the blacklist.

Once under way, the Revere readings were a smashing success, at least until Gately invaded the UAW stronghold of Detroit. Here, Gately established contact with the officers of left-leaning Dearborn Local 600 at the giant Ford Rouge plant, which employed many African-Americans. His task was eased by an advance visit from Mine-Mill's African-American regional director, Asbury Howard, who persuaded the Local 600 executive board that *Salt* was a "strong labor film" that deserved an audience. Before the scheduled presentation occurred, however, the strongly anticommunist UAW president, Walter Reuther, intervened to stop the booking. The Ruetherites communicated their opposition through union committeemen and stewards. But later, after several Local 600 officers had attended another Detroit reading, Revere met with the executive board and entertainment committee. Following this conference, the leaders of the Rouge local agreed on a January reading in spite of Reuther's objections. Gately regarded the promotional tour as a financial and public relations success, but acknowledged some difficulty in selling the readings. He reported skepticism "until they have once heard Anne," after which "everybody wants a reading."[35]

To Biberman, Jarrico, and Wilson, these doubts came as no surprise. Earlier attempts to halt production had made it clear that the film's critics had no intention of relenting in their assault. Recognizing that the "conspiracy to boycott" was likely to persist, IPC eventually organized IPC

Cover page of brochure promoting *Salt of the Earth*'s premiere, March 1954. Collections of the Wisconsin Center for Film and Theater Research.

Distributors, Incorporated, to circumvent the major motion picture producers who controlled 85 percent of the distribution outlets. Their marketing strategy was based on previews for selected labor, religious, educational,
and cultural leaders well in advance of theatrical runs. On October 17,
1953, a company press release appealed to civic leaders and "citizens with a
stake in civil liberties" to counter the "anticipated pressure of the would-be
censors." Based on the response to the *California Quarterly* screenplay, IPC
predicted that the completed film would "have more boosters than the
enemies of free culture dreamed existed."[36]

Before long there was reason to doubt this sunny forecast. One week later,
IPC attorney Charles Katz learned that independent theater owners in New
York had "*already* been visited" by American Legion representatives, who
announced their intention to picket any theater bold enough to book *Salt of
the Earth*. Based on information from an East Coast associate who was
scouting New York marketing outlets, Katz was aware of early resistance to
the film among potential exhibitors, as well as the danger of IATSE "sabo-
tage." It now seemed likely that Red-baiting would cause any theater that
ran *Salt* to lose its respectability, which meant that a New York contract
would be hard to come by.[37] Although Katz's informant wished to broker a
deal for *Salt* with the Stanley Theater in Manhattan, an art house that
contracted with Artkino, his analysis of the challenge was accurate.

Conscious of the problems ahead, ASP refocused West Coast attention
on the censorship issue with a Los Angeles rally billed as "The People
against the Book Burners." In December 1953, an audience of one thousand cheered speeches by CP activists, labor leaders, artists, and civil libertarians who assailed a variety of assaults on free speech. Featured speaker
was screenwriter Michael Wilson, who attacked the "book and film burners" and "McCarthyite forces" who had unsuccessfully attempted to kill
Salt of the Earth in the production stages. But since *Salt*'s enemies had failed
to prevent production, he warned, "obviously they would try to 'burn' it at
the box office" by intimidating exhibitors. The boycott could be defeated,
however, with

> The solid foundation of an organized working class;
> A group of cultural workers who will make the moods and needs of
> that class the touchstone of their creative contribution;
> The audience who will see the picture itself, a special kind of audi-
> ence — one which is ready to organize a search for outlets for this kind
> of film, so that a union picture can reach an audience.[38]

In a complementary address, Los Angeles Mine-Mill business agent Rito Valencia warmly endorsed the "new unity and coalition being formed by the worker and the intellectual," symbolized by the *Salt* project. When released, he asserted, the film would "make a lie out of the press and the distortions" that had colored previous debate over its production. Endorsing the film as the union's greatest contribution to workers' education in many years, Valencia described *Salt* as a "real slap in the face to big business," which had assumed that it "controlled the film making." To Valencia, Red-baiting by management merely demonstrated that business leaders feared the power of the moving image to communicate truth. Far from being destroyed by the corporations, he vowed, IUMMSW would remain alive "as long as they [took] ore out of the ground."[39]

The ASP rally confirmed left-wing awareness of the challenge ahead as IPC prepared for distribution in 1954. An early casualty was the Vincents' San Cristóbal Valley Ranch, which closed its doors in December 1953. Confronted by the ravages of McCarthyism, Craig and Jenny Vincent concluded that "in all fairness to [their] guests and [themselves]," they could no longer expose people to the danger of being framed on false charges of Communist associations.[40] While the *Salt* episode was only part of a wider attack on the ranch and its proprietors, the Vincents' fate boded ill for the project that had begun at San Cristóbal. Biberman, Jarrico, and Wilson understood that a fight loomed before them, but even the most hardheaded realist could not have anticipated the viciousness or comprehensiveness of the attack they were to face. As the film neared completion, IPC Distributors, under the direction of Sonja Biberman (the director's sister-in-law and an active leftist), readied itself for New York previews. The real boycott was yet to come.

SIX

The Suppression of *Salt of the Earth*

Inter-Union Conflict and External Pressures

As *Salt of the Earth* neared completion, promotional activity intensified. Since no distributor was willing to handle it, Independent Productions Corporation Distributors (IPCD) assumed responsibility for the task. While IUMMSW could help with labor union audiences and dissemination within Mine-Mill ranks, the hard work of advance preparation fell to Herbert Biberman and Paul Jarrico, whose task took them on a national tour filled with frustration. The booking process in major metropolitan areas brought home the wide reach of movie industry and union figures bent on killing the film. In the end, the boycott was near-total, so extensive that IPC legal counsel Ben Margolis viewed it as a clear violation of the antitrust laws — a "complete breakdown of law and order."[1] Optimism prevailed in early 1954, but hope soon slipped into despair.

The First Test: A New York Premiere

By late January 1954 Biberman and Jarrico were again fighting the International Association of Theatrical Stage Employees' boycott, this time in New York, where union technicians refused to participate in final processing of the film. IATSE had "passed the word" to its locals that "no one was to work on it," Biberman recalled, persuading him that a "knock down and drag out fight" was in the offing. With the assistance of skilled film editor Carl Lerner, an experienced technical crew made significant progress on developing the film. However, IATSE eventually tracked them down, and work ground to a halt. At this point, Jarrico turned to Haskell Wexler, a

Chicago technician, who helped assemble a team that succeeded in outsmarting the IATSE watchdogs and finishing the task. Only by using pseudonyms was it possible to induce a Chicago laboratory to complete this work, including the fine grains, duplicate negatives, and prints. A similar subterfuge was necessary in order to record the musical score. Introducing himself as Paul Jacobs, Jarrico succeeded in arranging for Sol Kaplan to score a film entitled *Vaya con Dios*.[2] In March, the job was finished and the film ready for exhibition; but the theaters were not.

In February, the promoters followed a dual-track strategy of holding previews for selected audiences while negotiating bookings at first-run theaters. On February 6, Biberman wrote his wife that three theaters were interested, "eager for what they suspect[ed] might be a large business. . . . They know of [the film's] nature and its character and its problems. But its problems and its box office are also clearly aligned in their minds." Before long a pattern began to emerge: tentative bookings or expressions of interest from class houses, followed by cancellations and apologies. Jarrico later asserted that these reversals were motivated by either fear of IATSE reprisal or pressure from the motion picture industry. While the private showings were an unqualified success and trade unions were enthusiastic, the previews failed to translate into prime bookings. By March 1954 Jarrico was urging that a lawsuit be filed against IATSE, but Biberman resisted this dramatic step, unwilling to be drawn into "minor engagements" that might force them to lose sight of their main objective.[3]

Meanwhile, lawyer Ben Margolis urged legal action if IATSE persisted in its obstructionism. President Richard Walsh, under pressure from his rival Roy Brewer on the Communist issue, had ordered IATSE projectionists to contact the International office before handling *Salt*. Margolis was convinced that Walsh was merely fronting for the major producers, and that only a lawsuit could "break through" the deal that had been made. Coupled with legal action, Margolis argued, immediate exhibition would be important to building support among unionists and civil libertarians. Labor's backing was essential, he noted, since IPC would be taking on a labor union; it was therefore important that the fight be waged as a civil liberties battle rather than an anti-labor action.[4]

Anxious to exploit the civil liberties issue, Biberman and IPC's New York legal counsel, Martin Popper, approached Morris Earnst of the American Civil Liberties Union. What they failed to realize was that Earnst was an FBI informant close to J. Edgar Hoover. While his role in the *Salt* boycott is unclear, he did little to advance the IPC cause. Earnst, who was at first convinced that a lawsuit was the answer, agreed to attend a preview showing though he maintained that film content was not an important consideration. Biberman resisted legal action, however, and was more interested in ACLU mounting a national publicity campaign than in Earnst's proposal. Both Biberman and Margolis saw value in ACLU participation in such "top maneuvering," but from the outset the cost of the Earnst plan was prohibitive.[5]

Four ACLU representatives, including Earnst and legal counsel Herman Levy, were present for the preview, after which Levy prepared a detailed memorandum for the organization's legal staff. While he thought *Salt* was "awful" from an artistic viewpoint, he insisted that it was not "outright Communist propaganda" but was likely to "elicit support for unions." Film quality and content aside, Levy decried the "attempt at censorship" apparently under way. *Salt*, he argued, was a "prime example" of a film that critics "should not attempt to suppress" because the effort to censor would merely "give it unwarranted publicity."[6]

Unaware of Levy's analysis, Biberman pressed the issue. On February 22, he urged New York ACLU officer Elmer Rice to intervene in the controversy, which by this time had been complicated by IATSE's threat to deny exhibitors projectionists. Biberman recited the already long list of sins committed against *Salt* and informed Rice that several lawyers saw IATSE's actions as an illegal conspiracy. While reserving the right to legal action, he argued that public pressure on Richard Walsh and the union would be "more efficacious." Biberman suggested that if the ACLU Censorship Committee and the Author's League were to impress Walsh with the potential damage to labor union interests in the boycott, IATSE might relent.[7]

In response to Biberman's entreaty, ACLU moved to explore the allegations of censorship. Legal counsel Clifford Forster disclaimed interest in *Salt*'s content but expressed concern about the possibility of prior restraint. As a result, he contacted Walsh, who denied that any orders to projectionists existed. Moreover, Forster concluded, because IPC had not yet applied for a license to exhibit, there was no "real issue of boycott" to resolve. He also informed Biberman that Congressman Donald Jackson had assured ACLU that "censorship was not his intention."[8] In sum, ACLU saw no censorship in operation.

ACLU's assurances were small comfort, as were Walsh's denials. Although Biberman was convinced that Walsh was "only the front," he was determined that he and his colleagues must "use their heads" in dealing with IATSE. Biberman preferred to avoid a direct counterattack against Walsh, not wishing to make him the "final or individual enemy"; he rather sought to portray Walsh as "part of a whole plan" to squelch the film. Unless IPC dealt carefully with Walsh, it would be "difficult" for AFL and

CIO trade unions to "take a position of attack against a trade union and its leader." At this stage of the project, Biberman essentially restrained Jarrico and Margolis, who were ready to fight it out in the courts. He successfully urged a combination of "diplomacy" and the "patience of Job."[9] Biberman prevailed.

Meanwhile, previews went forward with encouraging results. Religious leaders, labor figures, minority group representatives, and civil libertarians responded to *Salt* enthusiastically. An overly optimistic Biberman maintained that people who had seen it became "crusaders" and New Yorkers who had refused to support the film financially were now "sweet" because they had "heard the rustling wind and want to see." Among the most supportive viewers were women, who identified with the sexual politics central to the film's meaning. At one showing, Biberman was nearly overcome by their response:

> Women, how wonderful are women. For the wives of the distinguished personages who came were not hesitant in speaking of their tremendous enjoyment of the picture   and there was surprising applause at the end from such a small group . . . led by the women . . . The [theater] owner's wife was there and was very, very moved. And she was giving it to her husband . . . And good.[10]

The labor union response was equally encouraging. While leftist unions, including the UE, Furriers, and Marine Cooks and Stewards, were most active, many mainstream AFL and CIO organizations lent their support to the promotional effort. A special Carnegie Little Theater preview for three hundred representatives of twenty New York unions ended with "spontaneous applause." Trade unionists, "big, tough, even cynical guys" left "with tears streaming down their faces." Mine-Mill president John Clark reported that many unionists had concluded that they were obligated "to support the showing of this picture so it will be seen all over the country." Since his first viewing of the rough cut in early January, Clark had embraced the film and used his influence to promote it within Mine-Mill. On January 4, he stressed the pride in sponsorship that came with active participation in the production process. Stressing *Salt*'s realism, Clark told his members that once they saw it, they would immediately "understand the impact of this picture" as well as the "fight of reaction to bar its showing."[11] His warm endorsement reflected the closer working relationship that had developed since Jencks had prodded Wilson into involving the International leadership more directly.

ESTA PELICULA FUE HECHA PARA UD. TRAIGA A SUS FAMILIARES Y AMIGOS.

La película que nos realza como hispanos y nos inspira como humanos

La película que Hollywood no se atrevió a producir . . .

Por primera vez en la historia de la cinematografía americana se ha hecho una película por, para y sobre los trabajadores y sus familiares . . . Una cinta cinematográfica que se atreve a decir la verdad sobre la importancia de las uniones. Una película que nos presenta realista y dramáticamente el punto de vista de los trabajadores y las organizaciones a las que ellos pertenecen.

SAL DE LA TIERRA nos enseña la vida real de los mineros de origen mexicano en la minas de zinc en el suroeste de los Estados Unidos. Vemos y sentimos sus tremendas luchas por conseguir igualdad.

"LA SAL DE LA TIERRA"

(Salt of the Earth)

ROSAURA REVUELTAS
JUAN CHACON

86th ST. GRANDE
East of Lexington Ave.
AT 9-7720

NEW DYCKMAN
207th St. - East of B'way
TO 7-6770

Spanish-language handbill distributed in New York Hispanic community, March 1954. Collections of the Wisconsin Center for Film and Theater Research.

While Mine-Mill and mainstream unions momentarily edged toward rapprochement, internal disagreement surfaced within IATSE as the contradiction inherent in a labor union boycott of a pro-labor film became more troublesome. On February 17, Biberman privately expressed optimism on the IA situation, which he was convinced had been handled well. As a result of IPC's careful diplomacy, any precipitous action by Walsh seemed likely to divert anti-labor sentiment against IATSE. *Variety* reported that many in the movie industry were voicing reservations over any union action focusing on film content, which "constituted a worrisome precedent." These reported fears of censorship led Biberman to speculate that IATSE might simply "ease itself out of the leading position here and try to have the good old reliable American Legion take it on."[12]

Walsh and the IA were clearly becoming concerned about the publicity and costs associated with a high-profile lawsuit. *Variety* reported the union's determination to avoid violation of the antitrust laws, which caused them to be "very cagey." In Biberman's view, IATSE leaders "know they have to tread on eggs . . . and are doing so." He correctly predicted that the union would "pretend their people are doing it on their own and not on orders," which is precisely what Roy Brewer later claimed. At the same time, Biberman was convinced that the ACLU pressure was "paying off" in the form of Walsh's shifting position. On February 22, labor columnist Victor Riesel reported a reversal of IATSE's official policy, permitting union projectionists to run the film for preview performances. Denouncing Mine-Mill as "notorious," Reisel defended the latest twist in Walsh's reasoning, which now justified projecting the film in order to avoid "labor censorship over a means of communication and expression." The softening of IATSE's position coincided with a benign response to *Salt*'s exhibition from the movie industry's Production Code Administration. Although IPC never applied for a PCA seal, the New York office approved the film on February 28, 1954, "without restrictions."[13] It began to look as if Biberman had been right.

Meanwhile, Biberman and Jarrico intensified the search for a first-class house for *Salt*'s New York premiere. The results were not encouraging. Negotiations with the Schubert Theater chain proved fruitless, reportedly due to both IA pressure and the unwarranted financial risk. The choices were sharply limited because most exhibitors flatly refused to book the film due to fears of IATSE reprisals and retaliation by the motion picture industry.[14] By March the IPC promoters were desperate for a breakthrough.

What happened next is a matter of dispute. In Biberman's account, a sympathetic theater owner suggested a non-IATSE house as a last resort.

After exploring the options, they agreed on the Grande Theater on Eighty-sixth Street, which was run by Philip Steinberg. Following an acrimonious negotiation, the parties struck a deal to premiere the film at the Grande, with a follow-up booking ten days later at Steinberg's New Dyckman in the Bronx. Despite threats of retaliation by IATSE projectionists, allegedly made by Local 306 business agent Steve D'Inzillo, IPC proceeded with plans for the opening. Although disappointed over a scheduled premiere at a third-class non-IA house outside the quality theater district,[15] Biberman and Jarrico had a theater and an agreement.

As told by D'Inzillo, who occasionally clashed with Richard Walsh, the story is a bit more complex. He openly acknowledged Walsh's fierce anti-communism and confirmed receipt of an IATSE "directive" instructing union projectionists not to show the film. D'Inzillo regarded this decision as a "shame," because *Salt* was a "fine labor film." But he later denied making any threats concerning interference with the film's exhibition, and insisted that Biberman's account of the incident was inaccurate. Far from working to "squelch" the film, D'Inzillo recalls helping Biberman find the Grande Theater. As union business agent, D'Inzillo knew the New York theater owners well enough to "know which ones would be willing to run the film just to make a profit." He agreed with Biberman that Steinberg was essentially interested in the bottom line.[16]

Both D'Inzillo and Biberman concluded that Steinberg upped the ante for use of his theater as the controversy over *Salt* intensified. Biberman asserted that the theater owner demanded a cash payment as compensation for the pressure he was getting from other exhibitors and representatives of the motion picture companies. After being gouged by Steinberg, Biberman "plunked down an offer" that was accepted, and he had a theater again. When the "melodrama" was over, Biberman told his family that he was adjusting to "this slimy business," which he could tolerate as long as it kept the *Salt* project "in the tracks of this opening."[17]

As opening day drew near, the anxiety level increased. Biberman busied himself with last-minute promotional activity, including a plan to import Juan Chacón and Henrietta Williams from Silver City for the premiere. Final previews went off without serious disruption, while efforts to reach the union and Mexican-American audiences continued. Advertising material placed heavy emphasis on labor issues. *Salt* was billed as "an honest movie about American working people" that dealt with a labor conflict "from the point of view of labor" and "with a minority from the point of view of a minority." Finally, publicity materials promised a film that dealt with women as the "heroic equals of men," whose "worth, dignity, and beauty" were recognized. *Salt of the Earth*, its promoters claimed, honored the true "builders of our country — the American working people."[18]

To Biberman's and Jarrico's surprise, the premiere went forward without incident. Chacón, Williams, and Wilson were on hand for a successful opening, marked by an "enthusiastic" audience response. With fifteen thousand advance tickets sold to local unions, *Salt* played to full houses, while many disappointed viewers were turned away. To Biberman, the filmmakers were rewarded with "normal, peaceful living" for the first time in three years. And they had created "eight thousand feet of freedom in America."[19] For a brief period it seemed that the moment of victory had arrived.

The illusion of success remained for several weeks, reinforced by positive reviews and a ten-week run at the Eighty-sixth Street Grande, which broke all previous attendance records. Several reviewers saw no evidence of subversion in *Salt*. In the *New York Times*, film critic Bosley Crowther had high praise for Wilson's "taughtly muscled script," which developed "considerable personal drama." To Crowther, *Salt* was "simply a strong pro-labor film." While the film was "loaded," Otis Guernsey of the *Herald Tribune* argued, it did use "semi-documentary technique" effectively "to dramatize human dignity and courage in harsh circumstances." *Variety* summarized the reviews as generally in agreement that the film reflected "high craftsmanship," though it saw problems in "story line and angle." And from the Left, the *Daily Worker* predictably lauded *Salt* as a "remarkable achievement" soon to be "the talk of the nation." Similarly, Samuel Sillen reported in *Masses and Mainstream* that *Salt's* "overpowering beauty and realism" provided viewers an "exalting experience." Impressed with the very achievement of release, Dalton Trumbo wrote that whatever the reviewers' verdict, "they have done it, and good, bad, or indifferent I bow to them."[20]

Like Biberman, Jarrico was exultant; "Well, we're in! We licked them," he asserted. Momentarily, the New York premiere and the initial response seemed to presage a "breakthrough on distribution." Further encouragement came, of all places, from the commander of the Yorkville district American Legion. Although his initial reaction was to demand the film's cancellation, he consented to view the picture before launching an attack. Once the legionnaire had seen *Salt*, he surprised the filmmakers with an expression of approval and a promise to halt any plans to picket the theater. According to Biberman's account, the legionnaire told Steinberg:

This is in no sense an un-American picture. It has nothing socialistic, communistic, or anti-Catholic in it. The only propaganda is pro-feminist and I'm for that. Sure it deals with poor working people and shows their hardships . . . So what? Such hardships ought to be shown. I like the picture.[21]

Ever the optimist, Biberman now believed that his troubles were nearly over. Assuming the Legion's tolerant attitude would prevail, he concluded that "only the I.A. [was] left" and "without the support of such organizations," they would not "get to first base." All that remained, or so it seemed, was a successful opening at the New Dyckman in the Bronx. If all went well, the filmmakers would "have comparative freedom to do [their] job." But the New Dyckman was an IATSE house, and union policy was on the line. With the advantage of historical hindsight, Biberman later acknowledged that IA success in blocking *Salt's* exhibition there meant that the union possessed a "formula for the rest of the country."[22]

Even before the New Dyckman opening, signs of trouble began to appear. Despite solid reviews and financial success, Jarrico recalled, other New York exhibitors fell silent and no distributor would touch the film. Those who eventually expressed interest learned that if they played *Salt*, they would be cut off from the major motion picture companies, unable to get their films in the future. One by one, theater owners fell by the wayside and IPC was left with a promising film that nobody would take a chance on.[23]

Since their initial contact, Biberman and Steve D'Inzillo of Local 306 had been able to communicate well. As previously noted, D'Inzillo did not share Walsh's militant anticommunism. Indeed, he saw *Salt of the Earth* as a valuable pro-labor film and believed that Biberman had every right to exhibit it. However, as the local's business agent, he also had a responsibility to the International, and he most certainly did not make union policy. When asked by Biberman if Local 306 projectionists would be permitted to run *Salt*, D'Inzillo said he would be forced to pull his man. At least one group of projectionists was not opposed to showing the film and told the *New York Post's* Arthur Winston that D'Inzillo had ordered them to refuse service. And these discussions did not occur in a vacuum. Substantial debate had occurred within Local 306 before the film had reached New York, and union projectionists had taken a position permitting individuals to act on their own consciences if asked to show *Salt*.[24]

In the end, it was national union policy that determined the outcome at the New Dyckman. On March 26, after one showing, the union projectionist refused to continue running the film. His refusal brought D'Inzillo and two colleagues to the theater for a discussion with Biberman and Steinberg. Biberman remained "cool and rational," D'Inzillo later recalled, though he

was "irate" over responsibility for the crisis. Biberman eventually acknowledged that he had vented his anger at the wrong man, as Walsh had called
the shots. This analysis was later confirmed by D'Inzillo's lawyer, Harry
Sacher, who asserted that his client had "received instructions from the
very top, from 'Dick' [Walsh]." After Steinberg angrily threatened to employ a nonunion projectionist, D'Inzillo conferred with the International
office. The end result was the IA's decision to provide a union projectionist
to run the "subversive" film. According to Biberman's memoir of these
events, Walsh chose to protect IATSE's jurisdiction. His version was confirmed by the Alliance's Hollywood international representative, George
Flaherty, who, in April, announced that Walsh had reversed the union's
original decision and established a new policy.[25]

With the latest crisis behind them, the IPC principals savored a "momentary victory." *Salt* was running in an IATSE house with an IATSE
projectionist. But what did this small success really signify? Because of
start-up promotional expenses the company had spent thirty thousand dollars in New York, while receiving fifteen thousand dollars as its share of the
gross from the Grande (the New Dyckman had been a financial disaster).
Still, as Jarrico later observed, launching a film could be very expensive; yet
the investment was necessary because subsequent bookings and terms often
depended on the strength of the first run. Despite an excellent initial showing at the Grande, however, *Salt of the Earth* never caught on. The opening
run "did not pave the way for anything resembling normal distribution."[26]

But the chimera of victory was seductive. The New York experience had
demonstrated that a "large and enthusiastic audience" for *Salt* existed,
Biberman told Travis, but, he added cautiously, it was not "an automatic
one." Union legal counsel Nathan Witt agreed, as did Jarrico, who now
disclosed ambitious national distribution plans to David Platt of the *Daily
Worker.* He emphasized mounting national interest in the film, which had
run successfully in New York without picketing incidents. While impressed
by the early results, IPC legal counsel Ben Margolis told Biberman that
despite their success in New York, the union promotion scheme had limits. To Margolis, IPC needed to dispel the notion that *Salt* was solely a
"special interest" picture addressed to "certain sections of our people." *Salt
of the Earth* was a brilliant labor film, but it was much more. He insisted that
it was time to introduce the "conception" that "this picture is exciting
entertainment."[27]

While undoubtedly aware of the film's entertainment value, Biberman
was mindful of the need for coordination with his union sponsors. As a
result, his report to Travis stressed *Salt*'s potential for unifying an audience,

its "uncanny capacity for turning its audiences into a single homogeneous group." Sketching an ambitious program for nationwide distribution, Biberman assured Travis that there was "social gold in these frames," but reminded him that it "had to be sweated out by hard organizational work." He appealed to Mine-Mill for its cooperation, starting with a planned screening at the union's upcoming national wage conference, designed to ignite interest in *Salt* throughout the IUMMSW organization.[28]

Biberman and Jarrico were on their way, or so they thought. In April, Jarrico returned to Los Angeles to help prepare for West Coast distribution while Biberman, hoping to build support in the industrial heartland, shifted his base of operations to Detroit and Chicago. Without a national distributor, IPC was on its own. The result was a midwestern campaign based on the New York model, which had produced a semblance of success. Looking back at the New York experience ten years later, Biberman ruefully admitted that, in truth, they had "accomplished exactly nothing."[29]

National Distribution: Dreams and Realities in the Industrial Heartland

As Biberman moved into the industrial Midwest, his hopes for a strong worker response to a militantly pro-labor film seemed plausible. Certainly, labor strongholds like Detroit and Chicago would provide a receptive environment. Since January, plans had been under way to launch a program of previews in selected urban areas, designed to stimulate interest and prepare the ground for theatrical openings. Michael Wilson had worked closely with both John Clark and Maurice Travis to identify the target cities. He told Travis that IPC would "depend on Mine-Mill leaders" to select local audiences and approach independent exhibitors to arrange for suitable venues. Among the cities identified were Chicago, Salt Lake City, Los Angeles, San Francisco, Vancouver, B.C., St. Louis, Phoenix, and Tucson. In most localities, Anne Revere's readings were to provide a key first step in catalyzing a local support group.[30]

In Detroit, as we have seen, Walter Reuther had been unable to prevent the Local 600 General Council from hosting a reading. Once Reuther tried to "put the hammer on it," Jimmie Watts, editor of *Ford Facts* (the Local 600 newspaper), became "indignant" over the idea that anyone could tell the huge Ford local what to do. Watts, a graduate of the Detroit College of Law and an activist in the Michigan AFL-CIO Press Council, was at this time a spokesman for the anti-Reuther administration of Local 600 president Carl Stellato. His remarks underscored the fierce independence of the Rouge local. On January 10, Anne Revere presented a reading to an enthusiastic audience of three hundred, including council members and a large Ladies Auxiliary. At the subsequent meeting, several participants urged that Local 600 take over as producers of the film if Mine-Mill wanted to be relieved of the burden it had accepted. Mine-Mill's William Gately also arranged for *Salt* to be shown commercially at the Krim Theater, one of Detroit's best houses, while Local 600 assumed responsibility for locating suitable venues in the suburbs.[31]

Deeply impressed by the script, *Ford Facts* viewed *Salt* as a "remarkable and highly exciting portrayal" of the Empire Zinc strike. It recommended the film to the full membership as a "picture which vividly portrays the struggles of organized labor." Less enthusiastic was the ever-watchful labor columnist Victor Riesel, who blasted Revere as the "lady in Red politics" who was touring the nation for unions exposed by SAG as sources of "sheer Soviet-line propaganda." In a parting shot, Riesel also pilloried Local 600's leftish president Carl Stellato, who came under attack for his alleged "hate for the capitalism and anti Commies." What he missed was the free speech issue. To militants like CP activist Dave Moore, Local 600's determination to screen *Salt* symbolized the members' "freedom to speak [their] minds" as members of an autonomous local union that seemed an "island of democracy surrounded by the seas of [Reutherite] reaction."[32]

The early response in Chicago was equally positive, though financially unrewarding. Three city committees were established, composed of unionists and community leaders. Three hundred people attended the readings, which also resulted in invitations for return engagements from the Packinghouse Workers and the United Electrical Workers (UE) local. Here, Gately found a 750-seat theater, as well as a distributor who agreed to line up theaters throughout Illinois. In both Chicago and Detroit, then, preliminary contacts had reactivated a Popular Front coalition and prepared the ground for Biberman's appearances in April.

On the basis of his eastern swing, Gately concluded that problems existed in several communities. First, he argued, there was an unwarranted "separation of the labor movement from the progressive elements in the cultural and professional groups." Like Jencks, Gately had noticed a gap between "cultural workers" and a labor movement that had "deserted them." A second concern lay in the large number of rank-and-file union members and local leaders, both AFL and CIO, who wanted to have "contact with our people" but had not yet become involved. To Gately, the film offered the perfect medium to bring these forces together in a progressive alliance. His report helped persuade the International officers of the "broad support possible for this movie."[33]

Given the optimistic reports, Biberman had reason to feel encouraged as he departed for the Midwest. Before leaving New York, he arranged a preview theater in Detroit and informed UAW that five hundred members could be invited to a showing. Biberman fully expected UAW's enthusiasm to "count for a great deal" in persuading a theater owner to exhibit the picture. Naive with regard to UAW infighting, he thought that the union would become the "mobilizing center" for the run of the picture. He saw a "ferment in the UAW, which properly organized [could] be terrific." Biberman's assumption that a union close to the Reuthers and their anticommunist liberalism could become "the heart of the operation"[34] demonstrated his limited grasp of the impact of Cold War politics on the internal struggle for control of the UAW.

Biberman's correspondence suggests that he confused the warm enthusiasm of the left-leaning Dearborn local with the predictably less sympathetic views of the UAW International organization. He was convinced that if Local 600 would "truly devote itself to this operation," they could "make a new mark" that would make IPC's achievement in New York seem "puny." Biberman was right about one thing, at least. He understood that Detroit was critical because it represented the "jump from New York."[35] What he failed to grasp was the size of the gap to be breached.

Once settled in Detroit, Biberman showed *Salt* to Paul Broder, who owned and operated a chain of thirteen Detroit area houses. After agreeing to exhibit the film at one of his theaters, Broder was subject to immediate pressure from the area's American Legion, which threatened him with "extinction" were he to screen the picture. Alarmed by the Legion's initiative, the harried exhibitor urged Biberman to "straighten it out" so he could run the film. Within two days, Biberman had organized two previews for clergy, lawyers, unionists, educators, "art people," and "community leaders" — the usual suspects. And as usual, previews went well. Among those present were representatives of the UAW Education Department, AFL, the Conference of Christians and Jews, other UAW locals, and the Detroit Mexican-American community. Also in the audience were the city and state commanders of the American Legion, who had been invited in an attempt to defuse the growing controversy.[36]

At the theater, Biberman made a speech describing the film's checkered history. Standing near the legionnaires and addressing them directly, he told the audience about the threats without identifying their source. Biberman warned in his "loveliest voice" of censorship and the danger of dictatorship. Following these remarks, a successful screening of the film resulted in a "joyous" response. Deeply moved by what they saw, the UAW International leaders, who had come "to deny," agreed to discuss the film's further exhibition, while a Mexican-American priest reportedly "danced with pleasure."[37] Prospects seemed to improve.

The labor leaders present urged Broder to run the film. Indeed, it appeared that Detroit labor had been won over. The *Federated Press* news bureau reported that the preview had made a "universal hit" with union people, as well as with some of their enemies. One CIO veteran likened the story to the GM sitdown strike of 1937, while a Local 600 committeeman observed that "Old Henry Ford couldn't teach that company nothing [*sic*]." Even an AFL building-trades representative pronounced it a "good film." Aware of the picture's sexual politics, however, a nervous Italian-American CIO member did think it would "raise hell in some families . . . if the women folks see it." He was certain that "women [would] love it," but expressed doubts about "some of the men." *Ford Facts* summarized Detroit labor's reaction with the simple judgment that *Salt* was a "great film . . . on a par with anything presently coming out of Hollywood." The independent (and racially diverse) Rouge local identified with the film's theme of "a minority people fighting for their day in the sun." To Local 600 activist Dave Moore, this reaction was an "expression of the spirit of brotherhood" that had been "present in the local since its beginning."[38] Once again, *Salt* had deeply impressed a skeptical audience, and galvanized the spirit of interracial class solidarity.

Although union viewers endorsed the picture's wide exhibition, the key guests were those numbered in the Legion contingent. The legionnaires learned that the Bayard strike reflected the aspirations of the union local and its people, rather than the International union's alleged machinations; moreover, they were reminded of the New York Legion's decision against picketing a film that was "not communistic." Finally, the Detroit patriots were present while the unionists and other audience members argued in favor of free exhibition.[39]

Emboldened by the forceful endorsement from the preview audience, Broder then invited Biberman, the Legion delegation, and an FBI informant to join him for a late evening drink. Relaxed by the informal social environment, one Legion leader agreed that *Salt* was a "great film." Nonetheless, he insisted that it could not be permitted to run. The rationale was simple. There were two serious problems: Herbert Biberman and Mine-Mill. After recounting the whole story of Hollywood anticommunism, the strike, and the film's production, Biberman assured the legionnaires that they could do what they wished but that they "would never stop the film." And in response to the attack on his own role in *Salt*'s production, he defiantly stood his ground:

Who are you? What do you mean by cross-examining me? I went to jail for American freedom! I love this country and would die happily for its freedom. I have made sacrifices all my life, my fortune and my sacred honor for this country's freedom — and freedom of cultural communication. Do you think you people frighten me? That's silly![40]

Biberman's strong defense of himself, Mine-Mill, and the protection of civil liberties caused his critics to shift ground. Citing articles, documents, and editorials from *Counter-Attack* and *Alert*, they fell back on higher authority: Herb may have been a "nice guy," but they had their orders from above. And as one Legion man later told him, "when we move, we move." Biberman was especially offended by the man's appeal to him "as a Jew." Confronted by a threat to a Jew by a Jew, he broke off the conversation and told his companion to carry out his orders but stop "posing as a Jew."[41]

Chastened, yet enraged by the conversation, Biberman soon began to feel the weight of external pressure from organizations bent on protecting innocent Americans from the Red menace. The next day it became clear that theater owner Broder was wavering, which led Biberman to explore alternate outlets, only to discover that exhibitors had been warned to beware a film that had become a hot item. Theater owners wanted the film, Biberman wrote, but "then they get their heads beaten in and surrender." As he left Detroit for Chicago, he informed his family that it was "going to be a good fight" in the Motor City. He still hoped to sign with Broder, unless the censors had "eaten into him" before he returned. To Biberman, one thing was certain: "We must open in Detroit . . . and we will."[42] Time would prove him wrong.

As the situation in Detroit deteriorated, another struggle developed in Chicago, where Biberman had inked a contract with the Schoenstadt theater chain's Hyde Park Theater. Since January, Mine-Mill had counted on the Cinema Annex, a large art house known for screening "progressive" films, as a backup venue. By late April these arrangements had been confirmed and additional plans for a Hyde Park preview went forward. But on May 1, when nearly one hundred guests assembled at the appointed hour, they learned that no *private* preview would be permitted by IATSE until the theater signed a long-term contract covering Saturday showings. Furious over the setback, Biberman told his family, in a moment of frustration, that

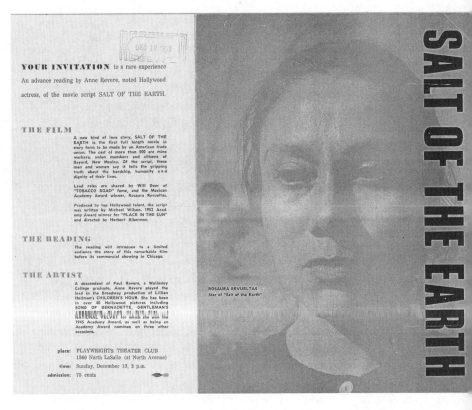

YOUR INVITATION to a rare experience
An advance reading by Anne Revere, noted Hollywood
actress, of the movie script SALT OF THE EARTH.

THE FILM

A new kind of love story, SALT OF THE
EARTH is the first full length movie in
story form to be made by an American trade
union. The cast of more than 500 are mine
workers, union members and citizens of
Bayard, New Mexico. Of the script, these
men and women say it tells the gripping
truth about the hardship, humanity and
dignity of their lives.

Lead roles are shared by Will Geer of
"TOBACCO ROAD" fame, and the Mexican
Academy Award winner, Rosaura Revueltas.

Produced by top Hollywood talent, the script
was written by Michael Wilson, 1952 Academy Award winner for "PLACE IN THE SUN"
and directed by Herbert Biberman.

THE READING

The reading will introduce to a limited
audience the story of this remarkable film
before its commercial showing in Chicago.

THE ARTIST

A descendant of Paul Revere, a Wellesley
College graduate, Anne Revere played the
lead in the Broadway production of Lillian
Hellman's CHILDREN'S HOUR. She has been
in over 40 Hollywood pictures including
SONG OF BERNADETTE, GENTLEMAN'S
AGREEMENT, for which she won the
1945 Academy Award, as well as being an
Academy Award nominee on three other
occasions.

ROSAURA REVUELTAS
Star of "Salt of the Earth"

place: PLAYWRIGHTS THEATER CLUB
        1560 North LaSalle (at North Avenue)
time: Sunday, December 13, 3 p.m.
admission: 75 cents

SALT OF THE EARTH

Invitation to Anne Revere's advance reading of *Salt of the Earth* script in Chicago, December 1953. Archives, University of Colorado at Boulder Libraries, Clinton Jencks Collection.

the "worst organizers [he had] ever met [were] the union organizers" who were guilty of "more double talk" than "action." Following a "big whoop and holler" from labor, there had been silence. As far as he could tell, as of May 1, "not one blessed thing had been done by the unions in Chicago," who were still busy "girding their loins." And the IATSE interference continued. On May 5, another disappointed preview audience was turned away due to the projectionists' union's refusal to cooperate. Meanwhile, Hyde Park Theater owner Kermit Russell responded to unspecified "pressures" with a request that the contract with IPCD be voided.[43]

Biberman's unwarranted tirade against union organizers revealed a gap between "cultural workers" like himself and unionists and their leaders, some of whom worked to bring *Salt* to Chicago audiences. In his frustration, he underestimated the hard promotional work of IUMMSW's Chicago international representative, James Durkin. Even more active in the union offensive was Patrick Gorman, secretary-treasurer of the Amalgamated Meat Cutters and Butcher Workmen of North America, who protested the Chicago boycott to both the projectionists and the Schoenstadt theater chain. In a letter to Gene Atkinson of the projectionists union, Gorman insisted that the film told a "human interest story" in a "manner such as no other labor film . . . shown before." He argued that *Salt* was a "factual picture" and that "we should never run away from facts." Gorman's plea to the exhibitor was more urgent. While the picture contained nothing "that could be construed as Communist propaganda," it was certain to "create controversy." As a "special film," *Salt* deserved to be seen, lest the national audience be at the mercy of "a group of autocrats moulding [*sic*] our opinions as others desire them to be molded." And in an unusual break with inter-union protocol, an angry Gorman protested directly to Local 110 after the cancellation of a scheduled preview for the AMCBW Chicago wage-policy conference.[44]

Equally active on behalf of *Salt* was Richard Durham, program coordinator for the United Packinghouse Workers of America, who later praised Gorman's stand and asserted that those who saw the picture considered it "the most outstanding labor film yet produced." While Durham was unable to act in time to assist Biberman in the Chicago market, UPWA Local 347 promised to "see that [its] entire membership receives its dynamic message." Simultaneously, Durham worked to promote national exposure for the film among packinghouse workers. So vigorous were these efforts that by late July, Biberman looked to UPWA in Des Moines and Sioux City to lead CIO unions in a nationwide campaign for the film, which would break a puzzling pattern of timidity on the part of most industrial unions.[45]

Meanwhile, an aroused Biberman countered the projectionist's obstructionism with a carefully reasoned formal protest to Local 110 president Clarence Jalas. He began by reminding Jalas that current national IATSE policy permitted the projection of *Salt of the Earth*, in accordance with Walsh's recent decision affecting both New York and Los Angeles jurisdictions. Beyond policy matters, however, Biberman argued that no theater, union, or private pressure group had any right to "act as censor of what all other Americans may and may not see." Threatening to publicize this free speech problem before the people of Chicago, he urged Jalas to "give this matter full consideration." One day later, Local 110 promised to run the film for any theater with a five-year union contract.[46]

Although Biberman's letter claimed no knowledge of the pressure's origins, he was fully aware of the changing political context in Chicago. At the heart of the censorship drive was the activist American Legion, which had recently featured an attack on *Salt* in *The Firing Line*, its membership publication (newsletter). In a special edition, readers were told of "one of the most vicious propaganda films ever distributed in the United States." Citing the Detroit police department's conclusion that the film would "incite to riot," *The Firing Line* detailed the backgrounds of and charges against all participants and IUMMSW. The Legion publication quoted anticommunist columnist Howard Rushmore, who decried "movie critics who should know better" and claimed that communists throughout the country had been ordered to "guarantee the film wide circulation and attention." And citing *The Sign*, a national Catholic magazine, *The Firing Line* asserted that the film script "steers a straight course for Latin America," where it was certain to become part of the " 'hate America' campaign." The Legion agreed with those who saw in *Salt* "pro-Communist Anti-American propaganda." As a result, steps were required to ensure that "no loyal American theater owner will touch it." To complement *The Firing Line*'s attack, the Chicago-area Legion took action. On May 8, the Legion's A. W. Togtmoyer condemned the film and urged Russell to cancel future showings. Alarmed by alleged subversion close to home, Edward Clamage, chairman of the Illinois Legion's Anti-Subversive Commission, also urged the Schoenstadt theater chain to halt the Hyde Park engagement. It was the Legion campaign that forced the decision to ban *Salt* at the Hyde Park Theater.[47]

Successful in this effort, Clamage now began to exert pressure on the Cinema Annex to cancel its showing, scheduled for May 21, 1954. Noting the Hyde Park cancellation, Clamage told Cinema Annex owner Mandel A. Terman that it was beneath the dignity of his theater "to indicate cooperation with the Communistic elements of our city and nation." He also asked the Chicago police to revoke *Salt*'s exhibition license and threatened a protest demonstration. While Terman's theater had not been Biberman's first choice, the Hyde Park failure had led him back to the Cinema Annex. Not only was Terman cooperative, but he also fired off a stinging rebuke to Clamage denouncing his letter as "McCarthyism in the world of art," which would mean the "death of art." He further endorsed *Salt* as an "absorbing, entertaining and plausible story of real people . . . building a better America, here in America." Terman scolded the Legion for its prejudgment of the film and told Clamage that his judgments of creative art were his own, not those of others. Terman closed by rejecting the "confidential smears and the pretty obvious intimidation implicit in [Clamage's] letter." Not long thereafter, Terman's audacity earned him a personal citation in *The Firing Line*, which attacked him for his chairmanship of the allegedly "subversive" Chicago Council of Soviet-American Friendship. In this way, the Legion said, his position on *Salt* could be "easily explained."[48]

By this time, the Illinois branch of the American Civil Liberties Union had become interested in the growing controversy over *Salt of the Earth*. Anxious to guarantee "freedom for the movie industry under the protection of the first amendment," the organization had recently participated in the legal battle over the *Miracle* case and that film's proscription in Chicago, which meant that it was very sensitive on the issue of movie censorship. Alarmed by the implications of Local 110's action on *Salt's* exhibition in Chicago, Chicago ACLU executive director Edward H. Meyerding warned Jalas against censorship of *Salt*, which, he argued, constituted a "serious infringement" on First Amendment freedom of expression. Meyerding simultaneously lodged a protest of the Hyde Park decision with Arthur Schoenstadt of the Schoenstadt theater chain and offered him ACLU assistance in the battle "to ensure freedom of the screen in Chicago." Attacking the "infantile thinking" of the film's critics, he asserted that someone had to "stand up to the would-be censors" and told Schoenstadt that ACLU was "ready and anxious to do this." To complement Meyerding's initiative, IPC Distributors urged *Salt's* friends in Chicago to exert pressure on the theater chain and union through direct contacts and organizational action.[49]

Despite the momentary unpleasantness, Biberman believed that he had his theater. Previews ran smoothly and the Cinema Annex opening was rescheduled for May 28, 1954. After a new publicity campaign, Biberman prepared for another premiere. It never happened. Under intense pressure from the union, the Cinema Annex projectionist failed to appear. With no union replacement, the Chicago premiere was again canceled and two thousand disappointed ticket holders went home. By Monday, a reported six thousand had been turned away. When the projectionist finally turned up, he claimed to have been locked in a union office and then admitted he had been sent to another theater; and at this point, he wanted no more of *Salt*.[50]

Now an angry Biberman and an insulted Terman prepared for legal action. They issued a press release detailing the entire correspondence with the American Legion and the duplicity of the projectionists union. Charging Clamage and Jalas with attempted censorship, Cinema Annex and IPC argued that the guilty parties were acting as a front for motion picture producers who feared the rise of independent film production (a questionable assertion). These "Hollywood monopolizers of thought" were responsible for "actions destructive of every right of the artist and the public audience" protected by American "traditions of individual liberty." They

urged interested parties to contact IPC if they wished to join as *amicus curie*
in a lawsuit. By mid-May lawsuits had been filed against both IATSE Local
110 and the Hyde Park Theater, which had broken its contract with IPC.
The company asked twenty-five thousand dollars in damages incurred as a
result of unrecovered promotional costs inflicted by the breach of contract.
In June, the American Civil Liberties Union lent its support.[51]

Meanwhile, Biberman and Terman worked to maintain the pressure on
IATSE's local leadership. In an open letter to Local 110 members, Terman
denied that the boycott was a labor dispute. The Cinema Annex owner
asserted that he had observed all provisions of the current union contract,
charging Jalas with injecting politics into an economic relationship. Reminding union projectionists that IATSE members were currently running
the film in New York, San Francisco, and Los Angeles, he underscored the
recent shift in the International's policy on *Salt*. Moreover, he insisted, the
Chicago union's censorship effort was poor public relations and a "disser-
vice to every operator" and to the "cause of trade unionism." Complement-
ing Terman's effort, Biberman wrote to other Chicago-area unionists to
expose Jalas's censorship effort as an expression of "private" views that
promised to "throttle communication" in Chicago. He repeated Terman's
observation that the union's action could "only bring discredit to the trade
unions," whereas the picture presented the "worth, dignity, and contributions of trade unionists" and could "serve the cause of working people
valiantly."[52] But the damage had been done, and no union could reverse the
course of action that had already killed *Salt* in the Chicago market.

As May slipped away, the Chicago debacle loomed large. Even before the
Cinema Annex disaster, Biberman knew that "Chicago is in a mess." Richard Walsh would certainly have endorsed this assessment. Steven D'Inzillo
later remembered that Walsh had "twitted" him with the charge that he
"hadn't done nearly so well" as the Chicago union's business agent had in
"keeping *Salt* out of Chicago." And "as Chicago went," Biberman reluctantly concluded, "so would go the entire Midwest."[53]

Events in Detroit supported this analysis. Here, promotional efforts were
crippled by the local Association of Theaters, which advised its members
against booking *Salt*. Biberman was still struggling to get the Krim Theater
for a summer opening, but he privately acknowledged that given the Legion
attitude, he would have to "battle that town to a finish." Moreover, he
predicted that the fight would be "acrimonious" and probably set back the
effort in ways that could "spill over into other areas." In an effort to reassure
his wife and family, Biberman speculated that if he could find time to ade-

quately prepare for an August 1 opening, the tide might turn and "Detroit [might] turn out to be a sensational success." But he knew better. As of mid-June, *Salt* was still "getting the silent treatment" in Detroit. Despite Biberman's cheery forecasts, the Chicago and Detroit cancellations were the beginning of the end; and he could not avoid the conclusion that failure lay ahead. In a later retrospective, he noted that when those two engagements were "summarily broken," he "knew we were through" and that only a miracle could reverse the "heavy, heavy damage that had been inflicted on us."[54] By summer 1954 Biberman was in no position to produce a miracle.

The Struggle on Home Ground:
Distribution in the Rocky Mountain West

While Biberman fought a losing battle in the Midwest, the West seemed at first glance a more promising field for a sympathetic reception of the *Salt* story and its cinematic re-creation. Not only was the struggle depicted rooted in the western economic and social experience, but also the Rocky Mountain West was the home base of the militant Mine-Mill union. Beyond this advantage, California, with its strong radical and liberal communities, held the potential for a favorable response. If the film failed in the West, its prospects elsewhere were dim indeed.

For months the International officers had prepared to make *Salt of the Earth* a Mine-Mill organizing tool, especially in the Rocky Mountain field. A key dimension of this plan was the use of its annual wage-policy conference in Denver to showcase the film and energize IUMMSW locals for the promotion of its wide exhibition. Biberman recommended that Travis acquaint the conference delegates with the progress made in New York, Detroit, and Chicago (the resistance in the Midwest had not yet solidified). He told the Mine-Mill officers that the film would go first to those communities that had organized well. And in a questionable diplomatic lapse, he asserted that communities had to "earn the right to have this film." By all union accounts, the conference screening was an unqualified success. The delegates responded to the preview with an enthusiastic endorsement of a resolution that embraced the film and praised its producers, screenwriter, director, actors, and technicians for a "wonderful job." On April 6, President John Clark informed Biberman that the conferees had gone on record in favor of an "all out fight for public showing in all Mine-Mill local areas." *Salt*'s "best promoters," Clark reported, would be the rank-and-file delegates, who had been "tremendously moved by the film." Publicity man Morris Wright characterized the screening as the "high point" of the entire conference.[55]

After consulting with Mike Wilson, Maurice Travis and the Mine-Mill leadership moved quickly to implement the conference resolution. Recalling the "warmth" and "great pride" stimulated by the conference presentation, he informed local unions of the obstacles overcome in New York. Travis pilloried employer interests for the "contemptible" methods used in their effort to prevent production and distribution of *Salt*. To bring these events closer to home, he noted that six Denver theaters had refused to screen the picture for the IUMMSW conference, largely due to pressure from "outside interests." And he acknowledged that "every enemy" of the union movement would continue to fight to silence "this dramatic and effective weapon of organized labor."[56]

In words that echoed Biberman's letter, Travis warned that only through diligent organization work could Mine-Mill ensure that the film was shown to a wider public. He then quoted Biberman's explanation of the process by which communities might get an early booking. Travis urged locals to secure theaters and organize a "guaranteed audience." Never underestimating the resistance the union faced, he exhorted members to use their cinematic weapon to promote the "message of democracy and unionism." Simply stated, Travis said, "the picture *is* Mine-Mill and everything we stand for."[57]

The promotional experience in Denver, home of Mine-Mill, was characteristic of the struggle unionists faced in the effort to support the film in the West. From the beginning of his search for a theater, Wright had encountered obstacles. The owner of the World Theater, where the conference preview was originally scheduled, backed out of his agreement after being warned that screening *Salt* would put him out of business. Pressed for details, he expressed fear of Red-baiting in the press, whispering campaigns, and problems with distributors. Another reluctant exhibitor told Wright that an IATSE operator had objected to running the film on instructions from his business agent. The operator of the Cameron Theater, Walter McKinney, also feared complications with IATSE, though he had been told by Jarrico that union projectionists in New York had capitulated because the IA had "no legal leg to stand on and they [knew] it." After a telephone call from a Denver AFL official, appealing to him on the basis of free expression, McKinney relented at the last minute and the wage–policy conference showing went ahead.[58]

Encouraged by the successful showing and the enthusiasm of the viewers, McKinney next consented to a commercial run, starting in May. But he soon reversed himself under renewed pressure from IATSE business agent Charles Webber, who warned of Red-baiting in the press and promised to obstruct weekend showings at the Cameron by strict enforcement of union rules. Counterpressure came from a city-wide union committee that promised heavy attendance. When McKinney consulted the *Denver Post* concerning its attitude, he learned that while freedom of expression would be respected, the *Post* wanted him to know that any proceeds paid to IPC would "go to the Communist Party" and be used to "aid the enemies of our country in their effort to destroy us." Under "heavy pressure," McKinney canceled and, in mid-May, Wright resumed his search for a theater.[59]

The most interesting innovation in the Cameron negotiations was the emergence of a novel nuance in IATSE policy. Because of the threat of legal action, as well as the specter of nonunion projectionists, the IA had formulated a subtle new approach. Its latest strategy was to harass, obstruct, persuade, and threaten exhibitors, but to avoid outright refusal to furnish an operator. In Denver, Webber told McKinney that he had nothing against *Salt*, which was a good movie, and that he personally opposed censorship; but he was following orders from the International union to "do everything possible to prevent showing the film." If all else failed, on the other hand, he was to "give in and handle it."[60]

As the struggle wore on, Wright encountered a firm refusal to negotiate from other Denver-area exhibitors, though reasons varied. Some feared negative publicity, others the IATSE treatment; and still others confronted pressure from distributors who threatened to deny future bookings. For example, the manager of the Welton, a downtown burlesque house, was interested in a booking, but knew that if he ran *Salt* he would be "ruined" because the "distributors would run [him] out of town."[61]

Angered by the blackout, the Colorado state AFL spoke out in support of free expression. After seeing the film, *Colorado Labor Advocate* editors attacked the "anti-Red hysteria" that had produced a "black silence of fear." *Salt* was "*not* Communist propaganda," but simply "good social commentary and good movie-making." Without endorsing Mine-Mill, the AFL organization did support the union's right to produce a film expressing its point of view. Moreover, the *Labor Advocate* insisted that the film be "judged on artistic ability and content rather than on its producer." The voice of the state Federation urged that some Denver exhibitor "take his courage in his hands (and in the current hysteria courage [was] needed) and show the film."[62]

Other liberal organizations joined in the protest. Both the American

Civil Liberties Union and Women's International League for Peace and Freedom urged that *Salt of the Earth* be "widely shown." The ACLU's Colorado branch expressed concern over the pressures exerted on exhibitors by private groups and "possibly government agencies," which were "intended in effect to suppress the movie." Incensed over the denial of the "right to see," the ACLU criticized Denver theater owners for creating a new criterion for exhibition — "movie orthodoxy" — and challenged them to accept their responsibility to screen controversial films.[63]

Indignant over the rising pressures, Mrs. Allie Jay, owner of the Arvada Theater in the Denver suburbs, took the chance. Warned by her son that the distributors would cut her off, she insisted on honoring her contract because she "did not like censorship of any kind." Besides, it was a business proposition and she needed revenues. After a successful four-day run at the Arvada, *Salt* closed in Denver. So did the Arvada Theater, shortly after Mrs. Jay's act of courage.[64]

Confronted by formidable odds, Mine-Mill proceeded with its promotional campaign. On April 18, Wright and Biberman met to discuss strategies for a sweeping public information campaign. At this point they still assumed substantial commercial exposure in the Denver area. Biberman's advice was to rely on personal contacts with opinion leaders and major organizations. Responding to Ben Margolis's recommendation, Biberman also counseled greater emphasis on *Salt*'s entertainment value at the expense of the narrower focus on labor. Moreover, he suggested that promoters stress the film's effort to grapple with the problems of the Mexican-American population and women. And in the Southwest, he argued, it was especially important to stress the positive reaction to previews in Mexico, which indicated the film's potential contribution to "the understanding of our country," as well as "our own understanding of the Mexican people." Finally, union support would be required; and Biberman was sure that *Salt* could "do more to win friends and community support than anything else ever put in Mine-Mill's hands."[65] What Biberman could not control was the ongoing collusion between IATSE and the distributors to close off access to theater space. In the face of intimidation by the major motion picture companies and their distributors, no public relations program was likely to succeed.

In contrast to the sputtering Denver campaign, Mine-Mill mounted an impressive effort in Silver City, where local reaction seemed most unpredictable. While Juan Chacón's role in the film had been exploited elsewhere, Silver City was his home territory and he worked hard to promote its showing. Chacón prepared a description of the production process that was widely disseminated throughout IUMMSW. Focusing on the role of Mexican-Americans in Local 890's filmmaking venture, Chacón emphasized their activism in artistic decision making and the importance of the union community's capacity for portraying the lives of members. Eventually, concerns developed in Local 890 because Chacón had "been called out too often" to promote the film, often at the local's expense. The International later defended its use of Chacón as worth the sacrifice because he was a "valuable asset to the film company and the promotion of the film." His work on *Salt* was typical of what some union members saw as Chacón's tendency to shoulder responsibility personally rather than work "collectively"; the result, they argued, was the rise of "bad feeling" that "culminated at the [Silver City] showing."[66]

Local 890's internal disagreement was insignificant, compared to the community disruption occasioned by *Salt*'s Silver City premiere. Arturo Flores later asserted that the film raised issues that some local citizens preferred not to discuss, such as the Mexican-American drive for equality and the women's struggle for respect within the union family as well as in the larger community. Local critics attempted to divert attention from these problems by alleging Communist influence within Mine-Mill and on the film. One important adversary was Reverend Sidney M. Metzger, the Roman Catholic bishop of El Paso, who bitterly attacked "Communist leaders who dominate a union." On other occasions he was more specific, denouncing Juan Chacón and Local 890. It was not surprising, therefore, that Metzger opposed the film or that priests in Santa Rita and Hurley urged parishioners not to see *Salt* when it played in Silver City. Although one priest in Bayard bucked the trend, recalled Virginia Chacón, most church officials opposed Local 890 and its efforts for political reasons: "We were Communists. How were they going to support us?" Similar concerns persuaded local theater owners E. W. Ward and Tom Wallace not to book *Salt of the Earth* when it became available. Ward conducted his own local poll, which convinced him that "the best interests of the community would be served by not exhibiting it." But H. D. McCloughan, owner of the Silver Sky-Vue Drive-In theater, read the numbers another way. Despite pressure from the local chamber of commerce, American Legion, cattlemen's association, and Silver City officials, McCloughan concluded that 90 percent of Grant County residents wanted to see the film. His decision to show *Salt* reflected both a perception of widespread local interest and personal friendship with the Chacóns and other Local 890 members.[67] There was to be no blackout in Silver City.

Although the Hollywood "cultural workers" chose not to attend the

Silver Sky Vue drive-in theater playbill, Silver City, N.M., May 1954. Archives, University of Colorado at Boulder Libraries, Clinton Jencks Collection.

Newspaper advertisement for *Salt of the Earth* holdover engagement, Silver City, N.M., May 7, 1954. Miller Library, Western New Mexico University, Juan Chacón Collection.

May 5 opening in Silver City, they sent a telegram commending the local
people who had "inspired the film and worked so hard to make it." The
filmmakers reminded the union community that the whole world now
knew that they were indeed the "salt of the earth." From the Hollywood
Hills, they "embraced [them] all." Perhaps more meaningful was the message from the deported Rosaura Revueltas, who expressed "joy in knowing
that this motion picture will bring us together." Revueltas asserted that the
future belonged to "the kind of people depicted in this film." Unable to
secure a visa for the occasion because of INS obstructionism, she lauded
Salt as a "flag of friendship above the confusions that surround us." A
disconsolate Virginia Jencks saw IPC's failure to send a delegation to Silver
City as a "bad mistake of appreciation and evaluation," which communicated a lack of enthusiasm for the entire project. She observed that there
was "bitter feeling against Paul and Herbert," who had gone elsewhere for
showings; but "nobody came here."[68]

Despite the disappointment, the Silver City opening was a smashing
success. In the community that had reviled the production company a year
earlier, cars lined up for blocks waiting for an opportunity to see the results
of the company-union collaboration. The local press underplayed the film's
appeal. The *Silver City Daily Press* attributed large crowds to "local curi-
osity," while the *El Paso Herald Post* insisted that audiences were "not inspired" by a picture that presented a "false" impression of mining conditions in New Mexico. To counteract these assertions, Local 890 took to the
airwaves, using its regular radio broadcast to underscore the unprecedented
turnout for *Salt* and to cite favorable reviews in the national press. The
reality was that *Salt* played to capacity crowds at the Silver Sky-Vue Drive-
In. An audience of five thousand saw the film during six days of exhibition,
which eventually returned more than one thousand dollars to IPC; the
turnout was remarkable for a county of fifteen thousand people.[69]

This success led IPC to seek Local 890's assistance in promoting the film's
exhibition in New Mexico and the Southwest. In a report to Chacón and the
local executive board, the filmmakers emphasized their progress against
great odds, which had enabled 100,000 people to see the picture. And they
claimed, somewhat disingenuously, that union pressure on behalf of *Salt*
had broken the IATSE boycott and begun to open the market. With Mine-
Mill backing, they argued, the "same thing [could] be done in New Mexico." To achieve this goal, IPCD had persuaded the reliable liberal activists,
Craig and Jenny Wells Vincent, to handle distribution in the state, assuming
Local 890 approval. Within ten days the local union consented to the arrangement and the Vincents were on board as coordinators of New Mexico

distribution. Although Local 890 was prepared to work with them to bring "more power to *Salt of the Earth*," the distribution plan was stillborn.[70]

Plans soon took shape to screen the picture in New Mexico, Texas, Arizona, and elsewhere in the Southwest. Ambitious publicity programs were advanced, often in connection with Mine-Mill organizing drives or representation elections. In most instances, they came to naught, as the spreading conspiracy of suppression extended into many remote areas. For example, from El Paso, Mine-Mill International representative Alfredo Montoya reported that exhibitors had been intimidated into "refusing to discuss the matter." At least one theater owner reported that his chain office in Mexico City had advised him not to handle the film. As an alternative to commercial exhibition, several union showings took place; and Montoya launched plans for screenings in Ciudad Juárez. Meanwhile, in Denver, Walter McKinney, who had originally proposed booking *Salt* throughout Colorado and New Mexico, was cowed into submission. As an alternative, the film was shown to Mine-Mill audiences in Clifton, Morenci, Bisbee, Miami-Globe, Ray, and Hayden-Winkelman, all in Arizona; Bayard, Miniturn, Carlsbad, in New Mexico; and Laredo, Texas. Because these were mining towns, the showings had an impact on entire communities. Despite demonstrable enthusiasm in the area, distribution in the Southwest was effectively contained as the result of heavy pressure from the major distributors and intimidation by community organizations such as the American Legion. Union stewards promoted *Salt* among workers, ad hoc worker committees "interviewed" exhibitors, and Mine-Mill officers sponsored public screenings; but "even sympathetic theater owners could not withstand that kind of pressure."[71]

Beyond Colorado and the Southwest, the northern Rocky Mountain area was Mine-Mill's other major field of activity. Here the story was depressingly similar. The International's assigned coordinator, William Gately, reported broken commitments in Helena, Butte, and Anaconda, typically after a distributor in Salt Lake City had warned theater owners of possible future discrimination. In Helena, for example, a prospective exhibitor "completely reversed himself," having been told that *Salt* was controversial and "dangerous." Although IPCD's Sonja Dahl wondered "who belong[ed] to that long arm" from Salt Lake, Jarrico knew full well that the reason theaters were closed off was that the major studios had told exhibitors "if you play that film, you'll never get another." By June, Gately was convinced that it would be a "tough fight to get the picture shown in these communities." It was no different in Seattle, where no theater owner would "take a chance on booking *Salt of the Earth*." When one theater manager dared to express interest, he was deluged with warning calls urging that he "stay away from it." These developments persuaded him that it would be "dangerous for him to show this picture." Gately concluded that "they've put a hammer on him," which suggested that Seattle would be the "worst town we've hit."[72] Although noncommercial showings went forward, the Northwest was a closed market by late summer and IPC prospects were fast diminishing.

Coming Home: California as a Last Opportunity

An important reason for IPC's absence from the Silver City opening was the key figures' immersion in the crucial promotional effort in California. Two days after the Silver City premiere, *Salt* opened in San Francisco, without incident and with IATSE projectionists. Bay Area labor groups rallied support for the beleaguered film. The leftish ILWU and its blacklisted journal editor, Alvah Bessie, plugged the film with the membership, while the San Francisco Labor Council endorsed the picture as "a good deal less than a Communist tract" but "a good deal more than a routine movie." The film also drew strong approval from R. L. de Cordova of Latin-American Democrats, who (in Spanish language leaflets) urged San Franciscans to see a film that portrayed the fight to "bring alive" the slogan "all men are created equal." Moreover, the local reviews were excellent. In a largely favorable comment, Luther Nichols of the *San Francisco Chronicle* invited readers to pretend that the Red-baiting had never occurred and judge the film "without preconceptions." What viewers could expect, he argued, was a "forceful human document" that succeeded by offering "starkly real portrayals of individual character."[73] After a solid four-week run, *Salt* broke even, a result that promised better things in the Los Angeles area.

As the Los Angeles premiere approached, IPC worked feverishly to assemble a strong interest-group coalition behind the film. As always, labor unions were at the center of the effort. IPC Distributors wrote directly to one thousand Los Angeles union officers, business agents, and shop stewards, confident that *Salt* would bring them "new pride in being part of organized labor." Among the area's strongest labor advocates were Mine-Mill, ILWU, the Amalgamated Clothing Workers, the Packinghouse Workers, the Retail Clerks, and the Labor Committee of the Independent Progressive Party. While they pursued top officials, *Salt*'s promoters operated on the assumption that it was the "rank and filers and lower echelon leaders who do the real selling job." Their stealth approach was so successful that the Los Angeles–area AFL and CIO leadership eventually intervened with public

Official Publication of Hotel and Club Employees Union Local 6, AFL
April 10, 1954

Every motion picture that comes out of Hollywood is Union made. The actors, designers, carpenters, electricians, cameramen and all other workers who help to produce the picture are members of one or another union affiliated with the American Federation of Labor. But the product that is sent out for exhibition on the screens across the land by the major Hollywood studios has ignored the existence of unions in their scripts and scenarios.

So it took a labor union to write, direct, enact.and produce a motion picture of, by and for workers. "The Salt of The Earth," playing at the Grande Theater on East 86th Street is the story of a strike in New Mexico that involves a scarce 100 metal miners. Yet, the simplicity and sincerity with which the story is told and the patient suffering of the workers involved makes the "Salt of Earth" the story of union everywhere and the struggle of the metal miners becomes the struggle of workers everywhere. It is a very moving drama which every member of a union who has ever had to face the stubborn refusal of an employer to come to a settlement, will be able to appreciate and understand. We recommend it highly.

D.H.

SALT OF THE EARTH — now playing
MARCAL THEATRE
6025 Hollywood Blvd. • HO. 7-0811 and DU. 4-2157

Editorial endorsements from the western labor press suggested potential union support for *Salt of the Earth*, May 1954. Archives, University of Colorado at Boulder Libraries, Clinton Jencks Collection.

attacks on *Salt*, a response interpreted by Leonard Titelman of IPCD as evidence of the company's significant "inroads to [the] labor movement."[74]

In early May, both AFL Central Labor Council secretary W. J. Bassett and CIO Council secretary Albert T. Lunceford warned union workers to "beware of Communist-inspired efforts to enlist labor support" for the film, which had allegedly been produced by nonunion labor. Lunceford, a conservative business unionist, also charged that *Salt* proceeds were earmarked for the Communist Party. With this action, the AFL and CIO establishments closed ranks in support of the conspiracy to spill *Salt* before it opened. As a follow-up, the Hollywood AFL Film Council added its voice to the chorus of criticism with a warning that all union members should be "on guard against" the picture and its "clever and deceitful manipulation of fact." With these attacks, business unionism sided with the forces of repression. While IPCD denied all allegations immediately, the damage had been done. The company's only recourse was to insist that *Salt* was an "artistic and powerful instrument" that would be useful to unions in their efforts to "solidify and strengthen their ranks."[75]

The IPC arguments were not persuasive to IATSE leaders, who still schemed to find a way to kill the film without violating the law. In early May the International launched a full investigation "to determine whether it's possible to keep the union's projectionists from working *Salt of the Earth*." IATSE International Vice President Carl Cooper of Hollywood announced that if the Alliance could "stop it within the scope of the law," the union would act. Meanwhile, an FBI informant reported that Walsh was prepared to order union projectionists not to handle the film and make it a test case, if challenged in court. While no open directive had been issued, Walsh did register "strong opposition to the film" in a public statement that promised to "throw stones in the way of the Communists." However, when the chips were down, IATSE acknowledged that it could not order its members to boycott *Salt* because such an action would violate the secondary boycott provision of the Taft-Hartley Act. This admission drew immediate fire from Hollywood American Legion Post 43, which registered concern over the union's unwillingness to place the film on the AFL Central Labor Council's "unfair" list.[76]

While the labor wars raged, IPC faced another obstacle when the Los Angeles press refused to take paid ads for the *Salt* opening. After a preview showing for the press, representatives of the major local papers decided by majority vote to reject IPC's advertising (though the *Daily News* refused to go along). Similarly, radio advertising was sharply restricted. The press boycott brought a protest from an ACLU delegation and a flurry of telephone protests. But the advertising problem was but one of several blows against *Salt*. By July, IPC distributors learned that no second features would be made available by the usual Hollywood providers. Sonja Dahl described the action as "hot and heavy in Los Angeles." To the IPCD executive, it seemed that "only Silver City and San Francisco [were] lands of the free and democratic." There was a similar touch in Jarrico's dry congratulatory message to Dore Schary, a recent appointee to the ACLU advisory council: "could you use your good offices to persuade local metro exchange to stop illegal discrimination" and "allow us to book metro shorts to run with 'Salt of the Earth'"?[77] No answer was forthcoming from one of Hollywood's foremost showcase liberals.

Although IPC faced formidable opposition, the company was not without friends in the Los Angeles area. Since Wilson's November speech attacking the "film burners," John Howard Lawson and the Hollywood Council of the Arts, Sciences, and Professions had been mobilizing support for *Salt* on the Left. After a private preview for ASP insiders in March, the organization acted on Lawson's suggestion that it cooperate with IPCD by distributing six thousand announcements and invitations for the Los Angeles premiere showing at the Marcal Theater. While ASP worked to stimulate attendance, radicals focused attention on Lawson's recently published *Film in the Battle of Ideas*, which featured the *Salt* experience as an illustration of the problems and possibilities of committed independent film production. Lawson regarded the film as a "vital contribution to the development of people's and working class film art in the United States." As one Los Angeles FBI informant observed, communist watchers firmly believed the *Salt* project to be a party initiative; at least one Hollywood communist-turned-informer thought that the production "probably represent[ed] the principal effort of the Communist Party cultural groups in the past several years."[78]

The friends of IPC overlooked no possible means of mobilizing support for the film. Because the Mexican-American population was assumed to be an important part of the market for *Salt*, a special promotional effort targeted Chicano/Chicana consumers. Spanish-language reviews and leaflets proclaimed the importance of the picture for the Mexican-American community. To bring this point home, the Los Angeles branch of the American Committee for the Protection of the Foreign Born sponsored a guest appearance by Chacón in connection with a major Cinco de Mayo celebration held at Los Angeles Armenian Hall. In this way, promoters sought to link *Salt*'s major themes to the commemoration of Mexican independence. The Committee for Protection of the Foreign Born continued to proselytize for *Salt* throughout its Los Angeles run. Its outspoken executive director, Rose Chernin, exhorted supporters to work for *Salt*'s widespread exhibition as an antidote to the "racist aspects of the Walter-McCarran Act" and its mass deportations of Mexican nationals. To Chernin, these efforts would strike a "blow at the Justice Department and their McCarthyite treatment of the foreign-born." A final component of IPCD's appeal to the Los Angeles Mexican-American community lay in the widespread use of a message from the absent Rosaura Revueltas, who, on the occasion of the premiere, wrote of her work on the production in glowing terms. Emphasizing a new appreciation for the "struggles and aspirations of the Mexican-American people in your country," Revueltas maintained that, like Esperanza, her life "[had] changed from what [she] learned in making this picture."[79]

Although IPCD expended great effort to attract a large Mexican-American audience in Los Angeles, the response from the barrio failed to meet expectations. Many Hispanic leaders "loved the film," but the promotional campaign "was not a very successful operation" in box-office terms. Helen Slote Levitt, an active leftist and one of the moving forces behind the radical *Hollywood Review*, wistfully recalled that "the people didn't come." Levitt, who worked tirelessly as a member of IPCD's Hollywood staff, concluded that the explanation was simple; Mexican-Americans "just don't come to Hollywood just to see a movie" because "it's not where they feel comfortable." And due to the problems already encountered in securing theaters, IPC gave little serious thought to booking an east-side house.[80] The failed attempt to fully mobilize *Salt*'s most receptive audience again dramatized the difficulty of sustaining a cross-class alliance in support of the film.

When *Salt* opened at the Marcal, huge crowds appeared despite the comprehensive radio and television press blackout. Though the reviews were mixed, Ray Ringer of the *Los Angeles Daily News* welcomed the film's focus on serious issues like the woman question, worker aspirations, and race relations. He noted that if propaganda had crept into the picture, it involved issues that needed to be aired and ideas that could be supported. An enthusiastic *Daily Worker* reported the opening as a "distinct triumph for the long-awaited film." Despite sporadic picketing by the American Legion and the film's other opponents, the opening represented a real, if modest, victory for IPC. To Biberman, the event was merely the beginning of the fight to "haul down the pirate flag of blacklist, boycott, and conformity in Hollywood."[81] *Salt*'s very appearance marked an important milestone in the development of independent film production.

The film's eleven-week run in Los Angeles, which grossed thirty thousand dollars, was a small shot in the arm for a struggling organization. Promotional efforts sputtered on during the summer, with discouraging results. Typical was the report from a Chrysler plant literature distribution: "reaction sharply divided—men either Red-baited and refused leaflet or smiled and said, 'Oh, Salt of the Earth' and took the leaflet." The good news was that all workers had heard of the film; the bad news was the sharply divided reaction. As the summer passed, the harassment continued. Picketing occasionally became disruptive, spot announcements were canceled, distributors refused to supply second features, the technical boycott persisted, and sniping from the press went on unabated. Despite several brief runs in California cities, none was financially significant. *Salt's* last theatrical booking in the United States occurred in Menlo Park, California, in September 1954. From that time on all efforts to arrange domestic commercial exhibition ended in "complete failure."[82] For the moment, it appeared that the grand experiment was doomed.

SEVEN

Another Chance

Overseas Markets and Domestic Limitations

By summer 1954, Herbert Biberman and Paul Jarrico sensed that the end was near. The Independent Productions Corporation had exhausted the available options, and there was no relief in sight. Both men were heavily in debt, as was the corporate organization they had brought to life. After brief successes in New York and Los Angeles, the national market had closed up due to the effective boycott engineered by the International Alliance of Theatrical Stage Employees and its allies. Since domestic exhibition seemed a dead end, only foreign distribution remained as a potential safety valve to relieve the financial pressure building against the *Salt* group; and realistic assessment of prospects for the overseas market led to a grim conclusion: the project could not be salvaged. In the absence of miraculous intervention, the venture was over. But just as hope seemed to evaporate, a second chance for IPC to recoup its heavy losses came from an unlikely source. This initiative was also to end in disappointment, but not before Biberman and Jarrico made one last attempt to chase the dream.

Critical Acclaim: Foreign Distribution and Artistic Credibility

Since the beginning of the *Salt* controversy, labor opponents, industry critics, and government figures had worried about the film's potential impact on audiences outside the United States. Roy Brewer, IATSE's Hollywood proconsul, was especially concerned over the damage allegedly inflicted by the picture in Latin America, where, he insisted, nationalists were likely to use the film to generate opposition to American imperialism. Because of these fears, the film's entry into the foreign market was a matter of serious concern for its most committed enemies.

These reservations were shared by other, more detached parties as well. As early as March 1954, Arthur Mayer of the Independent Motion Picture Distributors Association in New York cast his lot with the critics. *Variety* reported that Mayer had not only refused to handle the film, but had also urged in a public statement that its export be strictly prohibited. He declared his personal opposition to censorship, but maintained that "somewhere one must draw the line" and that *Salt of the Earth* was that place. Mayer claimed to speak for New York film executives and critics, who feared that the picture would "fall into the hands of Russian or satellite Communists" and be used to portray "life in capitalistic America" as a "tooth and fang struggle of oppressed poor people against monsters who own everything but hearts." Ignoring the factual basis of the events depicted in the film, Mayer denounced *Salt* as a potential "weapon in the hands of the Communists," who were certain to "make out that these [were] true conditions."[1]

To the dismay of the picture's enemies, IPCD went ahead with an aggressive foreign distribution program. Major market areas included Canada, Mexico, the Soviet Union, China, and both Western and Eastern Europe. The results varied, depending on geographical proximity to and ideological distance from the United States. The foreign distribution process also revealed the extensive reach of the boycott movement.

Because Mine-Mill had a strong Canadian organization, a vigorous campaign developed north of the border. By the end of June 1954 a Toronto booking had been arranged, while Sudbury, Ontario, and Vancouver, British Columbia, planned fall showings. William Longridge of the Canadian Mine-Mill Council reported that a union promoter was already on the job and that the creation of an AFL-CIO committee was under way. Within three weeks, reality had set in. Longridge described a campaign of intimidation strikingly similarly to the model previously established in the United States, particularly the pressure applied by distributors. The "blackout of the motion picture industry," he told Sonja Dahl, was "very extensive." Mine-Mill knew that Canadian theater owners, linked as they were to chains in the United States, had been "told not to book it" and denied shorts to play with *Salt*. Moreover, IATSE projectionists balked at screening the film. Longridge was astonished at the resistance in a heavily unionized town like Sudbury, where the "Canadian lackeys" in the theater business were "bending over backwards to carry out the wishes of their American bosses." While the pressure had also escalated in Toronto, theater owner Herman

Canadian unionists promote exhibition of *Salt of the Earth* in Toronto Labour Day Parade, September 1954. Archives, University of Colorado at Boulder Libraries, Western Federation of Miners and International Union of Mine, Mill and Smelter Workers Collection.

Shawn had "not in any way been intimidated or shown any sign of weakening." A two-week run at the Toronto Variety Theater began in early August, following IATSE's decision to run the film rather than face legal action. Although the picture was relegated to a second-rate house, critical response was positive. In free Canada, a CBC reviewer devoted a fifteen-minute broadcast to *Salt*, which he recommended to listeners in glowing terms. Nathan Cohen of CBL-Canada regarded the film as a "deeply-human drama," in the vein of such classics as *The Bicycle Thief* and *Open City*. Despite the pressures emanating from the States, free expression had not been obliterated in Canada.[2]

The result south of the border was in some respects discouraging. When *Salt* was first screened for Mexico's largest distributor, his response was enthusiastic. In anticipation of booming business, he planned to handle the picture's exhibition in his country. One day later, the arrangement was abruptly canceled, and the film eventually opened in a Mexico City art house specializing in opera film and Soviet pictures. After substantial obstructionism and delay, partly due to Mexican government fears of American reaction, *Salt* finally premiered in October 1954.[3]

The Mexican reaction to the film surpassed anything Biberman had experienced in the United States. Laughter, applause, and raw emotion greeted *Salt* in Mexico City. Every city newspaper was effusive in praise of IPC's achievement. In an unexpected move, the Catholic Legion of Decency awarded the picture its second highest rating. And for a short time, at least, Rosaura Revueltas was lionized as the accomplished artist she was. *Tiempo* cited realism and social content in comparing *Salt* to such great international films as *The Grapes of Wrath* and *Open City*, while *Novedades* recommended it "without reservation" for its "pace, sharpness, and power" in presenting a "piece of reality." Likewise, *El Universal* endorsed the film's "indisputable realism" and *La Afición* saw in it the achievement of "values of spiritual power" through its emphasis on "indestructive [*sic*] faith in a just cause." Even the government news organ *El Nacional* dismissed the "hostility of certain elements in the United States" and their "labeling it Communist," with the observation that insistence on "equal treatment for American citizens of a different race is not a Communist demand." The government recommended that *Salt* be seen by all who had "not lost their sense of solidarity with brother Mexicans, harassed and exploited on the other side of the border by forces which do not truly represent the American people or their government." This solidarity surfaced at the premiere in the spontaneous singing of the Mexican national anthem at the film's conclusion, as Rosaura Revueltas was overwhelmed by emotional demonstrations of affection. Present for the occasion, Biberman reported widespread amazement that North Americans had made "the first *Mexican* film." Artist Diego Rivera summarized the Mexican reaction in a word: "stupendo!"[4]

More restrained, but nonetheless enthusiastic, was the reaction of Eastern European audiences and leaders, whose ideological commitments predisposed them to welcome *Salt* as an expression of socialist realism. Jarrico maintained that IPCD wanted Communist United Nations delegations to see the film "not simply for political reasons," but rather because the company "wanted to sell the picture to these countries." To ease the task, diplomat Andrei Vyshinsky and the Soviet delegation invited several hundred Communist-bloc representatives to a special showing at Soviet quarters on Park Avenue in New York. When the screening ended, there was a "long silence" followed by a "loud standing ovation." A beaming Vyshinsky pumped Jarrico's hand and predicted: "A billion people will see this film.

You will make a lot of money." Because *Salt* played in China for fifteen years as well as the Soviet Union, the foreign audience was large; but in financial terms, Jarrico later recalled, "we lost our shirt."[5]

One year after foreign distribution began, *Salt* had yet to repay production costs. The ongoing struggle confirmed a company statement, made in September 1954, that it would take "gallons of sweat and much patience" to ensure that foreign audiences gained access to the film. The extended reach of the boycotters guaranteed that problems would continue to plague distribution efforts. Because American labs refused to produce copies, for example, Polish distribution was achieved only after a print had been shipped to Poland, where the printing and fitting were completed. And as of September 1958, *Salt* was losing money in the key South American market, where no reputable distributor had been found. In Mexico, Jarrico later recalled, it "disappeared" after one week. Later, when IPCD closed a deal with the Chinese government, the United States government nullified the sale. China simply appropriated the film, and no money reached the company. Finally, in 1959 the United States Information Agency blacklisted *Salt* for foreign distribution, which meant that IPC was unable to convert blocked foreign currency into dollars by exhibiting the picture overseas.[6] The practical consequence of these difficulties was the company's failure to successfully exploit the foreign market to offset losses sustained during production and domestic distribution.

Though disastrous financially, *Salt* won critical acclaim in Eastern Europe. In East Germany, the only nation to provide cash in advance, it "opened with the greatest success." Even more satisfying to Biberman was its receipt of the grand prize at the 1954 Czech International Film Festival at Karlovy Vary. While *Salt* earned recognition as best picture, Rosaura Revueltas won the award for best acting performance by a woman. The citation for the film prize recognized *Salt* as a "work of great artistic and ideological value." One Czech reviewer later compared the picture favorably with the George Gershwin opera *Porgy and Bess*, which had also been performed in Prague. Critic Norbert Fayd regarded *Salt* as a "better-executed work of art" that successfully represented "American reality."[7]

The Czech award did not go unnoticed in the United States, where Biberman's nemesis, Congressman Donald Jackson, again attacked *Salt* as Communist propaganda. Jackson interpreted the recognition as further evidence of the film's Soviet inspiration and IPC's subversive intent. And in a parting shot at Revueltas, who had accepted the award in Prague, Jackson dryly expressed the hope that the film's star had "had an enjoyable and productive visit in the Kremlin." He declared that *Salt* was "doing the job it was designed to do" by "carrying distortion, inaccuracy, and American-made Red propaganda to millions of human beings," who were likely to accept the picture's images as "a true expression of American life." Jarrico found in Jackson's diatribe evidence that the anticommunist congressman was on the defensive, because Jackson had also complained bitterly that some deluded American film critics had reacted favorably to the picture.[8]

But it was not only American and communist reviewers who saw merit in *Salt of the Earth*. As the film became well-known in Europe, the plaudits continued to accumulate. From France came reports of a "unanimously enthusiastic" response in both press and public forums. Critical reactions ranged from "great" to "masterpiece" and even "classic." Several reviewers applauded the film's social realism, which, *Paris Soir* observed, Zola would "have loved." *Le Monde* noted that a long time had passed since the French had "seen such a forthright American film." And more credible than the Czech award was *Salt's* receipt in 1955 of the International Grand Prize for best film exhibited in France, awarded by the *Académie du Cinema de Paris*. At this moment of artistic triumph, Biberman later asserted, both he and Jarrico felt free to break their business ties with the company to "secure [their] personal and family livelihoods."[9] Vindicated, though financially devastated, they were at last psychologically able to make a new start.

The recognition received in France was more positive than was the response in England and Canada, where *Salt* produced a mixed reaction. About half of the British press reaction was favorable, though critics tended to comment on the political controversy surrounding the film, including charges of propaganda content. Most appreciated *Salt's* stark realism and many credited the filmmakers with truthfulness in portraying the dark side of American capitalism. The *Glasgow Herald* observed that the film "roars against the brutalities of Big Business," while the *Western Evening Herald* found *Salt* "powerfully moving" and "sadly true." Much of the London press praised the picture, which "touch[ed] greatness" and had "the power to move" an audience. Acknowledging the difficulty of making an unbiased judgment, *Punch* described a "perfectly good story, propagandist but ably and ingeniously worked out, well acted and quite gripping." And the *Catholic Herald* described a "challenging" picture that was a "human document in which the people [were] real and likable." These reactions were consistent with the high praise for *Salt* at the Edinburgh film festival. Despite substantial endorsement in the press, the film was not financially successful in England, a result that Biberman attributed to the British distributor's insistence on emphasizing the strike rather than the picture's entertainment value (this at a time when London was paralyzed by two strikes). Jarrico later agreed, noting IPC's forced reliance on a "third-rate distributor."[10] These problems notwithstanding, foreign distribution in England and elsewhere held more promise than did thwarted domestic exhibition in the United States. Despite that potential, however, the residual impact of the American boycott ensured *Salt*'s financial failure abroad.

Because of *Salt*'s considerable critical success overseas, FBI watchdogs redoubled their undercover work in late 1954 and 1955. Although the bureau had previously come up empty-handed, in August 1954 the Justice Department reiterated its interest in "any information that would indicate the film was originally financed or subsidized by foreign sources." In September 1954, a Hollywood informant reported that consistent with prior investigations, his information still indicated that domestic funding was drawn primarily from the Los Angeles and New York areas. Not only was there no "Moscow gold" behind the project, but the Soviets' hard bargaining on prices helped seal IPC's fate as a business operation. Three years later, the United States government was still obsessed with *Salt*'s success in the foreign market. USIA officials confirmed that it was one of a very few films that "were giving the United States trouble overseas." Despite the strength of the foreign market, Jarrico asserted in 1955 that the "domestic conspiracy" had hampered international distribution. Even after foreign outlets were found and *Salt* gained a "big reputation abroad," he recalled, IPCD "had trouble getting the money that was owed."[11]

Never a financial success, *Salt of the Earth* had nonetheless emerged by 1955 as what an IPC progress report deemed an "honored, respected, prize-winning film," extolled by some critics as an "American masterpiece." The company weakly claimed to be confident of the "ability of this film to win its way" into American theaters. Bolstered by *Salt*'s extraordinary worldwide reception, IPC looked forward to the day when it would be able to demonstrate that the company could "not only make good films," but "make them pay off as well."[12] What the report failed to say was that IPC's last chance to crack the domestic market in the United States had already been lost.

Last Opportunity: The "Big Thing" and the Boundaries of Collaboration

So confident were Biberman and Jarrico of the film's "inherent value" that they persisted in a search for a miracle that would "lift [them] above the damage wrought by the conspiracy." And at a low point, when prospects looked bleak, the miracle did appear in the persons of three AFL union leaders from Pennsylvania who, in April 1954, came to the Grande in New York to see *Salt of the Earth* for themselves. Deeply moved by what they saw, these men (a Teamster, a UE representative, and a United Mine Workers officer) immediately recognized the picture's potential value as a tool in labor education and union organizing. With an eye to the film's instructional use, these union men approached New York labor lawyer Seymour Baskind with a proposal to have the AFL assume responsibility for *Salt's* national distribution, beginning with Pennsylvania bookings. Aware of the picture's checkered history, the unionists were "not troubled by it"; the Federation's imprimatur would silence any such criticism. One of the Pennsylvania union leaders told Biberman at a New York meeting that he had been persuaded by the film that the allegation of subversive content had no merit. Baskind closed the New York discussions by asserting that the more he had "heard about the gang-up on this film," the angrier he had become. Like most union enterprises, the scheme would take time to develop, but as a "partisan and fan," he meant to "put this through."[13]

Biberman was stunned, then elated, by the plan. He saw the country as one step away from liberation—a new "democratic self-realization, of peace, reasonableness, and fraternity." He wrote his family of his excitement, though he tried to restrain optimism with an acknowledgment that all these ideas could easily "vanish in thin air." But he insisted that the underlying principle would not be denied: "working people cannot ignore this film" and it was "up to [IPC] to find the right way to bring it to them."[14]

The important question soon became how best to approach the AFL national leadership with the idea. Baskind first spoke to Jack Levin, who had been working to locate theaters for IPC, and then to James L. McDevitt, director of Labor's League for Political Education (LLPE, AFL's political arm) at AFL headquarters in Washington. While Baskind and Levin understood *Salt's* value to the labor movement, they were motivated primarily by the potential for personal profit in its successful distribution. An old friend of Baskind, McDevitt agreed to see the film, which impressed him as a means by which big labor might move into the field of theatrical distribution. Convinced that *Salt* was a "pro-labor film," McDevitt recommended that other national AFL leaders be brought into the discussions.[15]

Meanwhile, Biberman began to consider the AFL initiative in a wider context. Convinced that part of IPC's problems lay in inadequate national awareness of the entire undertaking, he concluded that a comprehensive plan for the future was essential. The AFL opportunity held the potential for such coordination and organization, which Biberman hoped would develop from the labor leaders' plan to start with Pennsylvania and move gradually onto the national union scene. The LLPE scheme was more important, he thought, than opening at new theaters in New York or anywhere else. Biberman remained convinced that *Salt* was financially viable, but that true economic success required "the involvement of others than ourselves . . . and we have not achieved this because *we have not been working on it.*"[16]

While IPC was involved only indirectly in the courtship of AFL, Baskind and Levin worked feverishly to bring about a liaison; and with some encouraging results. By mid-June they had built substantial interest in the plan, now referred to by Biberman as "the big thing," among Federation leaders. If LLPE agreed to take on the film, Biberman wrote, IATSE would be "out-flanked." Hoping to accomplish this goal, he followed Baskind's advice and temporarily shelved the Chicago lawsuit so that no public conflict between IPC and AFL would be evident. All was in readiness for a top-level decision, once a private screening for Education director John D. Connors and his entire department could be held. Convinced that a major breakthrough was imminent, Biberman could barely contain his optimism, especially after he learned that McDevitt "loved" the film and wished to "move ahead with it."[17]

So overwhelmed was Biberman that he was prepared to meet any demand AFL might make; and there was a big one. In order to avoid inter-union conflict, McDevitt asked that Mine-Mill's name be removed from the film credits. Biberman favored accommodating this request, which he regarded as reasonable, especially since certain IUMMSW leaders in New York had once made the same suggestion. He noted that "there are Mine-Mill signs all through the film," so the credits were actually unnecessary. His true views were clear in his expanded rationale:

> I have no qualms about dropping Mine-Mill's name — (it was a romantic notion to begin with) — too filled with a bravado by people who did not think sufficiently about what other people think . . . I am a little tired of dragging un-businesslike gestures along at the cost of my fortune and *our* fortune. We live and learn. I feel no debt to Mine-Mill that is not repaid implicitly in the film. The desire on our part to repay it explicitly at the cost of vast possible support seems to me to be silly. It is sectarian and should be recognized as such.[18]

While Biberman was making a business decision, there is a tone of condescension in his remarks, a tone that suggests that the bond among "cultural workers" and manual laborers was weaker than the *Salt* group had once proclaimed it to be. Because he had worked so long and so hard on the film project, Biberman was understandably ready to do all in his power to bring the LLPE scheme to fruition. Full of doubt and conscious of the obstacles ahead, he confided to his family that he really didn't expect it to develop, but that he had "never, never wished so hard for anything material — as for this to transpire."[19]

As the decision date drew near, Levin wrote Biberman to reassure him of McDevitt's steadfast support. Levin described the AFL's reaction to the first showing as "beautiful" and the response "enthusiastic," especially among the women present, who argued that the film was a "great picture, not alone for trade unionism but for theater entertainment." McDevitt, who remained convinced that *Salt* "could mean a lot for trade unionism," now insisted that the final screening be held in Washington the following week, so that he could be present for the final discussions. Once Connors, the Education Department, and Federation president George Meany had seen the film, AFL approved McDevitt's plan and promised that negotiations on terms and procedures would follow. On July 1, Biberman reported that patience had produced a spirit of "unanimity and readiness." An elated Biberman looked forward to the dissemination of *Salt* under the aegis of the "most conservative men in the American Federation of Labor,"[20] whose endorsement guaranteed the film's credibility and legitimacy. It was a naive hope.

The AFL offered to purchase forty prints and distribute perhaps one hundred through theaters, if all releases and agreements could be secured. For a moment, Biberman glimpsed "normal right of way into the American audience." To his family, he wrote that negotiations were "nearing a climax." Two days later Levin reported that progress had been "exceptionally good" and that thus far, the film stood "on its own feet." Despite uniformly encouraging reports from the matchmakers, Levin and Baskind, nagging delays throughout the month of July[21] suggested that all was not well.

Sensing complications, Biberman worked to strengthen the AFL connection in any way possible. One aspect of the offensive involved a *Salt* screening for the Cleveland Clearing House on Civil Liberties, an informal group of Ohio organizations concerned for civil rights, racial justice, and labor interests. The key figures in Cleveland (from IPC's standpoint) were AFL leaders, who created a coalition of supporters "even broader than the Washington picture." As a follow-up to the private showing, Sam Pollock, president of Meat Cutters Local 427 wrote McDevitt to endorse the film and to urge LLPE to take over its distribution, a step that, in his view, would "educate more people and stimulate a pride in the union that one thousand speeches could not do so well." Dismissing the political controversy over the picture, Pollock asserted that there was "nothing in the film that any AFL union could not subscribe to."[22]

Despite encouragement from Cleveland, the AFL deferred action for six weeks. The Federation's delaying tactics concealed an internal struggle that was eventually to doom IPC's hopes for LLPE sponsorship. The hidden complication lay in IATSE's position on *Salt*, which was itself the subject of an intense intra-union battle. The fate of the LLPE plan was inextricably linked to the outcome of the fight between Richard Walsh and Roy Brewer for the Alliance presidency, a feud that had been brewing for months, and was aggravated by Brewer's rabid anticommunism.

Ever since May, when IATSE had decided against a complete projectionists' boycott of *Salt* in Los Angeles, New York, and elsewhere, Brewer had leveled a barrage of criticism against Walsh and IATSE for their refusal to take bolder steps to kill the film. However, the root of this attack may be traced to Walsh's refusal to act on Brewer's 1953 proposal to reorganize IATSE, with greater autonomy for the West Coast locals. On May 3, a national committee to "Draft Roy M. Brewer for President" issued two broadsides to IATSE members, charging Walsh with creating "mistrust" between Hollywood and other Alliance locals and harboring a "soft attitude on Communism." Ten days later, Brewer took aim at Walsh's refusal to keep IATSE projectionists from showing *Salt* in New York. Although Brewer later asserted that *Salt* was a minor issue in his campaign, Biberman recalled that he consistently attacked Walsh for softness on the film. Brewer also argued for "reform, not revenge" against former communists in the entertainment industry, but disingenuously denied playing a role in "clearance" procedures. While he rejected "excesses" in communist hunting, Brewer's remarks left little doubt that he presented himself to the union membership as the stronger anticommunist.[23]

As his campaign against Walsh picked up momentum, Brewer took the anticommunist crusade well beyond the movie capital. Most dramatic was his foray into New Mexico, in July 1954, for an appearance as self-appointed Hollywood ambassador to the people of Silver City. Convinced that "most Mexican-Americans were well-intentioned good people who were being manipulated," Brewer resolved to go to Silver City to show the people of New Mexico "that there was no hard feeling between Hollywood and the people of that community." In this instance, the initiative had first come in March 1953 from Silver City through Denver, where movie distributor Charles R. Gilmour (claiming to speak for New Mexico movie exhibitors) had set out to repair the damage that the "whole mess" had done to the community's reputation. Gilmour, who operated the Denver-based Gibraltar theater circuit, proposed a scheme to dramatize Grant County's Americanism. If a Hollywood delegation came to Silver City to "speak for the industry" and for "Americanism," Gilmour argued, it could "kill the growth of the Commie seed right here." Nervous about the negative reaction to the Revueltas arrest, Gilmour also suggested that a Mexican-American star be sent to assist community leaders in their anticommunist campaign. Local theater owners insisted that because the Hollywood Ten had "moved en masse to the Silver City area," a response became "a matter of industry support." Concerned about falling box-office receipts, the exhibitors called on the producers to coordinate "concerted action against this spread of Communist activity." In June 1954, the Silver City Chamber of Commerce revived the plan, with the support of several local committees and Seaborn P. Collins of Las Cruces, who was then a candidate for national commander of the American Legion. Once invited to participate in a Fourth of July celebration, Brewer seized the political opportunity thus offered him. He promised the chamber of commerce that he and other Hollywood personalities would join them as a reminder that "all good Americans reject[ed] everything for which *Salt of the Earth* [stood]."[24]

Once apprised of the invitation, the Screen Actors Guild swung into action with a request that Pat O'Brien, Ann Doran, Pedro Gonzalez-Gonzalez, Marian Carr, and Ann Robinson represent Hollywood. On July 1, 1954, SAG president Walter Pidgeon and board member George Murphy urged their attendance in anticipation of national press coverage that would result in "great propaganda for the United States in Latin America" by correcting the "distorted picture of race relations" allegedly created by *Salt of the Earth*. More to the point, SAG assumed that their "very presence" was certain to correct the "myth that Hollywood is full of Reds." Participation was, in the words of "Buck" Harris, an "excellent public relations move" for the Guild. In response to the board's initiative, Gonzalez-Gonzalez and Doran joined Brewer and local dignitaries for a July 3 patriotic observance designed to cleanse New Mexico's image. Among those present were Governor Edwin Mecham, Major General C. G. Sage (New Mexico's adjutant general), C. M. Custer (grandnephew of George Armstrong Custer), Seaborn Collins of the American Legion, and Catholic Church representatives, including Archbishop Edwin V. Byrne of Santa Fe.[25]

Of the many speakers, none was more colorful than Brewer, who told the assembled patriots that Hollywood and Silver City had something in common in that each had been "victimized by the Communist Party." He maintained that the two communities were stronger because they had faced the

"Americans for Americanism Day," Silver City, N.M., July 3, 1954. Second from left, Archbishop E.V. Byrne; at microphone, Pedro Gonzalez-Gonzalez; right, Harold Welch of Silver City Chamber of Commerce. Courtesy of Silver City Museum.

challenge in a "realistic fashion" and were fully aware of the danger from American Communism. More nationalistic rhetoric filled the air as speaker after speaker elaborated on the program theme, "all out for America."[26]

Another view prevailed in the Mexican-American miners' community. Workers generally boycotted the event after Local 890 blanketed the mines and plants with leaflets warning them that the rally targeted them and their union. While some Hispanos attended, they were largely scabs and *"venditos"* (sellouts), and were certainly not representative of majority opinion in their ethnic community. Both Virginia Chacón and Arturo Flores recalled the Americanism rally as part of management's persistent attempt to break the union and as an affront to the Mexican-American population. As a result of worker suspicions, local "cowboys," *"venditos,"* and chamber of commerce supporters made up the bulk of a crowd of one thousand (far short of the thirty thousand predicted). Nonetheless, local officials and their Hollywood associates were well pleased with the day's proceedings. Ann Doran, a SAG board member, reported that her words and Pidgeon's message had been well received; and, she thought, Gonzalez-Gonzalez had done a "splendid job of public relations."[27]

Roy Brewer's role in the Silver City rally blended well with his challenge to Walsh for the IATSE presidency. The Brewer presidential campaign also meant that prospects for the LLPE scheme depended on the outcome of the IATSE election. By 1954 a leading force in the motion picture industry itself, Brewer now began to escalate his attack on Walsh for softness on Communism, oblivious to the International union's clear hostility to *Salt*, as well as to Communism in the entertainment field. The immediate impact of the Brewer campaign was to force Walsh further to the right. At the IATSE convention in August, Walsh reminded delegates that he had "opposed Communism in every possible way." In an important move for *Salt*'s future, he also pledged to "carry on that fight vigorously" with the expectation that all Alliance members would "do the same."[28] With these words, the prospects for AFL support of *Salt* diminished significantly.

McDevitt and LLPE did not capitulate to the anticommunist militants without a fight, but the obstacles proved insurmountable. Walsh was understandably prominent among the AFL leaders consulted when plans for Federation distribution of *Salt* were on the table in June and July. Moreover, according to Jarrico, McDevitt threw his support to Walsh in his successful reelection race against Brewer. Jarrico mistakenly believed that Walsh had been a party to the development of a momentary consensus in favor of AFL distribution as a pilot program for further Federation film ventures. Therefore, Jarrico thought, his decisive reelection in August promised to free *Salt* from the paralysis that had prevented IPC from realizing the financial rewards of independent production. Biberman was equally confident that with Walsh "no longer under the gun," the company's problems would be solved.[29]

In the wake of Walsh's reelection, Biberman attempted to restart the planning process initiated by AFL in June. Convinced that with Brewer out of the way "one of the problems [was] apparently solved," he urged Levin and Baskind to proceed with negotiations as soon as possible. Biberman also suggested that AFL consider the original Pennsylvania plan, which would permit LLPE to engage the steelworkers and UMW as partners in promotional activity. Finally, he asked Baskind to discuss lifting the IATSE ban with Walsh before the AFL's upcoming national convention.[30] Biberman's impatience with the pace of deliberations was painfully obvious.

Baskind, in turn, counseled patience, pending neutralization of the

IATSE resistance, which, he argued, was a foregone conclusion. Once this "formality" could be dealt with, the project could move forward, but with a novel twist. Baskind no longer contemplated adoption by the AFL, but he did propose to create his own independent distributing corporation that might lease the film to LLPE. The new distributing company was to purchase the film at cost, thus severing formal ties with IPC and IUMMSW. In addition, IATSE would have to lift the ban so that future commercial distribution might proceed without obstruction. Finally, Baskind sought a twenty-five thousand dollar fee for his services as midwife.[31]

Desperate for a solution, Biberman warmed to Baskind's proposal. He especially welcomed the idea that the lawyer intercede with Walsh to request removal of the ban against the film. Biberman wrote that he "passionately" wished to see the "consummation of this undertaking," which could become a "notable achievement in the history of communications." Accepting the Baskind proposal, he predicted that its success would be a "potent step in the direction of recovering sanity in our land." Not only would successful distribution become a "unifying force," but it was also likely to be financially rewarding. Only one problem remained: because of past losses, IPC was in no position to provide a twenty-five thousand dollar fee. Baskind would have to settle for compensation based on future profits. Biberman hoped "with all [his] heart" that this contingency arrangement would not deter Baskind from his goal or from "further association with the film."[32]

Unmentioned, but still a matter to be considered, was the need for Mine-Mill to assume a lower profile by becoming a silent partner in the venture. In September, Jarrico told Travis that LLPE insisted on the removal of both IPC and IUMMSW from not only the credits, but "any further relation to the film." Moreover, AFL wanted to be able to say that "Mine-Mill never owned any part of the film." Jarrico assured the International that the filmmakers could find a way to make such a statement truthfully but still make personal contributions to the union strike fund and to Local 890, all out of anticipated profits. Nervously anticipating a positive reaction from Mine-Mill, Jarrico asked Travis for some insider response to the new plan.[33]

By mid-September it was clear that Jarrico and Biberman intended to move on the Baskind proposal. It was, after all, their only option. Biberman was more frank with his family than in his public statements or in his correspondence with Mine-Mill. On September 1, he admitted that "the arrangements are not glorious — but they are arrangements." Not only would the Baskind distribution plan "give the film its chance," but it also promised financial rescue. The AFL wanted a divorce from the IPC and Mine-Mill, as well as complete control of the picture. Aware that his IPC colleagues would "yell," Biberman nonetheless accepted a price of 400,000 dollars which meant a company profit of 160,000 dollars. Most important, he thought, a "real distribution company" would be in place and *Salt of the Earth* would finally "become part of our American movie fare." To Biberman, "these people [meant] business," and they had "solid support,"[34] With no alternative before them, Biberman and Jarrico embraced the last-chance solution.

But what of Mine-Mill? The union that had stood firm with the "cultural workers" through troubled times had a moral claim on the product of their collaborative labor. Resolved to put the case in blunt terms, Biberman began his approach to Mine-Mill by announcing that the company and its officers found themselves "stone broke." He uncharacteristically admitted that because the obstacles had been "too much to overcome," the company and its principals had "not had quite enough to tip the scales." When approached by the AFL, he added, they "saw a beam of light," which had finally led to an agreement, for which the IPC sought union consent:

1. Film purchase at cost for a five-year lease, with deferred payment.
2. IPC and IUMMSW names removed from title
3. Creation and funding of a national distribution organization.
4. Guarantee that Mine-Mill held no stock in or ownership of film.
5. World market revenues not covered by the agreement.

Biberman assured Travis that the IPC had fought against the bill of divorcement, but finally accepted the proposal because they "had to buy it" lest the film be buried. He also argued that it was impossible to completely disassociate Mine-Mill from the picture because future viewers would know of its origins. Furthermore, he insisted that no "greater compliment" could be paid IUMMSW than adoption by bodies like AFL and LLPE. Through the proposed agreement, *Salt* became "the film of all American labor," even though "certain things must be given up." Biberman noted that with the acceptance of the deal, the film would move "from the dog-house into normalcy and honor in one step," as would the IPC and IUMMSW. Were this the case, their sacrifices would be justified. The IUMMSW concurred, agreeing, in Jencks's words, that "the message was more important than the union's self-interest." Understanding IPC's desperate financial position and hoping for national distribution, Mine-Mill agreed to sign releases from their original agreement once a contract was signed. In late October, IPC reported to the members of Local 890 and the Ladies Auxiliary that *Salt* had become an international success and the company stood on the verge of a "major breakthrough."[35]

Reality was much more complex. From the beginning of the LLPE negotiations, Baskind and Levin were engaged in the project primarily because they anticipated substantial profits from the enterprise, the success of which was absolutely dependent upon IATSE's willingness to lift its ban on *Salt*'s exhibition. The Alliance's relaxation of its policy was in turn predicated on the assumption that, relieved of the pressure exerted by Brewer's candidacy, Walsh would adopt a more moderate stance. The outcome now hinged upon the results of negotiations among Levin, Baskind, McDevitt, and Walsh, conducted in October during the AFL national convention in Los Angeles. At this time McDevitt, Jarrico, and Biberman met to discuss *Salt* and its usefulness for the labor movement. Baskind and Levin also secured support from officers of several Hollywood AFL Film Council unions. Meanwhile, McDevitt reiterated his conviction that the film was "moderate" and consistent with an approach to its subject "which any AFL union might have employed." For a time, both Biberman and Jarrico thought that they would get "serious big labor support."[36]

But Walsh's intransigence meant that their optimism was unwarranted. Biberman later recalled that Baskind's conversations with Walsh in Los Angeles had not gone well. On a bright note, however, Baskind's contacts with other IATSE officers in Los Angeles revealed "unqualified opposition to the boycott." But Walsh remained adamant in his belief that *Salt* was Communist-inspired and that "it wouldn't be a beneficial story to the United States if it got outside of the United States for exhibition." Undaunted by Walsh's reaction to the LLPE proposal, Baskind arranged for a follow-up meeting in New York, by which time he expected Walsh's opposition to be "dissolved."[37]

But Walsh was unmoved. At the New York meeting, he told Baskind that "under no circumstances would [he] recommend the picture" to LLPE and that if its use ever came up for consideration, he would advise McDevitt "not to have anything to do with the picture." Moreover, Walsh threatened to attack any AFL leaders who "in any way associate[d] themselves with this film." Biberman later asserted that Walsh threatened to "make a scandal" if LLPE persisted in its plans for *Salt*. Since Walsh was an AFL vice president and a key member of LLPE, his words were not taken lightly; it is clear that he killed the Baskind-LLPE scheme. In Biberman's view, Baskind dropped the plan because it threatened his personal interest in an ongoing working relationship with the AFL.[38]

By November even the politically naive Biberman saw the handwriting on the wall. In a letter to Baskind, he pessimistically noted that a negative decision by LLPE and Baskind would be a "serious blow," but that the plan had been "right, good, necessary . . . and worth the effort." He added an assurance that even if it failed, the lawyer would retain his "respect, affection, and gratitude." Biberman then floated several alternative proposals for union involvement in nationwide distribution, in the hope that Baskind would continue his association with IPC. He weakly expressed his hope that there was not a "quality of 'all or nothing' in respect to this film."[39] These were the words of a desperate man.

When the bad news from New York arrived, few were truly surprised. Given Walsh's attitude and McDevitt's unwillingness to proceed further, Baskind's decision to abandon the project was predictable. More difficult to account for, as noted by Chicano historian Juan Gómez-Quiñones, is the mainstream labor movement's failure to capitalize more effectively on *Salt's* obvious instructional value in labor education. The answer lies in an appreciation of domestic anticommunism's awesome power. *Salt's* appeal to mainstream unions was insufficient to overcome the hostility of conservative union leaders like Walsh. To Biberman, it was all very clear — and quite simple: "Richard Walsh had refused to permit it and had made his opposition so frightening that Mr. Baskind and his associates determined to give up the project entirely."[40]

Biberman's disappointment in the result was evident in a lackluster note to Travis, in which he feigned satisfaction with the new union friends he had made. He wearily solicited Mine-Mill's assistance in a new IPC effort to manage national distribution itself. Biberman suggested that the International work to gain the support of all other independent unions.[41] The pro forma aspect of his letter bore the earmarks of despair.

The failure of the LLPE plan came as no surprise to Travis. He told Biberman that despite his own past criticisms of the film's handling, he "profoundly" understood the value of the picture. Most important, Travis commended IPC's behavior as a "marked lesson in courage and adherence to principle" for his union, as well as for "progressive people generally." For Mine-Mill, he added, the most valuable use of *Salt* would be its employment "in defense of the union" and perhaps for internal noncommercial showings. Nonetheless, he fully understood IPC's need for more commercial exhibition, with IUMMSW assistance.[42] The balance between the two approaches was yet to be established.

As a first step toward a new distribution campaign, Biberman and Jarrico now moved to rekindle the IPC–Mine-Mill collaboration. As early as August 1954, Jarrico had met with the Mine-Mill executive board to discuss the more effective union use of the 16-millimeter print. Although they had long feared that the International might use *Salt* as a weapon in their many jurisdictional battles and thereby alienate other unions, in November IPC moved to assist Mine-Mill by providing copies for internal use. Expressing the hope that Mine-Mill would work to promote new commercial showings, Biberman made a renewed pledge of cooperation. In agreement with Biberman's conciliatory gesture, Jarrico urged that the International move immediately to "mobilize its locals and representatives behind an intensive effort to get theatrical bookings."[43] The tenor of these communications clearly implied that a new start on both union and commercial distribution had been made.

No amount of renewed planning could conceal the gloom that set in with the failure of "the big thing." While Biberman had doggedly pursued an elusive dream, he emerged from the battle convinced that the collapse of the AFL-LLPE distribution scheme transcended the petty concerns of Walsh or IATSE. Reflecting upon the summer's experience, he concluded that the outcome involved the entire motion picture industry "and a lot more . . . industry, committee, and IATSE." In a similar vein, Jarrico later speculated that the "same focus in the labor movement" that had doomed the CIO's left-led unions and inspired the CIO's role in vanquishing radical European unions had also "managed (with no great difficulty) to kill the plan." To Jencks, the plan's failure was symptomatic of corporate America's success in limiting the New Deal social contract through an accommodation with a domesticated labor movement. "Given the Cold War context," Jencks recalled, the AFL "was not going to take any chances."[44] The muzzling of Cold War critics, progressive unionists, and Hollywood leftists was part of the larger social compromise that locked business unionists and corporate managers in a grim embrace. The failure of the LLPE plan and the decisive suppression of *Salt of the Earth* were directly related to that socioeconomic and political bargain, which contributed to the homogenization of Cold War culture in the United States.

Coda: End of the Road

The IPC principals could last only so long. As early as the summer of 1954, the financial strain became unbearable for some. In June, Jencks reported to Mine-Mill that a meeting with Jarrico made it clear that the man had "reached the end of the rope" as far as full-time work on *Salt* was concerned, and that he would soon be forced to "turn to the problem of making a living." Wilson had already refocused on the "problem of eating," while it was unclear "how much longer Biberman [could] last."[45]

By the end of 1954 *Salt* had run commercially at exactly thirteen theaters in the United States. In January 1955, an IPC report recapitulated the film's awards and the "extravagant praise" it had received outside the country. Earnings had been meager, but the company's "original hope for substantial income from abroad still seem[ed] justified." Though financially strapped, the filmmakers felt that they had been part of an "historic achievement" and claimed to be confident of "ultimate success." But off the record, Biberman was less optimistic. Frustrated by the ongoing IATSE boycott, he complained to Baskind that union technicians still refused to develop film and projectionists were not running *Salt* in Chicago. In a lengthy soliloquy, Biberman's pent-up anger spilled out:

> Is there nowhere within the greater body of the largest aggregation of trade unions in the United States, one voice strong enough to register moral objection and moral suasion in respect to such a situation? Is it possible that of the scores of influential leaders who have seen this film, and loved it, there is not one whose emotions, whose preacceptance of the honest, public, artistic effort, will rise above the small fears and petty "political" undertakings of less representative individuals? Is there no one who has sufficient love for our laws, not to speak of our traditions, who will be impelled to create sanctuary for a union film within our country? . . . Are the responsible leaders of the working people in the United States determined that this silly game of surreptitious maneuvering continue to be imposed upon us? Are they satisfied that the millions of members of their organizations shall be deprived the opportunity which they themselves wish might be afforded them of profiting from a viewing of this film because a few obstinate, unreasoning individuals are seeking dark satisfactions which will not stand discussion? .

While still professing his "unshakable faith" in the "moral stature of the leaders of the American union movement,"[46] Biberman regretfully concluded that they had utterly failed to grasp the issues at stake in the struggle. Yet he hoped against hope for the miracle that had continued to elude him.

During the long negotiations Biberman had frequently expressed self-doubts to friends and family. Many provided him with moral support in his darkest hours. Screenwriter Albert Maltz, his Hollywood Ten comrade, often reminded Biberman of the uncertainty inherent in the creative life. In late 1953, Maltz had acknowledged the possibility of failure after years of intellectual investment, but told Biberman that the "value of any creative endeavor" was not to be measured by its final outcome so much as by "its initial vision." This, to Maltz, was the "suffering and triumph in all creative work." He concluded that with *Salt* "the goal [had] been big and worth the terrible effort." Similarly, Biberman's wife, Gale, responded to her husband's despondency in the midst of the LLPE negotiations with an uplifting note insisting that he had "no right to assume any failure in Chicago — or anywhere else — as [his] own *personal* failure" simply because his efforts "didn't crack a huge machine." And when he returned to Los Angeles during the LLPE negotiations, Gale was a rock of support. She assured him that it had been a magnificent, courageous battle, and insisted that they stay with it to the bitter end. "Like Esperanza in the film," she told him, " 'I don't want to go down fighting! I want to win!' "[47]

But the negotiations stalled and the machine rolled on, crushing all in sight. By year's end, IPC seemed beaten by the IATSE–Hollywood-corporate-labor establishment. Biberman and Jarrico understood that because, at Baskind's urging, they had long postponed legal action, IATSE had come to assume that IPC was paralyzed and would never retaliate against its multiple provocations. But once the AFL distribution scheme had been derailed, other options took on new life.

The LLPE plan had come as a "miracle," as Biberman had seen it in April 1954. By 1955, he later noted, "the only miracle left" was a lawsuit "to cause American justice to open the channels to a free market . . . in communication of ideas." As an important preliminary step, IPCD again attempted to open *Salt* in Chicago. It came as no surprise that IATSE projectionists refused to run the film. For IATSE Local 110, the surprise occurred when the company filed a complaint naming officers, projectionists, and the union as defendants in an action seeking damages and injunctive relief.[48]

With the shift in venue to the Chicago courtroom, the *Salt* struggle for free expression entered its final stage. In a practical sense, the battle for open exhibition was already over, because the film's disastrous first run had come to an ignominious end. Since Jarrico, Biberman, Wilson, and the other IPC artists and leaders had been forced to seek other employment, the issue became part principle and part pocketbook. The suppression of *Salt of the Earth* had run its dismal course, but sorting out the residue would require many years of further struggle. The indirect effects of the ongoing controversy cast a long shadow over the lives of the men, women, and organizations who had worked to preserve free expression in Cold War America.

EIGHT

Legacies

The Consequences of Suppression

As Biberman and Jarrico awaited the results of legal action in Chicago, other momentous events signaled a relaxation of the domestic tensions that had dominated Cold War America. Coincidental with the collapse of the LLPE plan and the IPC shift to legal action, the United States Senate gained the courage to censure Wisconsin senator Joseph McCarthy, who had long hounded American intellectuals, artists, unionists, and political figures across the ideological spectrum. While the impact of this action may not have been immediate, a sliver of light penetrated what had been a dark corner of American life for the embattled Left. However, the change came too late to save IPC or its sole creative venture, *Salt of the Earth*. And because the specter of the Communist menace lingered long after the Senate's action, the lives of both the *Salt* activists and Mine-Mill leaders were to be influenced for years by the project. For some, the persecution persisted long after the film controversy had disappeared from public consciousness.

American Justice: Challenge in the Courtroom

In early 1955, the IPC filed suit against IATSE's Local 110 in Chicago federal district court and anxiously waited for a decision. With the support of the American Civil Liberties Union's Illinois division, which, in March 1955, joined the company with an *amicus curiae* brief, IPC alleged that the projectionists' boycott violated the Sherman Antitrust Act of 1890, which had outlawed combinations in restraint of trade. Disclaiming any interest in the film's merits, ACLU challenged Local 110's actions as a group attempt to "act as a censorship board for the entire community." Its *amicus* brief argued that the projectionists union held "monopolistic control over motion pictures in Chicago" and that an injunction would employ the Sherman Act to achieve the "ends served by the first amendment," which protected feature films.[1]

In response, the IATSE defense claimed that the Sherman Act was inapplicable because no injury had been inflicted on the public by the union's actions. Moreover, the union contended that it was not engaged in interstate commerce and therefore could not be sued under federal antitrust law. In sharp disagreement, Judge Philip L. Sullivan ruled that the film was "certainly" in interstate commerce, which the boycott clearly interfered with. More importantly, Sullivan declared that the public had as much right to see a film as it did to attend a meeting or read a newspaper. In support of the plaintiff on every point raised, the judge ordered IATSE to lift the ban or face triple damages of 316,500 dollars. With this injunction, IPC's legal battle appeared to have ended in success. The result was widely reported as an important victory for free speech and a crucial advance in the struggle to exhibit *Salt* in Chicago.[2]

Biberman reacted with great satisfaction to news of the legal victory, which ensured that "sooner or later the private censors will be defeated" and the American people would gain the opportunity to "judge this film for themselves." *Mine-Mill Union* reported the result with greater restraint, as a first-round victory in what was likely to become a long legal fight. Mine-Mill was also quick to note that Sullivan's decision was "not directed against trade union organization or activity," an important issue for a union struggling to remain independent in the face of the steelworkers' and mineworkers' raiding campaigns. For proponents of free expression, such as ACLU, it was a significant judicial curb on an egregious abuse of power, which threatened the "entire stream of one form of communication in a large area." To Biberman, the decision opened a window of opportunity, or so it seemed.[3]

In an attempt to capitalize on the legal victory, the IPC offered to waive damages in return for Local 110's agreement to permit *Salt*'s screening in Chicago. While IATSE failed to respond directly, it reaffirmed its initial position through informal channels. Biberman interpreted the union's delaying tactics as a message that the film would never open in Chicago. By fall, the IPC was again in court, seeking a temporary injunction prohibiting further interference with efforts to run *Salt*. The ACLU, concerned over Local 110's exercise of the "power over all of us to choose or not to choose," remained steadfast in its support. In November 1955, the company reported that with many backers in Chicago and a strong argument it stood a good chance of winning an injunction. To Biberman, the moment was "propitious."[4]

His optimistic assessment of IPC prospects was premature. For months, the litigation dragged on, after which Local 110 changed counsel. The union's decision was a devious move, designed to force Sullivan off the case. Because the new attorney was Sullivan's nephew, the judge agreed to transfer the case out of his court to avoid conflict. In Judge Samuel Perry's court, the union argued that because some of the filmmakers had been named before HUAC as communists and refused to confirm or deny the allegations, the projectionists enjoyed an "absolute right" to refuse to run their film. Moreover, Local 110 alleged that *Salt* had been made with nonunion labor (a false charge) and that, therefore, operators might refuse to touch the picture. As Biberman later asserted, "absolute rights" were, in fact, "rights to destroy." Even more damaging were Local 110's interrogatories, which Judge Sullivan had deemed irrelevant to the case. When Judge Perry ordered Biberman and Jarrico to respond to Local 110's questions concerning their political beliefs and activities, thus in effect overruling Sullivan, the IPC withdrew its complaint and the case was dismissed. As a matter of principle, they refused to "disrobe in public at the command of Jalas,"[5] but the price paid was high. The IPC attempt to fight IATSE as a separate entity ended in failure.

Since late 1955, however, Biberman and Jarrico had explored a more comprehensive alternative action, aimed at the major motion picture corporations and their partners in conspiracy, including Brewer, Hughes, Walsh, Jackson, and their collaborators. The result was extensive preparation for a sweeping antitrust suit aimed at the conspiracy to boycott the production and distribution of *Salt*. While Jarrico, Biberman, and lawyer Ben Margolis originally believed they had a good chance to succeed, with especially compelling evidence against Brewer, they faced severe limitations from the outset.

Not the least of these obstacles was the immense financial burden, complicated by the exhaustion of liberal financial resources after so many appeals to support the *Salt* project. Typical was the advice Biberman received from an old friend, who questioned yet another effort to resurrect the picture. While sympathetic to Biberman's plight, this financial "angel" was less impressed with the antitrust suit than he had been with the film, which he had supported generously. Biberman's correspondent, a lawyer himself, was convinced that the major distributors had deliberately refused to exhibit *Salt*; but to show conspiracy was "quite another matter, difficult of proof." Another picture or a more realistic battle, he thought, made more sense. Then came the heart of the message: "would it be too cruel of me, as your friend, to say let go of the tail? Let the problem turn around . . . the picture itself is a fine work of art and speaks for itself. Should you not, at last, throw away the whip?"[6] It was sound advice, but difficult to accept for one who had fought so hard and long for the right to be heard.

While aware of the obstacles, the IPC and IPCD nevertheless filed suit in New York on June 21, 1956, asking triple damages of 7.5 million dollars under the antitrust law as well as injunctive relief. Named as defendants and "co-conspirators" were sixty-eight individuals and organizations, including Brewer, Hughes, Walsh, Jackson, the Association of Motion Picture Producers, the Motion Picture Association of America, IATSE, all major motion picture companies, and several distribution chains. The complaint charged that the alleged conspiracy and boycott in restraint of trade prevented any corporation or individual employing blacklistees from engaging in the motion picture industry in this country or overseas. Not only did the plaintiffs assert the existence of the much-denied but unquestionably real Hollywood blacklist, but the lawsuit itself was stunning in its scope. And given the power and influence of the defendants, it was perhaps naive from the outset to hope to prevail.[7]

Quixotic though their action seemed, Biberman, Jarrico, and Margolis thought the suit might succeed. Simon Lazarus, announcing the move, expressed gratification at the film's critical success and optimism concerning legal action: the company had produced a film that "brought honor" to the United States and fully intended to "win the suit . . . and re-enter the motion picture field." While he railed against the "self-appointed censors," he also insisted that the defendants be held responsible for the economic consequences of their actions. Most important, Lazarus argued, were the two fundamental and interrelated issues at stake: the rights of free speech and free enterprise. His statement resonated with pride in the past and hope for the future.[8]

As Biberman's lawyer-confidant had predicted, the critical problem was to prove conspiracy. Jencks recalled the difficulty of demonstrating conclusively that the unions, studios, and distributors had worked together and acted in concert. In Jarrico's words, the studios and laboratories admitted, "Yes, we refused to help this picture. We even took steps against the picture. But we didn't do it in collusion with other companies." In short, they "denied conspiracy, and under the anti-trust laws, [IPC] had to prove conspiracy." On the contrary, the companies were able to show that they had not cooperated in an orchestrated boycott. A case in point was that of

Republic Pictures, which, shortly after the suit was filed, conducted an in-house records search to prepare for its defense. Lawyer Charles Oberle asked Republic to produce any files relating to Congressman Jackson's telegram of March 19, 1953, which had requested studio action on the production of *Salt*. A review of the Republic files revealed that studio executive Maurice Benjamin had asserted in 1953 that nothing be done, since the firm had "no control over the picture" and saw no "basis on which [it] could take or participate in the action." Like Brewer, Republic fell silent. Apparently, only Paramount, Columbia, and RKO even acknowledged Jackson's appeal, and there was no evidence of action or collusion.[9] All of which tended to discredit a conspiracy theory, though it did not demonstrate innocence of harassment.

Even Brewer, against whom the evidence was most compelling, succeeded in his denials of conspiracy. During the trial, he denied having issued orders to IATSE locals and affiliates not to process or project *Salt of the Earth*. Later, when interviewed for the documentary film *A Crime to Fit the Punishment* (1984), he did not recall any such directive. Brewer disingenuously insisted that he didn't know how the word got out to locals. He argued that "there was really no dissent, in any area of our union."[10] While the evidence contradicted his assertions, the plaintiffs were unable to demonstrate conclusively that he had engaged in conspiratorial behavior.

In short, there was no smoking gun to document a conspiracy. The plaintiffs initially believed that they had definitive evidence in the Hughes letter to Congressman Jackson, which had outlined in meticulous detail the steps to be taken to kill the film. In order to prove collusion, Jarrico later argued, it was essential that Howard Hughes be called to testify; but try as they might, IPC attorneys were unable to subpoena Hughes. As a result, the company was handicapped in its effort to show how the Hughes plan had been implemented.[11]

Confronted by the need to earn a living, both Jarrico and Biberman resigned from their positions as IPC officers in June 1956, just as the antitrust suit moved forward. For Biberman, the company had become a "luxury which [he] could no longer afford." Moreover, he was determined to devote more attention to his wife and children. Finally, when New York lawyer George Brussel, Jr., a strong civil libertarian, agreed to accept the lawsuit, Biberman decided that a "climax" had been reached in his relationship with the company, and felt free to leave. Jarrico, too, severed his ties with IPC and attempted to recover his financial losses, eventually moving to Paris. Similarly, Michael Wilson disengaged from the *Salt* project and turned his attention to screenwriting, sometimes using fronts to market his work. In December 1955, an exhausted and emotionally drained Wilson urged Biberman to move on to other challenges. While grateful to Biberman for his tenacious defense of *Salt*, Wilson told him that "no one . . . expect[ed him] to make a life work of it."[12]

As the lawsuit dragged on for years, defense lawyers used another weapon against IPC, the issue of the principals' political beliefs. As a consequence, when asked to give a deposition, Biberman agreed only after making it clear that he would hold to the position he had maintained since 1947, which meant a firm refusal to answer questions pertaining to his political beliefs or those of others. While he stood ready to answer all questions bearing on the facts of conspiracy, unlimited examination of constitutionally privileged matters were to be off limits. But, as Jarrico later noted, the studio lawyers "managed to deflect the issue to whether we were Reds and dodge the issue of whether the industry had combined to stop an independent production." When the Biberman deposition was taken, defense lawyers asserted that IPC had been "organized, financed, and supported by Communists, Communist sympathizers, and fellow travelers for the purpose of espousing the cause of Communism and spreading the Communist propaganda." Their tactics clearly hinged on attacking the plaintiffs' political ideas and practices, rather than responding to the IPC allegations. Moreover, defense lawyers consistently sought to undermine IPC's case by linking Biberman to the company's ongoing operations long after he had resigned his position. Six years after his departure from IPC, the opposition was still trying to label him a managing agent for the corporation.[13]

In his summation of the case against the industry, attorney Ben Margolis charged that even in an industry well known for its disregard of the antitrust laws, the defendants' actions were "heinous beyond parallel." They had destroyed a property, he argued, by blocking manufacture, paralyzing the filmmakers' movements, and vilifying them through accusations of treason. Even more reprehensible, he insisted, was the industry's willingness to employ the outcasts as long as they worked through thinly veiled fronts, thus gaining access to the pariahs' talents at "bargain-basement prices." But when the blacklisted artists "dared attempt independent production," Margolis argued, they were to be "ELIMINATED . . . EXTERMINATED," lest they succeed in altering the "climate of fear" suffocating creative expression in Hollywood. Despite this harsh penalty, Biberman maintained to the end that the "American miracle" was still possible, with "justice in a free market — governed by law." In 1964, he asserted a continuing belief in that justice without which there could only be "chaos in a jungle — where accusation replaces truth — and cowardice *becomes the national virtue*." His words reflected the naivete perceived by Jencks and also revealed Biberman's romantic idealism, which marked his role in the *Salt* story to the bitter end. The *Salt* case went to trial in September 1964, and on November 12 the jury handed down a verdict of not guilty. In the absence of a smoking gun, no other result was possible. Jarrico later asserted that most jury members were sympathetic to the plaintiffs, but that conspiracy had not been conclusively documented.[14] *Salt of the Earth* and its creators, it seemed, were thus consigned to the dustbin of history.

Self-Defense and Survival: Mine-Mill in the 1950s

While the *Salt* group struggled in the courtroom, IUMMSW fought a spirited rear-guard battle in the workplace. In the wake of Mine-Mill's expulsion from the CIO, a scramble developed among other industrial unions hoping to replace its beleaguered leaders. By the early 1950s the remaining Mine-Mill loyalists found themselves courted by the UAW, the USWA, the Machinists, and the Teamsters. Ironically, this intense rivalry enabled Mine-Mill to survive as an independent union with a membership variously estimated to be from 75,000 to 100,000. In view of the steady political attack on IUMMSW, its survival as a successful union throughout the decade of the 1950s was a remarkable achievement. An examination of the generally unsuccessful raids on Mine-Mill's membership underscores the strength of WFM history and tradition in preserving an island of militant unionism in the sea of a rapidly bureaucratizing union movement, particularly among Mexican-American workers in the Southwest, the majority of whom supported IUMMSW to the very end in 1967.

While Mine-Mill had many suitors, the steelworkers were undoubtedly the most active. Starting in 1953, USWA-CIO undertook a double-edged campaign to attract Mine-Mill adherents to their organization: at the top leadership level, exploratory discussions examined common interests and affiliation by negotiation, while in the western field, aggressive raids sought to contest IUMMSW control of local unions. In both cases, a key point of contention was the desire of Mine-Mill loyalists to retain local control and separate identity in the event of affiliation with the gigantic steelworkers union. The USWA appealed to non-ferrous metal workers with assurances that their identity would not be lost by affiliating with the larger organization. Rather, the steelworkers argued that their diverse composition guaranteed that affiliates would retain their uniqueness and independence. As a bonus, the steelworkers pledged that new members would regain the organizational strength and bargaining power lost as a result of Mine-Mill's recent political difficulties.[15]

Side by side with promises of independence and new bargaining strength, the steelworkers openly and clumsily tried to exploit the Communist role in Mine-Mill's affairs. Misreading member loyalties, the CIO castigated Mine-Mill's left-wing leadership for allegedly adhering to the Communist Party line and practicing a "rule-or-ruin" policy that had nearly destroyed their union. In the belief that the IUMMSW membership wanted to halt the disintegration of their union and "return to the mainstream of American industrial trade unions," the CIO urged non-ferrous metal workers to bring their organizations into the steelworkers union and "reestablish their great traditions of unionism." In many parts of the Rocky Mountain West, Red-baiting went hand in hand with the steelworkers' organizing drives of 1954 and 1955. For example, in 1955, USWA-CIO attacked the Travis leadership with broadsides asserting that it was simply truthfulness to "call a spade a spade," and that it was not "Red-Baiting" to "call a Communist a Communist."[16]

USWA International representative Nicholas A. Zonarich discounted Mine-Mill claims of unwarranted raiding in IUMMSW jurisdictions. To Zonarich, the steelworkers' incursions were not raids; they represented a "revolt of Mine-Mill members against Communist leadership." A prime area for these inroads was the Montana field, where the "revolt in Mine-Mill" appeared to have reached an advanced stage by 1954. The struggle here was "important to American labor unions and to [the] country for security reasons," Zonarich argued, since Mine-Mill was "controlled by the Moscow toolbox." Convinced that the local leaders in Montana supported the steelworkers, he urged President David McDonald to target them in the renewed campaign. But after a dismal failure in Butte, Zonarich began to rethink the emphasis on the problem of radicalism. In April 1954, the chastened organizer noted that the "feeling of loyalty and pride toward the old WFM and its heir, the IUMMSW," had been mentioned by many observers as a "strong tie." Yet he found this idea "difficult to accept as a factor." Herein lay the steelworkers' blind spot: "condemnation of union officers for alleged radical tendencies" may well have "added to the solidarity of the union to withstand attacks."[17] The importance of the radical tradition to western mineworkers never quite sank in with the steelworkers in the 1950s.

In no area was Mine-Mill more entrenched than in the Mexican-American mining communities of the Southwest; and no local was more steadfast in its loyalty to the International than the Amalgamated Bayard District

Union. Local 890 was subject to the same pressures from the steelworkers and other competitors as those which had influenced Mine-Mill loyalists in the Montana field. Moreover, in the wake of the *Salt* controversy, the local battled incessant Red-baiting that focused on the film's creators. So intense were these pressures that, in 1953, Secretary Adolfo Barela spoke out against the attacks on the picture to calm member fears. He assured his union brothers and sisters that "what was going on in Grant County [was] similar to the Steel raids in Bessemer and in the Coeur d'Alenes," including the use of "open terror and great propaganda." Barela reminded union members of their friends in the community and solidarity within the membership, which made the organization strong. The Empire strike and the *Salt* episode had drawn the Mexican-American community together and created a bond that would enable Local 890 and Mine-Mill to withstand the steelworkers' onslaught, at least for the short run.[18]

In Grant County, the steelworkers' campaign employed the *Salt* controversy as a weapon in a drive to replace IUMMSW as the organization of choice. In response, Barela stressed the idea that Local 890's enemies were not worried about the film, so much as they wished to use it as a "union-busting move." He informed Mine-Mill members that the movie's harshest critics were the same individuals who had called in the steelworkers during the strike. With a parting blast at the "union-busters," Barela asserted that Local 890, which had "come a long way" under Mine-Mill leadership, refused to be "driven into company unions." In contrast, the steelworkers' district director, Charles J. Smith, claimed to have many supporters in Bayard who were anxious to affiliate with the CIO. Unwilling to identify with the craft-conscious AFL, they were reported to be equally disillusioned with the "Red label" at the top of Mine-Mill.[19] On balance, Barela's sense of solidarity between union, worker, and community was the more accurate measure of Grant County union sympathies in 1953.

As historian James Foster has noted, the Empire strike gave IUMMSW its "last breath of life" in the 1950s. The *Salt* project and the publicity surrounding it was part of that revival. At the national level, merger talks with the steelworkers, machinists, and laborers began in 1955, but no agreement resulted. Nevertheless, in the same year, during Mine-Mill's national strike against Phelps-Dodge, Kennecott, and American Smelting and Refining, Local 890 worked in cooperation with AFL craft unions and railroad brotherhoods to forge firm solidarity. Similarly, in 1956, discussions with the Teamsters led to a mutual-assistance pact authorizing joint organizational efforts, legislative work, defense against raids, and support of bargaining and authorized strikes. Their goal was to "organize the unorganized" and

promote the "mutual well being of the membership of the two organizations." Hoping to undermine this arrangement, the steelworkers saw to it
that the Teamsters received a report on the Communist connections of
Mine-Mill's top leaders, but the pact remained in effect and was renewed in
1961. After increasingly futile efforts to maintain an independent identity,
IUMMSW was swallowed up by the steelworkers in 1967, and a long
tradition of radical unionism seemed at an end.[20]

While Mine-Mill was able to turn back the steelworkers' raids for many
years, the accumulated pressures of constant representation elections, government harassment of officers, congressional hearings, and charges of
Communist infiltration had finally overwhelmed the heir to the WFM
tradition. As in many left-led unions, the leadership had concluded that
they simply had to make the best accommodation possible by merging with
a mainstream union.[21] It was the only way to protect the workers they
represented. The most remarkable aspect of Mine-Mill's struggle was not
its eventual disappearance, but the length of its survival as an independent
organization.

Following nearly two decades of bitter jurisdictional warfare, a new team
of International leaders, headed by Mine-Mill's new president, Al Skinner,
concluded that collaboration with the steelworkers was the only feasible
course of action for the struggling organization. The 1967 merger finally
ended the sometimes vicious Red-baiting featured in the years of competi-
tion. And twenty years after the merger, the steelworkers were ready to
boast of the radical tradition brought to the marriage by IUMMSW and its
predecessor, WFM. By 1986, a USWA fiftieth anniversary commemorative
brochure spoke with pride of the long and contentious Empire Zinc strike,
as well as the critically acclaimed film *Salt of the Earth* and the French
international prize it had captured in 1955.[22] Having won the bitter jurisdictional battle, USWA could afford to be magnanimous since the bitter
memories of the early Cold War had faded. Gone were the rancorous
charges of Communist domination leveled against Mine-Mill in its years of
defiant independence.

The residual strength of IUMMSW in Grant County reflected a long
history of Mexican-American unionism dating from the rise of Mine-Mill
in the 1930s and 1940s. In 1961, then–vice president Al Skinner reported
to the IUMMSW executive board that although widespread raiding had
caused serious inroads in many localities, the Southwest remained intensely
loyal to Mine-Mill. His analysis of Local 890 indicated that while the
USWA continued to staff an office in Silver City, steel's progress was nil and
"the raid was dead in this area."[23]

The dedicated unionists of Local 890 had built an organization in the 1950s that was more than a labor union. These men and women—some communist, some noncommunist, and others apolitical—had created a worker community that coalesced during the Empire strike and the *Salt* struggle to challenge the social, racial, and political values of their time. By fighting job and wage discrimination, they broke the economic bonds forged through generations of inequity. And their willingness to question inherited gender roles anticipated dramatic changes that were to transform American society a decade later. Furthermore, the people of Grant County pioneered a new brand of unionism that opened opportunity to talented leaders regardless of ethnicity or sex, which established a model the union movement has yet to replicate as it strives to modernize in response to new demands in a new era.[24] Finally, the boldness and initiative displayed by the worker community enabled its people to play a key role in the *Salt* story as artists, critics, and, by their example, strong civil libertarians. For without the courage of the local union, as well as the determination of the more ideologically driven International, the IPC challenge to the blacklist could not have been raised. Their legacy is a motion picture that still bears witness to the stultifying impact of the Cold War on civil liberties in the fearful America of the 1950s.

Aftereffects: In the Wake of the Storm

The suppression of *Salt of the Earth* occurred within the context of the federal government's broader assault on the left-led unions in the 1950s; and central to the official attack was persistent harassment of "progressive" union leaders. His militance in the Empire strike and role in the origins and production of *Salt* marked Clinton Jencks as a target for special attention in Washington and from federal officials in the field. For Jencks, therefore, the strike and the film's production were only the beginning of a long nightmare that would profoundly affect his life.

As an international representative for Mine-Mill, Jencks was in a vulnerable position even before the Empire strike and the *Salt* controversy had inflamed public opinion and management thinking in the early 1950s. However, the root of his problems in the 1950s lay in Section 9(h) of the Taft-Hartley law, which required labor union officials to sign affidavits declaring that they were not Communist Party members. This provision became a weapon for anticommunists seeking to expel radicals from the labor movement, since unions whose officers refused to submit affidavits were denied National Labor Relations Board services and prevented from participating in representation elections. Jencks had signed his first Taft-Hartley affidavit in 1949, well before the government witch hunt had reached fever pitch. Despite later claims to the contrary by professional witness and notorious prevaricator Harvey Matusow, there is no firm evidence that Jencks was a member of the Communist Party. However, as historian Ellen Schrecker has demonstrated, he was associated with the Communist movement and was an active member of a left-wing labor union. He was, in short, immersed in a radical movement culture. Because he moved freely within party circles and was an outspoken advocate of workers' rights and racial equality in the segregated Southwest, Jencks was frequently the target of Red-baiting attacks. For his part, Clinton Jencks was convinced that the revolutionary implications of democratic unionism were so provocative that corporate interests sought to silence its adherents in IUMMSW, himself included. Mine-Mill was clearly a large and early target for communist hunters following its expulsion from the CIO. In 1952, when the Senate Judiciary Committee formed a "Task Force Investigating Communist Domination of Certain Labor Organizations," chaired by McCarthy's loyal ally, Senator Pat McCarran of Nevada, IUMMSW was the first union to be called before the body. Both Jencks and his union were under government scrutiny, not to mention FBI monitoring, a full year before *Salt* became an issue. Their story provides a textbook case of McCarthyism in action.[25]

Although Jencks had been questioned previously in Albuquerque, it was not until *Salt of the Earth* made the Empire strike a national issue that the government watchdogs and corporate management moved aggressively to curb Mine-Mill activists in New Mexico. After professional witness Harvey Matusow recited a fabricated tale about meeting Jencks at the Vincents' ranch in San Cristóbal, where he allegedly admitted party membership and his intention to cripple Korean War copper production, Jencks found himself under arrest in Silver City. In April 1953, Jencks was charged with perjury in signing the Taft-Hartley noncommunist affidavit.[26]

Most accounts describe Matusow as a congenital "hustler" and a chronic liar. By 1951 he had been fired from several Communist Party–related positions, often for petty thievery. In search of recognition and angered at the Party's failure to provide it, he turned informer in 1950. The following year, he identified Jencks as a CP member, largely on the basis of conversations allegedly held in 1950 at the San Cristóbal Valley Ranch. By 1952 the FBI had learned that Matusow had "never attended a meeting of the Communist Party in New Mexico," and that he had "never seen any direct evidence to prove" that Jencks was a party member. Though Matusow believed Jencks to be a communist, J. Edgar Hoover admitted that the evidence of his party membership was "not substantial." In fact, no FBI informer could link Jencks to the party after 1949, when he had signed the Taft-Hartley affidavit. In sum, the bureau knew its case against Jencks was extremely weak, a reality confirmed in late 1951 when Matusow admitted he had lied about the Mine-Mill activist.[27]

But, in October 1952, Jencks convicted himself in the eyes of some observers by taking the Fifth Amendment before Nevada senator Pat McCarran and the Senate Internal Security Subcommittee at its Salt Lake City hearings. With the mining industry urging action in the Jencks case and the statute of limitations running out, the Justice Department found itself under intense pressure for a Taft-Hartley prosecution. Within this emotionally charged atmosphere, Jencks's high profile in connection with the *Salt* project made him a logical target. In response to the charges made by Harvey Matusow, Jencks attacked the Senate committee's procedures and goals while claiming the protection of the Fifth Amendment.[28] The confrontation in Salt Lake City marked the beginning of Jencks's problems with a federal government determined to destroy Mine-Mill as an effective labor organization.

After the hearings, Jencks returned to his union duties in New Mexico, which included work on the filming of *Salt*. By April 1953 he stood accused of perjury after Matusow had repeated his charges before a grand jury in El Paso. Circling the wagons, Mine-Mill leaders argued that Jencks's persecution was part of a wider government campaign to kill the left-wing unions. Meanwhile, Local 890 protested that IUMMSW had been targeted because of the Empire strike and the production of *Salt*, which had been the subject of constant attack since the picture had been made. In a statement supporting Jencks, Local 890 shop stewards interpreted the arrest as "a continuing effort to keep our movie from being shown" and an FBI attempt to "get Jencks after the ruckus over Mine-Mill's right to make [it]." Reiterating their commitment to Jencks, the stewards asserted: "This is our fight, too." One month later the local executive board created a five-person Local 890 Jencks Defense Committee and authorized the transfer of fifteen hundred dollars from the treasury to the International's Jencks Defense Committee.[29] Their action was an extraordinary expression of solidarity from a financially strapped local union. The endorsement from Jencks's Mexican-American union brothers spoke volumes about their view of his long-standing dedication to Local 890's cause, as well as his commitment to full equality.

The Company says:

"WE ARE NOT TRYING TO DESTROY THIS UNION...

we are trying to give it <u>PROPER</u> leadership !"

THIS is the story of the Jencks case.

The story's plot is told in the two sentences quoted above. The speaker was Mr. Richard C. Berresford, manager of employee relations of New Jersey Zinc Company. He was testifying before the House Committee on Education and Labor in Washington, March 16, 1953.

He got results.

One month later, on April 17, one of the labor leaders with whom Mr. Berresford deals was indicted by a federal grand jury, charged with falsifying his non-Communist Taft-Hartley affidavit.

Mr. Berresford has run into some obstacles in his effort to bring "proper" leadership to the unions with which he deals. The following is quoted from the hearing record cited above:

Congressman Gwinn: *Well, the men should — if they exercised their proper rights to elect better officers, that would clear up the situation, wouldn't it?*

Mr. Berresford: *You would think it would, but it does not . . . they feel perhaps that these leaders give them good service . . . and therefore why change?* (Mine-Mill is the union Berresford is talking about.)

I do not think the average worker thinks very deeply on this nor realizes the implications. I suppose that is particularly true of the Americans of Mexican or Spanish background. They want good labor representation which they think this union is giving them, and they also want racial equality which we think this union has distorted.

IUMMSW attacks New Jersey Zinc Company as part of the effort to exonerate Clinton Jencks, ca. 1954. Archives, University of Colorado at Boulder Libraries, Clinton Jencks Collection.

It was this theme that dominated discussion of the case during the Mine-Mill national convention in September 1953, which adopted a resolution committing all local unions and the International to the Jencks defense. In support of the resolution, Local 890 president Juan Chacón reviewed Jencks's contribution to the creation of the amalgamated local, its growth, the Empire strike, and the production of *Salt.* To Chacón, the indictment was closely linked to the union's boldness in making the film, completed only thirty days before the government moved against Jencks. He argued that the companies were "out to destroy not only Local 890 but the labor movement as a whole." Even more eloquent was African-American delegate Asbury Howard, who had worked as a Mine-Mill organizer in the Deep South. Howard likened Jencks's work for racial equality to the freedom struggle in the South. He reminded delegates of management's efforts to separate Anglo and Mexican-American, in the belief that if they "[got] every Anglo leader, then the Mexican-American people [would] fold up." Calling for racial and economic solidarity, Howard insisted that "when we unite and show the bosses every member of Mine-Mill saying to the phonies — hands off Brother Jencks, they will keep hands off." Deeply moved by the display of affection and solidarity, Jencks closed his own remarks with a pledge:

> I believe, so long as I draw breath in my body, that I will fight in good faith for the traditions of this country that we love, for the traditions of this union that we love just so long as you are willing to carry your part in that same good fight.[30]

Jencks did continue to fight; and he continued to lose. Convicted in January 1954 on two counts, he was sentenced to five years and ten thousand dollars on each count. His case reached the Supreme Court on appeal, at which time Jencks's attorneys asked for the original FBI reports on Matusow and other witnesses. Meanwhile, the unpredictable Matusow had recanted his testimony and expressed remorse to Methodist bishop G. Bromley Oxnam, himself a target of anticommunist attacks. In June 1954, Oxnam publicly announced Matusow's recantation in a statement that undercut not only the Jencks conviction, but also the government's entire anticommunist program. Not long thereafter, the government's star witness published his confessions in *False Witness*, a book underwritten by Mine-Mill's advance order for several thousand copies. Nonetheless, in 1955 the Fifth Circuit Court of Appeals upheld Jencks's conviction, after which the case went to the Supreme Court in 1957.[31]

By this time the Supreme Court had begun to turn away from the anti-communist crusade. Since the Jencks decision had been based on perjured testimony, its reversal was not exceptional. Matusow had alleged that at the Vincent ranch he had had conversations with Jencks that in fact had never occurred. As a result, on June 3, 1957, the high court reversed the Jencks verdict. But more important was Justice William Brennan's opinion, which stated that the defense had a right to see the original FBI reports on Matusow, thus confirming the defendant's rights when confronted by awesome governmental authority. The Supreme Court ordered a new trial for Jencks, whereupon the government dropped the case. It was a rare victory for IUMMSW in a time of extreme difficulty, which subsequently included battles with HUAC, the Senate Internal Security Committee, and the Subversive Activities Control Board, all of them bent on demonstrating that Mine-Mill was a Communist front organization.[32]

During the course of the Jencks prosecution, the *Salt* group worked to assist the defense. There were two aspects of this activity: preparation of publicity materials and use of the picture as an organizing and fund-raising device. Particularly active on the pamphleteering front was Michael Wilson, who had developed a very close personal relationship with both Clinton and Virginia Jencks. Wilson's main activity involved the development of a publication describing Clint's contribution to the union, especially Local 890, and the reactions of his union brothers and sisters to his work. More important perhaps was *Salt* itself. In May 1954, Wilson told Travis that "where Clint's defense is concerned," the picture "is worth more than a score of articles." Subsequently, the article designed by Wilson was used in connection with fund-raising activities that featured exploitation of a 16-millimeter version of the film. And IPC initially pledged to do "anything [it could] to be helpful" to the Jencks Defense Committee.[33]

Starting with the earliest strategy discussions in April 1954, Mine-Mill pressed for extensive use of *Salt* as a "weapon in the defense," in the belief that "Jencks's part in the picture" and the strike would "rally outside forces to support of the defense." Travis urged the use of 16-millimeter prints as "indispensable to a successful approach . . . in our own local unions." In June, he told Wilson that more liberal use of the film in the mining camps was an essential prerequisite to widespread commercial exhibition. Finally, during the August executive board meeting, International board members again pressed Jarrico to assist in making the film an "effective weapon." At this point, the imperatives of the defense campaign clashed with the needs of the distributors, whose success depended on commercial showings. On August 31, Jarrico attempted to discourage any further use of the film that might "jeopardize the mobilization of the broadest possible support for theatrical exhibition." The IPCD now opposed using *Salt* to raise funds for Jencks or victims of anti-labor hysteria. While the company would permit *Salt* to be screened in more isolated venues, it urged that theatrical bookings remain the main focus of union promotional efforts, which in the long run would "increase its usefulness."[34]

The result of these discussions was a modus vivendi that enabled Mine-Mill to make extensive use of *Salt* in the mining camps, most of which were in remote locations. In October 1954, the executive board reaffirmed its intention to employ the film in the Jencks defense "because of the terrific impact" it made on union audiences and other sympathetic groups. Moreover, *Salt* also became useful as an "educational organizing weapon" to "build [the] union and make it more solid." While firm in his insistence on use of the 16-millimeter print, Travis acknowledged that the larger goal of both the distributors and the union was to screen the picture in as many theaters as possible so that it reached a "broad section of the American people."[35]

By 1956, when the Jencks case went to the Supreme Court, theatrical bookings were largely an academic question, and IPC was preparing for its antitrust suit. Equally problematic was Jencks's position within the union. Under intense scrutiny itself, in March 1956, IUMMSW forced him to resign his position as international representative "for the good and welfare of the union." Although Jencks preferred to retain his position, he had become too controversial for Mine-Mill. While Local 890 invited him to come home as local union representative, he refused to displace the Mexican-American then functioning as representative because to do so would have negated his earlier work to encourage Chicano/Chicana leadership. And so a loyal and militant organizer was eased out of the union he had grown to love. After leaving Mine-Mill, Jencks soon learned that he was on every blacklist in the Southwest. When he found work, it was very demanding, and Red-baiters consistently made life hard for him. Invariably, he would be dismissed for no identifiable reason. In the words of one California state unemployment official, he belonged in a new classification of "politically unemployable." As a result of continued harassment and frustration, Jencks finally earned a Ph.D. and began a new career teaching economics at San Diego State University, a position from which he retired in the 1980s. Always a solid union man, he retained great respect and affection for the union he once served. And he remained deeply interested in the modern revival of *Salt*, which, he asserted, reminded modern viewers of "a side of America a lot of people have not seen."[36] For Clinton Jencks, the struggle with corporate America never really ended.

Salt of the Earth argued persuasively that human equality was the central issue in the Grant County struggle. Publicity still, *Salt of the Earth*, ca. 1954. Collections of the Wisconsin Center for Film and Theater Research.

Jencks was not the only person whose life was changed by the *Salt* experience. For the people of Grant County, the strike and the film had long-term ramifications. While the solidarity of the crisis years was difficult to maintain, Local 890 remained one of the strongest Mexican-American locals loyal to Mine-Mill. Perhaps the most significant result of the Empire strike was the eventual end of the dual wage scale. Nonetheless, as of 1955, the better jobs still went to the Anglos, although the union was working to break down that distinction. And while housing accommodations had improved, including the introduction of inside plumbing, Mexican-Americans still occupied the least attractive quarters available to mine employees.[37]

The women of Local 890 failed to maintain the position achieved during the early 1950s. While their militance placed them squarely within the history of female activism in the Mexican-American community of the Southwest, many returned to more traditional roles as the years passed. Even after they had assumed responsibility for maintaining the strike, the women never became union "insiders" and decision makers. The power of cultural heritage and long-held assumptions concerning gender overwhelmed the new consciousness formed as a result of the strike and film-production experience. Deborah Rosenfelt accurately concludes that although the status of women improved over the years, the "old way" in gender relations had reasserted itself by the 1970s.[38] But as a consequence of modern Chicana activism as well as the publicity created by the *Salt* controversy, a sharper awareness of the options available to women as part of the worker community would eventually emerge. Moreover, as a result of the film's rerelease in 1965, new generations of Americans have been exposed to its argument. An important result of the filmmaking experience and the film's modern revival has been a clearer consciousness of an alternative model of interaction among men and women. *Salt of the Earth* is a living document that reminds today's viewers of a path not taken, but still open.

To Juan Chacón, the inactivity of the Ladies Auxiliary in later years was one of many disappointments in union affairs. For some time following the *Salt* controversy, he was reelected president of Local 890 and worked to keep it loyal to Mine-Mill during the raiding episodes of the 1950s. Defeated in 1963 in a presidential race, he returned to the workplace at Kennecott. After ten years in the ranks, he ran again in 1973, this time as a successful candidate for the presidency of Steelworkers Local 890. True to form, Chacón remained militant in voicing the needs of Mexican-American workers. Gómez-Quiñones notes that although Mexican-American membership in USWA had reached 10 percent by the late 1970s, the International sometimes failed to negotiate strong contracts that addressed their concerns. USWA's inattention to rank-and-file concerns led Local 890 dissidents in 1971 to attack I. W. Abel's administration for promoting "class partnership unionism." A preference for "class struggle unionism" was a central theme in Chacón's comeback presidential campaign in 1973, during which he pledged to address rank-and-file needs and to "clean up relations with the companies" by ending private meetings with "certain union leaders." Chacón's reelection presaged a revival of militancy in local labor–management relations. A case in point was Local 890's wildcat strike in 1974, designed to protest the International's extension of the standing contract on July 1 after discussions had led to an impasse over terms of a new agreement. Accusing Kennecott of stalling on the key issues, workers remained out until a new contract was signed on July 21.[39]

The walkout was consistent with Local 890's history of aggressive opposition not only to management, but also to the steelworkers' leadership itself. Angered because the local had not received International support on many local issues, especially matters relating to workplace safety, the union voted unanimously for the strike. As Chacón later noted, the International devoted less attention to the local than had been true under the militant Mine-Mill leadership of the 1950s. As a result, he complained, the labor movement had lost strength and "union leaders [had] a weaker attitude toward the companies" and were "willing to settle contract negotiations without a strike."[40]

Because of the strike, Kennecott fired both Chacón and Local 890 financial secretary Israel Romero. Chacón argued that the dismissals were the company's way of punishing union officials for "participating in an action voted unanimously by the membership." More significant, he thought, was the warning thus communicated to the rank and file that they did not have the "right to vote on acceptance or rejection of agreements" that were to establish the "very conditions under which they have to work." To Local 890, the firings were aimed at destroying the union they had worked so hard to build: "The issue is *slavery*. Will rank and file workers continue to have the right to vote on the acceptance or rejection of a collective bargaining agreement which will govern their pay and working conditions?"[41]

As Local 890 fought both Kennecott and the steelworkers' bureaucracy, they once again invoked the images projected in *Salt*. Both press releases and financial appeals for the Chacón-Romero Defense Fund reminded recipients that the union people who were once part of that "world famous movie" were again "fighting for safety, good-faith settlement of grievances and the right of rank-and-file members to vote" on national contracts negotiated by the International. Put more simply, the issue boiled down to the workers' "right to democratically control their own union." In support of Local 890, *Salt* actor Will Geer agreed to co-chair a fact-finding committee to investigate Kennecott's actions against Chacón and Romero. Others involved in the defense included Clint Jencks and Mike Wilson. Geer summarized their perspective on the dispute: "Things haven't changed much in 21 years. Men who live in New York are still trying to run the lives of people here in Grant County." The *Salt* group rose to the occasion one more time. And in October 1975, Chacón and Romero were finally reinstated.[42]

The battle signaled Juan Chacón's unreconstructed radicalism as a proponent of Mexican-American workers' rights. Even after his retirement, he retained the militant vision of his youth. Still committed to the Mine-Mill principle that since "labor produces wealth, wealth belongs to the producers thereof," a mature Chacón continued to welcome "constant struggle." Chacón remained steadfast in his endorsement of worker ownership of the means of production, which he saw as the only solution to the problems of the American labor movement. Moreover, he insisted that "workers themselves are going to have to direct their own lives." To the end of his life in 1985, Juan Chacón endorsed collectivism as the best means of helping the worker. And he was still committed to activist leadership: "I was born to be this way—mess around with people, help them if I can. I love it."[43] Like the leftist leaders of Mine-Mill, he still embraced the labor movement as a tool for the improvement of the human condition. Chacón thought he had found a better way to a better world.

While Juan Chacón retained his union position and then took his place among the rank and file, the talented Rosaura Revueltas encountered personal hardship in the years after her stunning performance in *Salt*. A young actress with a promising career in 1953, she paid a heavy price for her commitment to the film. When she returned to Mexico, she was greeted by a negative press and a skeptical movie industry. Blacklisted in her own country, she was also denied entry into the United States for either personal or professional purposes. Although the Mexican people were unconcerned about Communist influence in the film, the American motion picture industry placed her on a blacklist, which was enforced in her home country as well. While she remained professionally active in Cuba and Eastern Europe for a time, her movie career suffered irreversible damage. By 1960 this setback had produced serious financial problems for Revueltas. Desperate for income, she wrote Ben Margolis to inquire into the returns from *Salt*. Asking if there was "any money available" for her, she stated simply that "things here [in Mexico] are still mighty rough for me." Her financial problems aside, she later recalled the film as a "miracle" and "flag of friendship" capable of making the United States a "most beloved neighbor of all our peoples." Later in life, she resided in Cuernavaca, where she supported herself by offering instruction in hatha yoga. Not long before her death in 1996, at the age of eighty-six, she insisted that the penalty imposed on her was "too great a punishment, an unjust punishment."[44] Few would disagree with her analysis.

An exception to this generalization would be Roy Brewer, who remained militantly anticommunist despite the waning of the Cold War and the eventual collapse of the Soviet Union. As late as 1983, Brewer "freely and proudly" acknowledged his role in the suppression of *Salt*, although he was imprecise about the exact mechanism used to impose the boycott. At that time, he still insisted that the film was "out and out Communist propaganda." When Barbara Moss and Stephen Mack produced *A Crime to Fit the Punishment* (1984), documenting the making and suppression of *Salt*, Brewer threatened to obstruct the distribution of their work. Brewer told *Variety* that he never gave permission for the filmmakers to use his comments in their picture. His view of *Salt* had not changed: he made "no apologies" for his "stand against Communist infiltration in Hollywood," since "all the Hollywood Ten were on direct orders from Moscow." His threat against the Moss-Mack film was an eerie throwback to the age of the blacklist, which had given rise to the conspiracy against *Salt* and Brewer's pivotal role in engineering it. Despite his criticism of the documentary, normal distribution went forward. There was no return to the bad old days. But Brewer remained convinced that *Salt*'s suppression was in the national interest: he told the documentary producers that he "hated to see any more attention given" to the film.[45]

It was the irony of fate that Brewer's wish was not to be granted; equally ironic was the reality that Biberman's major contribution to film history never gained full commercial distribution. Biberman made one more film, *Slaves* (1969), which was artistically much inferior to *Salt*. As one of the blacklist's most persecuted victims, he had already seen the practical wisdom of an alternative career in real estate. When he died in 1971, the corpus of his work was thin indeed; nonetheless, Biberman's place in American cultural history had been secured by his direction and promotion of a film that grew steadily in stature following its suppression in the blacklist period.[46] *Salt*'s tortured history provides modern scholars with stark evidence of the great fear that paralyzed America in the days of the HUAC inquisition and McCarthyism.

Unlike Biberman, blacklistees Michael Wilson and Paul Jarrico managed to survive economically on the basis of their writing skills and the value of their work on the black market. Both resided for a time in France, after which they returned to California, Wilson in the mid-1960s and Jarrico in the 1970s. Wilson continued to write screenplays until his death in 1978, while Jarrico became involved in a variety of film projects. In 1997, at the time of his untimely death in a tragic automobile accident, Jarrico remained active in screenwriting and other motion picture pursuits. Long deprived of a normal Hollywood career, by 1990 he had regained the professional status he had enjoyed as of 1951. His was a long road back. Both Wilson and Jarrico were justifiably proud of their work on *Salt*; Jarrico in 1996 characterized *Salt* as a "pioneer film" because of its advanced interpretation of economic issues, race relations, and women's rights. Moreover, he concluded, the very completion and release of the film must be regarded as a triumph, in view of the forces arrayed against it.[47] Modern criticism and social analysis have strengthened the Wilson-Jarrico view of *Salt*'s historical significance.

The Financial Record: A Failed Investment

Despite positive critical reaction, *Salt of the Earth* failed financially. Because of the boycott, first-run commercial exhibition proved, in Ben Margolis's words, a "total fiasco" for the company, investors, and filmmakers. The film never came close to making a profit. At a total cost of 250,000 dollars, *Salt* was a relatively inexpensive production; but the film's backers never recovered their initial investment. And the modest revenues that did come in were immediately plowed back into the expenses incurred in the long, drawn-out antitrust suit. The financial record confirms Jarrico's assertion: the *Salt* group "lost [its] shirt."[48]

By 1956, it had become obvious that IPC's condition was perilous. Its then-current financial report pegged IPC/IPCD's outstanding debt at 226,115 dollars. The company informed investors of the obvious: the situation was serious. Although the officers still hoped to meet obligations, they could no longer promise repayment in the short run. The recent thaw in the Cold War and *Salt*'s warm reception overseas encouraged IPC to hope for tens of millions of new viewers; but it realistically noted that debt repayment lay years ahead.[49] The company's officers had glimpsed the future, and the prospects were dim.

The financial picture had not changed measurably by the late 1950s. In 1958, an FBI monitor observed that although the company had not been profitable, foreign distribution might enable it to recover some of its losses. The informant reported a conversation with Biberman, who told him that IPC and IPCD were not "active at the present time," nor did they "contemplate making another picture in the near future." In this instance, his account belabored the obvious. One year later, a disappointed Biberman cited "frightfully rough days" in reluctantly accepting an IPC settlement of 150 dollars, while releasing the corporation of all obligations to him for monies owed.[50] For Biberman, the financial venture was over. It was time for closure.

Although first-run commercial exhibition never materialized, *Salt* later gained substantial distribution in 16-millimeter form. Literally shut out of the domestic market for ten years, it was reissued in 1965 after the failed antitrust suit and rose phoenixlike from the ashes to become a cult favorite on university campuses and with "progressive" audiences in the 1960s and 1970s. Once it became "respectable," Jarrico recalled with pride, *Salt* had gained international recognition and belated domestic notice. The film played on public television and was released on video cassette; for a 1950s black and white picture, it has done well in its second life. In 1997, Turner Classic Movies screened *Salt of the Earth* in recognition of the fiftieth anniversary of the 1947 HUAC hearings and the blacklist's inauguration. Regarded by some scholars as a classic, *Salt of the Earth* was the only film Jarrico ever worked on that, in his words, "got better over the years instead of worse."[51]

Because *Salt* confronted the issues of racism, sexism, and economic exploitation in American life, it found a place in the iconography of the Left. Although its financial failure initially retarded the development of independent radical filmmaking in the United States, *Salt* later became an inspiration to New Left filmmakers and a teaching tool for historians, women's studies specialists, film scholars, and others committed to the study of the motion picture as primary source. Moreover, it remains one of the few feature films to portray American labor and worker culture in a strongly positive light.[52] Minority workers and women are endowed with agency and intelligence as they grapple with real problems against long odds. And finally, the hollowness of the "anticommunist consensus" of the 1950s is exposed by a film that dignified labor and working people, only to be reviled by powerful forces in American society and culture. *Salt of the Earth* provides a window into the past, a prism through which a new generation of viewers may glimpse the dark side of American life in the age of the great fear. Moreover, its suppression underscores the fragility of civil liberties in an open, democratic society. *Salt*'s message contains a lesson for all seasons.

Epilogue

An Afterthought: What Kind of Film Was This?

Modern scholars have been more generous in their evaluation of *Salt* than were many interpreters in the 1950s. While most find fault with its one-dimensional structure, romanticism, and lack of subtlety, few have failed to recognize the film's boldness in addressing problems typically overlooked in the barren film fare of its era. Labor historians have been deeply impressed by the picture's honesty and courage in embracing labor's cause and workers' issues, while film scholars applaud it as an attempt to reintroduce meaningful ideas into the filmmaking process and challenge the blacklist that lay like a pall over the movie industry in the days of HUAC and McCarthy. And scholars in many disciplines acclaim the prescience of Wilson, Biberman, and Jarrico in advancing women's issues by embracing a feminist position in a way that clearly ran against the predominant trends of the 1950s.[1]

As previously noted, contemporary critical reaction was mixed, but in most cases *Salt* received positive, often outstanding, reviews. Many commentators, while endorsing the film's gripping social realism, added disparaging remarks concerning stilted portrayals of management and alleged propaganda content. Among the skeptics, none was more outspoken than Pauline Kael. In an extended review, Kael, in 1954, blasted *Salt* as "as clear a piece of Communist propaganda as we have had in many years." Ridiculing the Left, she allowed that *Salt* could "seem true for those liberals and progressives whose political thinking has never gone beyond the thirties." For deluded leftists, she argued, "Depression social consciousness" was an "exposed nerve" which, if touched, became "the only reality." To Kael, the key danger in the picture lay in potential Communist exploitation of local grievances and principles that "no thoughtful American" could reject. Communist propaganda, she assured her readers, "captures the direction of groups struggling for status." In short, *Salt* constituted "shrewd propaganda for the urgent business of the U.S.S.R."[2]

Jarrico later asserted that Kael had harshly "Red-baited" the film largely on the basis of the *California Quarterly* script. Although he professed respect for her usually sharp critical faculties, he insisted that the renowned commentator had a blind spot on *Salt* that merely reflected the temper of the times. Jarrico was especially concerned about Kael's employment of "parallelism," a practice common among 1950s anticommunists. Her argument that *Salt*'s themes of labor, minority, and women's rights were Communist ideas was flawed, he insisted. The reviewer's equation of these themes with Communist ideas, and her simple assumption that they were inserted because the *Salt* group included CP members, was, in Jarrico's words, "not enough." He argued that effective analysis now required a "historical approach" that transcended one-dimensional charges of propagandist intent.[3]

In 1954, however, it was precisely such fears that haunted an army intelligence officer assigned to report on a preview showing at a Chicago Unitarian church. After providing a full description of the film's plot and its development, the watchdog provided his superiors with an analysis of *Salt*'s "Communist implications." Among them were: "working class strength and victory in unity; the strength a single union can portray against a large company; and the effectiveness of the picket line in the revolt against capitalism." True enough, but hardly news. The intelligence officer especially feared that to a person "unfamiliar with the . . . better Communist propaganda techniques, the film would appear as another excellent Italian film portraying 'life.'" Fortunately, he thought, the film would be "dull to the average movie-goer," though it could have a "strong appeal to the intelligentsia." But *Salt* "could be a strong instrument of class struggle propaganda" if screened for workers in union halls.[4]

It is possible, of course, to interpret the making of *Salt of the Earth* as primarily an expression of the Communist movement culture of the late 1940s and early 1950s. Historian Robert C. Hodges, for example, sees the *Salt* story as essentially a Communist project that momentarily reconstituted the traditional Popular Front coalition. However, this is not to say that the film was a CPUSA-directed project. Like the new historians of American Communism, Hodges acknowledges the importance of grassroots initiative in the activities of CP members, especially low-level cadre. Viewed in this light, *Salt* may be best understood as the outcome of an extraordinary collaboration among rank-and-file communists, independent leftists, and unaligned activists united by their common determination to challenge the blacklist and the wider political persecution that had stifled free expression in Cold War America.[5]

In reality, despite the film's persuasive power, its impact owed little to direct Communist Party influence. The Communist intellectual leadership in Hollywood had been largely frustrated in its attempt to significantly alter the film. If propaganda was to be found in *Salt*, it resided in the strong argument the film makes against unrestrained capitalism, which was hardly the exclusive property of the CP. Indeed, while John Howard Lawson commended Wilson, Jarrico, and Biberman on their work, he expressed disappointment in party efforts to mobilize mass support for *Salt*. The most militant party activists, Lawson argued, had clearly overestimated the "'spontaneous' welcome" that supposedly awaited the film, while party moderates had been foolish in "assuming that this film could compete with Hollywood in the commercial market." His many criticisms notwithstanding, Lawson embraced the idea of independent production and urged the creation of more works like *Salt of the Earth*.[6] But retrospective endorsement did not signify preproduction impact. In the final analysis, the picture was intellectual property belonging to the men and women who made it rather than the political party they adhered to.

Similarly, it was the moral and spiritual property of the men and women of Local 890, most of whom were apolitical or mainstream left. Although there were some communists among them, they tended to be old-line Popular Fronters who had little knowledge of CP ideology and thought of the party essentially as a reformist instrument. The vast majority of Local 890 members had no interest in the Communist Party, and their leaders always stressed the validity of democratic political institutions. What Mine-Mill communists contributed to the union cause was the spirit of militancy[7] that energized them during the Empire strike and the *Salt* struggle. Yet each battle was a grass-roots initiative more than an institutional development, and both reflected the activism of a socially and economically conscious Mexican-American community.

Juan Chacón always viewed *Salt* as the expression of the Mexican-American spirit, as well as an effective organizational tool. As noted by Jencks, moreover, the people of Local 890 had been desperate for equality and saw the film as a way to get their story to a wider public. To Arturo Flores, the film demonstrated that "struggle was not useless" and that the strike had elevated the Mexican-American people. And through the production committee, they made *Salt* their own. Further evidence of Mexican-American pride in the picture came in 1955, when a group of Los Angeles Chicano unionists proposed a Chicano/Chicana campaign to open the theaters of the Southwest to its exhibition. Because the film "belong[ed] to the Mexican-American community of the Southwest," they told Biberman, responsibility for its promotion "belong[ed] to them as Mexican-Americans and as trade unionists." Biberman expressed interest in the attitude that motivated them, which he saw as "profound self-interest" and a "compliment to themselves and the film." For Biberman, their initiative revealed *Salt*'s power as an instrument of self-identified value to Mexican-Americans seeking to achieve "cohesion as a minority" and "increased strength."[8] Because of his urgent need to market the film, Biberman's account must be viewed with caution; but the contacts he described were one more measure of the Mexican-American community's sense of ownership with regard to a film it clearly embraced.

Michael Wilson's analysis of the film's impact emphasized its importance in consolidating gains already made by the Mexican-American worker community, "especially concerning the roles of women." His view is shared by many of the *Salt* principals. However, modern scholarship has demonstrated that these advances for women were transitory and that traditional cultural values reasserted themselves over time. Even as sympathetic an interpreter as Deborah Rosenfelt acknowledged the power of long-held assumptions. When she visited Grant County twenty years after the *Salt* battle, she found no "enclave of socially conscious men and liberated women." Nonetheless, the feminist implications of the strike and the *Salt* controversy have continued to draw historians' attention. Charles Ramirez Berg, for example, stresses Esperanza's role as the female protagonist as a remarkable exception to the filmmaker's rule of the "absent Chicana." Even more emphatic is critic Ruth McCormick who, in 1973, asserted that no American film had ever dealt as thoroughly with the "issue of women's liberation, from the politics of housework to the myth of male supremacy."[9] The greater respect for women and sensitivity to their needs occasioned by the Grant County upheaval of the early 1950s was part of a progression of consciousness still in formation forty years later. The history of the women's crucial role in the strike cannot be erased; *Salt of the Earth* depicted changes and raised issues that were the wave of the future.

But men and women eat in the present. To deal with that reality, Biberman turned to the pedestrian details of real estate as a means of providing for his family's needs. Then, after several years of relative obscurity, something remarkable happened to Biberman and the film. Coincidental with the failure of the antitrust suit, the political climate in the United States underwent a change. As a result, a number of new options presented themselves. In 1965, Biberman published a penetrating memoir of the *Salt* experience and his wife Gale Sondergaard returned to Broadway in a one-woman show with strong feminist content. Each enterprise, in its own way, rekindled the *Salt* spirit. Moreover, as Biberman told Mike Wilson, the new social and political consciousness of the mid-1960s began to open new doors for the film, at least in 16-millimeter distribution. Biberman had always been pleased by the interest shown in the picture among university audiences, but he now sensed a "new chance." The Student Nonviolent Coordinating Committee arranged for several New York showings in 1965, events that opened an opportunity for a flurry of interviews. Biberman proclaimed that he was "pushing in the direction of 1954." He even allowed himself to hope for commercial exhibition. Elated by passage of the civil rights laws of 1964 and 1965, he also expressed satisfaction at "discrimination exposed" and outlawed. But above all, he was thrilled that *Salt* had been "asked for by the exhibitors because it looks like the theme of the Great Society." All things considered, Biberman thought that the "momentary feeling [was] good" and that he was "making it."[10] After eleven years, it seemed that he was starting the *Salt* promotion anew; and in an important sense, the film's time had indeed come.

Symptomatic of a revived interest in *Salt of the Earth* was the publication in 1965 of Biberman's account of the filmmaking experience. A long-standing labor ally, E. P. Gorman of the Meatcutters union, pronounced the book "a good story" and marveled at Biberman's bravery in developing the film and publishing the memoir. Left-wing criticisms varied considerably. While Robert Joseph of the liberal literary journal *Frontier* wondered if the *Salt* group had chosen "the right vehicle, the right background, the right auspices for their statement," he displayed some sympathy for their message. In an editor's note, *Frontier* reasserted its original position that *Salt* had always been entitled to a screening and expressed the hope that a rerelease would result in a more "democratic" reaction. Responding to Joseph, Biberman restated his personal commitment to resistance, even as he acknowledged his underestimation of the challenge *Salt* had presented to a motion picture industry that had "surrendered an American medium of communication to the scum of the country." He closed with an assertion that the end of his book could be the "beginning of the film" in a nation that seemed poised on the "verge of a resistance," in which *Salt* might "play a significant role."[11]

Less reserved than Joseph was Barrows Dunham of the left-leaning *National Guardian*, who (ironically adopting the language of Hollywood hype) pronounced Biberman's memoir a "thriller, a cinematic spectacular, a supercolossal epic of the idiocies of oppressors." He thought the book "wonderfully good" for contemporaries and "even better for posterity." Its truth was not just "stranger than fiction"; it was "more supercolossal." As for both the Hollywood "tyrants" and the "recanters," Dunham asked if they did not know that the Jarricos, Wilsons, and Bibermans were "themselves a portion of the salt of the earth." His answer: "They knew it, all the time, the bastards; they knew it all the time."[12]

From the hard Left, John Howard Lawson endorsed the book as an account indispensable to those who felt that American cultural and academic freedom were in danger. Lawson saw the *Salt* story as "virtually unknown" in a nation still crippled by the "damaging and continuing effect of McCarthyism on our culture and life." He also attacked the mainstream press for critical neglect of Biberman's book, which was itself subtle Red-baiting. Even the "generally courageous" *Frontier* was guilty, he argued, having criticized the IPC for collaborating with Mine-Mill and choosing to tell the Empire Zinc story. To Lawson, it was an "illiterate" attack on people who had followed their consciences. Biberman had given his answer to the critics in a memoir that was certain to be a "revelation and a warning to all Americans."[13]

While leftist critics worried that the *Salt* story would slip unnoticed into a past many wished to extinguish, Biberman ruminated on the meaning of the entire experience. Following the announcement of a verdict in the antitrust case, he wrote Ben Margolis of his own mixed reaction to the outcome. While disappointed, he also felt satisfaction because "the bastards did not stop us." While their opponents had "struck [them] foully," they "got it back to our hilt." Moreover, the *Salt* group had fought "as honorable left Americans . . . not for the left but for our country," which had "profited from that fight." Biberman also argued in a round-robin letter that "of such defeats, victory is made." Similarly, Simon Lazarus maintained that by coming as close to victory as it had, the IPC had "discouraged any repetition against other films of the boycott which strangled ours." For Biberman and his associates, the production of *Salt* had been an act of protest against an industry without moral compass. They had protested since 1947 and were "still protesting — in the black market — in the open in certain areas," and "in [the] court." Biberman defiantly concluded that "history is our judge."[14]

In many respects the judgment of history elevated *Salt of the Earth* and its makers to a status never reached in the fear-ridden 1950s. For all its limitations, writes Victor Navasky, the picture "anticipated both the feminist and independent film-producing movements by more than a decade (not to mention its premature concern for the Chicanos)." He speculates that without the blacklist, a "newly experimental cinema" could have produced more socially conscious films like *Salt*, which stands as a "crude specimen of what might-have-been." As late as the 1970s Michael Wilson lamented the movie industry's resistance to the exploration of serious and controversial ideas on film.[15] *Salt of the Earth* represented an alternative consciousness of the artist's social responsibility.

To historian Brian Neve, the film's uniqueness lay in the filmmakers' successful translation of a shared ideology into a purposeful script and film. Likewise, Larry Ceplair and Steven Englund emphasize *Salt's* conversion of firmly held beliefs into a forceful political statement. Moreover, the simple completion of the picture was a major achievement that rallied the persecuted and demoralized Hollywood Left. As Sylvia Jarrico noted, the film's production "refurbished [their] sense of political usefulness," by encouraging blacklistees whose futures had been blighted by Hollywood's capitulation to fear. Peter Roffman and Jim Purdy have viewed *Salt's* "very existence" as an "extraordinary assault on HUAC."[16] In short, the appearance of a provocatively independent film production offered hope to the outcasts of Cold War America.

Salt of the Earth was a revealing document from another perspective as well, in its sympathetic treatment of American labor and worker culture. As Francis R. Walsh observes, the film presented militant unionists and the strike from the workers' viewpoint. Moreover, the film effectively depicted the pivotal role of women in the working community, including the ambivalence in gender relations produced by assertive women who successfully established their claim to a position of parity in the union family. Walsh further stresses the film's exploration of agency on the part of working men and women liberated by unionism. A "clearly pro-labor" picture, *Salt* marked a departure from the "jaundiced" view of organized labor characteristic of most Hollywood fare.[17]

The portrayal of workers with dignity was only one of many extraordinary dimensions of a film that challenges long-held beliefs in several ways. *Salt of the Earth* is a historical document that reflects the social and economic tensions simmering below the surface of American life in an era once viewed as a period of bland consensus. Both the Empire strike and the film itself signify the deep divisions separating labor from capital and workers from management in the affluent society. The confrontation in Grant County revealed the harsh reality of class conflict in Eisenhower's America.

A no less significant reality was the social rebellion that unleashed not only women's agency, but also an explosive gender conflict that festered beneath the thin veneer of conformity expressed in the much-touted family values of the 1950s. The women and men of Local 890 and the IPC questioned the sex-role definitions ingrained in the received culture and revised, at least temporarily, the sexual division of labor assumed, if not lived, by many Americans. The women of the Grant County worker community were anything but homeward bound, caught as they were in a critical situation that propelled them into the public sphere in a dramatic lurch. In the process, the "old way" of gender relations suffered a severe jolt, from which it never completely recovered. While the "new way" was never firmly established, there was no way to close the door completely on the ideas that took root in the hearts and minds of the women whose lives had been affected by the strike and the film. A generation later, the readjustment of gender relations was still an incomplete process, and the new system with its altered consciousness constituted a structure still in formation.

Equally significant to Chicana and Chicano activists was the ambivalence created by a film that extolled their culture, but missed the long history of militance that preceded the Empire struggle and the production of the film. Some scholars believe that the long tradition of Mexican radical activism is lost in *Salt's* interpretation of the strike as a seminal event characterized by a new class awareness. Yet as previously noted, it is also clear that the Chicano/Chicana community of the Southwest embraced *Salt of the Earth* as an expression of Mexican-American cultural resilience and strength. Their supportive response to the film paralleled Mexican-American loyalty to Mine-Mill in the troubled union's years of greatest peril. The Mexican-American radical tradition in the Southwest fueled both developments.

For Chicanos, Hollywood leftists, mainstream liberals, and principled conservatives, the *Salt* controversy was significant as a call to conscience and a test for civil liberties. The battle for the film was, in the words of Simon Lazarus, an "honorable chapter" in recent American history. With the passage of time, Herbert Biberman, Paul Jarrico, and Michael Wilson reemerged as exemplars of the dissenting tradition. Their politics aside, the *Salt* group stood almost alone against thought control and censorship in a period of grave constitutional danger; and they emerged as people of courage who insisted that the Bill of Rights be honored, despite the pressures exerted by the forces of political conformity. As Biberman declared in 1970, the moral of the story was a warning to the oppressors: "Be careful whom you blacklist—he may be extolled as a hero in the next, if not his own generation."[18]

In the final analysis, then, *Salt of the Earth* remains an enduring document of Cold War America and an emblem of determined independence. A film little seen in its own time has become a symbol of an alternate vision of America in the 1950s, a view that emphasizes conflict and confrontation. The *Salt* story challenges the consensus view of race relations, gender roles, and class harmony and signifies a historical counter-trend, which existed side by side with a "culture of conformity." The age of McCarthy and "the Committee" also produced the dissent of the *Salt* group and its supporters among the friends of intellectual and artistic freedom in a nation under siege. For all the vicissitudes of its troubled history, *Salt of the Earth* remains a fragile celluloid monument to that culture of resistance.

Appendix 1

Howard Hughes Letter

March 18, 1953

Congressman Donald L. Jackson
House Office Building
Washington, D. C.

Dear Congressman Jackson: In your telegram you asked the question, "Is there any action that industry and labor in motion picture field can take to stop completion and release of picture and to prevent showing of film here and abroad?"

My answer is "Yes." There is action which the industry can take to stop completion of this motion picture in the United States. And if the Government will act immediately to prevent the export of the film to some other country where it can be completed, then this picture will not be completed and disseminated throughout the world where the United States will be judged by its content.

According to newspaper reports, photography of this motion picture has been finished at Silver City, N. Mex.

However, completion of photography of a motion picture is only the first step in production.

Before a motion picture can be completed or shown in theaters, an extensive application of certain technical skills and use of a great deal of specialized equipment is absolutely necessary.

Herbert Biberman, Paul Jarrico, and their associates working on this picture do not possess these skills or this equipment.

If the motion picture industry — not only in Hollywood, but throughout the United States — will refuse to apply these skills, will refuse to furnish this equipment, the picture cannot be completed in this country.

Biberman and Jarrico have already met with refusal where the industry was on its toes. The film processing was being done by the Pathe Laboratories, until the first news broke from Silver City.

But the minute Pathe learned the facts, this alert laboratory immediately refused to do any further work on this picture, even though it meant refunding cash paid in advance.

Investigation fails to disclose where the laboratory work is being done now. But it is being done somewhere, by someone, and a great deal more laboratory work will have to be done by someone, before the motion picture can be completed.

Biberman, Jarrico, and their associates cannot succeed in their scheme alone. Before they can complete the picture, they must have the help of the following:

1. Film laboratories.
2. Suppliers of film.
3. Musicians and recording technicians necessary to record music.
4. Technicians who make dissolves, fades, etc.
5. Owners and operators of sound re-recording equipment and dubbing rooms.
6. Positive and negative editors and cutters.
7. Laboratories that make release prints.

If the picture industry wants to prevent this motion picture from being completed and spread all over the world as a representative product of the United States, then the industry and particularly that segment of the industry listed above, needs only to do the following:

Be alert to the situation.

Investigate thoroughly each applicant for the use of services or equipment.

Refuse to assist the Bibermans and Jarricos in the making of this picture.

Be on guard against work submitted by dummy corporations or third parties.

Appeal to the Congress and the State Department to act immediately to prevent the export of this film to Mexico or anywhere else.

Sincerely,
Howard Hughes

Source: *Congressional Record*, Mar. 19, 1953, 83d Cong., 1st sess., p. 2127.

Appendix 2

Members of the Motion Picture Industry Council

Association of Motion Picture Producers
Artists Managers' Guild
Hollywood A.F.L. Film Council
Independent Motion Picture Producers Association
Independent Office Workers
Screen Actors' Guild
Screen Directors' Guild
Screen Producers' Guild
Screen Writers' Guild
Society of Independent Motion Picture Producers
Society of Motion Picture Art Directors
Unit Production Managers' Guild

Source: Biberman-Sondergaard Papers, Box 44.

Abbreviations

ACLU	American Civil Liberties Union
AFL	American Federation of Labor
AMCBW	Amalgamated Meatcutters and Butcher Workmen of North America
AMPP	Association of Motion Picture Producers
ANMA	Asociación Nacional México-Americana
ASP	Council of the Arts, Sciences, and Professions
CIO	Congress of Industrial Organizations
CSU	Conference of Studio Unions
HICCASP	Hollywood Independent Citizens Committee of the Arts, Sciences, and Professions
IATSE	International Alliance of Theatrical Stage Employees
ILWU	International Longshoremen and Warehousemen's Union
INS	Immigration and Naturalization Service
IPC	Independent Productions Corporation
IPCD	Independent Productions Corporation Distributors, Inc.
IUMMSW	International Union of Mine, Mill, and Smelter Workers
LLPE	Labor's League for Political Education
MPA	Motion Picture Alliance for the Preservation of American Ideals
MPAA	Motion Picture Association of America
MPIC	Motion Picture Industry Council
SAG	Screen Actors Guild
UAW	United Automobile Workers

UE	United Electrical Workers
UMWA	United Mine Workers of America
UPWA	United Packinghouse Workers of America
USWA	United Steel Workers of America
WFM	Western Federation of Miners

Notes

1. The studio strikes and the rise of anticommunism in Hollywood have received substantial scholarly treatment. Among the strongest accounts, upon which the foregoing summary is based, are Robert Sklar, *Movie-Made America: A Cultural History of American Movies*, rev. ed. (New York: Vintage, 1994), 256–60; Larry Ceplair and Steven Englund, *The Inquisition in Hollywood: Politics in the Film Community, 1930–1960* (Berkeley: University of California Press, 1983), 212–23; John Cogley, *Report on Blacklisting*, vol. 1, *The Movies* (Santa Barbara: Fund for the Republic, 1956), 60–73; Nancy Lynn Schwartz, *The Hollywood Writers Wars* (New York: Alfred A. Knopf, 1982), 220–25, 243–50; David Caute, *The Great Fear: The Anti-Communist Purge under Truman and Eisenhower* (New York: Simon and Schuster, 1978), 487–90; Richard M. Fried, *Nightmare in Red: The McCarthy Era in Perspective* (New York: Oxford University Press, 1990), 74–75; see also Denise Hartsough, "Film Union Meets Television: IA Organizing Efforts, 1947–1952," *Labor History* 33 (Summer 1992), 361; Lary May, "Movie Star Politics: The Screen Actors Guild, Cultural Conversion, and the Hollywood Red Scare," in May, ed., *Recasting America: Culture and Politics in the Age of the Cold War* (Chicago: University of Chicago Press, 1989), 139–40); IATSE, *IATSE, 1893–1993: One Hundred Years of Solidarity* (New York: IATSE, 1993), 44–49; Brian Neve, *Film and Politics in America: A Social Tradition* (London: Routledge, 1992), 107; Hugh Lovell and Tasile Carter, *Collective Bargaining in the Motion Picture Industry: A Struggle for Stability* (Berkeley: Institute for Industrial Relations, 1955), 19–25. For an arresting combination of personal recollection and scholarly analysis, see Mike Nielsen and Gene Mailes, *Hollywood's Other Blacklist: Union Struggles in the Studio System* (London: British Film Institute, 1995). Chapters 5–8 are especially rich in detail concerning the studio strikes.

2. Interview, Richard Walsh, July 30, 1979, Silver Spring, George Meany Memorial Archives, Oral History Collection, 11.

3. Ceplair and Englund, *Inquisition in Hollywood*, 224; Sklar, *Movie-Made America*, 258; Caute, *Great Fear*, 488–89; Fried, *Nightmare in* Red, 75. For comment on Brewer's collaboration with MPA, see Nielsen and Mailes, *Hollywood's Other Blacklist*, 136–37; Caute, *Great Fear*, 502.

4. See, for example, Ceplair and Englund, *Inquisition in Hollywood*, especially chaps. 10–12; Victor S. Navasky, *Naming Names* (New York: Penguin, 1980); Sklar, *Movie-Made America*, 260–68; Caute, *Great Fear*, 491–97; Fried, *Nightmare in Red*, 75–78; Cogley, *Report on Blacklisting*; Walter Goodman, *The Committee: The Extraordinary Career of the House Committee on Un-American Activities* (New York: Farrar, Straus, and Giroux, 1968), 207–16; Gordon Kahn, *Hollywood on Trial* (New York, Arno Press and *New York Times*, 1948); "Hollywood Blacklisting," *Film Culture* 50–51 (Fall-Winter 1970)(special issue on blacklisting); Peter Roffman and Jim Purdy, *The Hollywood Social Problem Film: Madness, Despair and Politics from the Depression to the Fifties* (Bloomington: Indiana University Press, 1981), 284–87; Stefan Kanfer, *A Journal of the Plague Years* (New York: Atheneum, 1973); and Bernard F. Dick, *Radical Innocence: A Critical Study of the Hollywood Ten* (Lexington: University of Kentucky Press, 1989).

5. Ceplair and Englund, *Inquisition in Hollywood*, 255; Sklar, *Movie-Made America*, 265; Fried, *Nightmare in Red*, 77–78; Caute, *Great Fear*, 499–500.

6. Waldorf Statement, Nov. 24, 1947, quoted in Sklar, *Movie-Made America*, 266; reprinted in its entirety in Ceplair and Englund, *Inquisition in* Hollywood, appendix 6, 455. The producers' concerns over censorship are discussed in Caute, *Great Fear*, 499; Ceplair and Englund, *Inquisition in Hollywood*, 297.

7. For discussion of the anticommunist films of the blacklist era, see Stephen J. Whitfield, *The Culture of the Cold War*, 2d ed. (Baltimore: Johns Hopkins University Press, 1997), 132–40; Terry Christensen, *Reel Politics: American Political Movies from the "Birth of A Nation" to "Platoon"* (Cambridge and New York: Basil Blackwell, 1987), 89–94; Andrew Dowdy, *The Films of the Fifties: The American State of Mind* (New York: William Morrow and Company, 1975), 20–31; see also Daniel J. Leab, " 'The Iron Curtain' (1948): Hollywood's First Cold War Movie," *Historical Journal of Film, Radio, and Television* 8 (1988); Leab, "How Red Was My Valley: Hollywood, the Cold War Films, and *I Married a Communist*," *Journal of Contemporary History* 19 (1984). The impact of the blacklist on its victims is described in Ceplair and Englund,*Inquisition in Hollywood*, 398–410; and Caute, *Great Fear*, 504–6, 515–18.

8. "A Communist 'Hate' Tribute to the Loyalty and Patriotism of the American Motion Picture Industry," July 1950; "Declaration of Principle Adopted at All Industry Conference," Chicago, Aug. 30–31, 1949, Motion Picture Industry Council Papers, Beverly Hills, Margaret Herrick Library, Academy of Motion Picture Arts and Sciences Library, Box 1.

9. Whitfield, *Culture of the Cold War*, 130–31; Ceplair and Englund, *Inquisition in Hollywood*, 213; "Screen Guide for Americans" (1950), Radicalism Collection, East Lansing, Special Collections, Michigan State University Library.

10. Nielsen and Mailes, *Hollywood's Other Blacklist*, 163. For Brewer's account of

his position in Hollywood, see Interview, Roy Brewer (unfinished transcript), Los Angeles, Archives, University of California at Los Angeles, 11, 17.

11. Douglas Monroy, "Fence Cutters, Sedicioso, and First-Class Citizens: Mexican Radicalism in America," in Paul Buhle and Dan Georgakas, eds., *The Immigrant Left in the United States* (Albany: State University of New York Press, 1996), 30, 33; Mario T. Garcia, *Mexican-Americans: Leadership, Ideology, and Identity, 1930–1960* (New Haven: Yale University Press, 1989), chap. 7, esp. 199; Juan Gómez-Quiñones, *Mexican American Labor, 1790–1990* (Albuquerque: University of New Mexico Press, 1994), 117–18; James C. Foster, "Mexican Labor and the American Southwest," in Foster, ed., *American Labor in the Southwest: The First One Hundred Years* (Tucson: University of Arizona Press, 1982), 160–61; Robert C. Hodges, "The Making and Unmaking of *Salt of the Earth:* A Cautionary Tale" (Ph.D. diss., University of Kentucky, 1997), 46–50; Ernesto Galarza et al., *Mexican-Americans in the Southwest* (Santa Barbara: McNally and Loftin, 1969), 41–42; James Burnhill, "The Mexican American Question," *Political Affairs* 32 (December 1953), 57; Lorenzo Torres, "Juan Chacón" (Tucson: Salt of the Earth Labor College, n.d.), 7. The development of Mexican-American ethnic awareness following the conquest is discussed in David G. Gutiérrez, *Walls and Mirrors: Mexican-Americans, Mexican Immigrants, and the Politics of Ethnicity* (Berkeley: University of California Press, 1995), chap. 1, esp. pp. 28–29; D. H. Dinwoodie, "The Rise of the Mine-Mill Union in Southwestern Copper," in Foster, *American Labor in the* Southwest, 54–55; Author Interview (telephone), Clinton Jencks, Nov. 17, 1997.

12. Juan Gómez-Quiñones, *Chicano Politics: Reality and Promise, 1940–1990* (Albuquerque: University of New Mexico Press, 1990), 50–51; Monroy, "Fence-Cutters, Sedicioso, and First-Class Citizens," 31–32; see also Garcia, *Mexican-Americans*, chap. 8; Gómez-Quiñones, *Mexican American Labor,* 167–68; Liliana Urrutia, "An Offspring of Discontent: The Asociación Nacional México-Americana, 1949–1954," *Aztlán: International Journal of Chicano Studies Research* 15 (Spring 1984), 177–84; "Report of Alfonso Sena, National Board Member from Colorado," ANMA, ca. 1952, International Union of Mine, Mill, and Smelter Workers Papers, Boulder, Archives, University of Colorado Libraries (hereafter cited as IUMMSW Papers), Box 206; Author Interview, Alfredo Montoya, June 25, 1998, El Paso, Tex.; *Peoples Daily World*, Oct. 19, 1950; Ellen Baker, "Gender Consciousness and Political Activism in New Mexico's Working Classes," Paper Presented at North American Labor History Conference, Detroit, Oct. 25, 1997, 4–5. An important personal account of ANMA activities may be found in Bert Corona, *Memories of Chicano History: The Life and Narrative of Bert Corona*, ed. Mario T. Garcia (Berkeley: University of California Press, 1994), 169–92.

13. Burnhill, "Mexican American Question," 57–58; Garcia, *Mexican-Americans,* 227. For evidence of the Communist Party's commitment to civil rights, social equality, and economic equity, see "Resolution on Party Work among the Mexican People," Aug. 3, 1948, and "Resolution on the Conditions of the Mexican People," Aug. 3, 1948, Labadie Collection, Ann Arbor, Harlan Hatcher Graduate Library, Univer-

sity of Michigan, Communism-United States-Communist Party–Mexican Americans File; see also Hodges, "Making and Unmaking of *Salt of the Earth*," 45–46.

14. Monroy, "Fence-Cutters, Sedicioso, and First-Class Citizens," 33, 31–32; see also Garcia, *Mexican-Americans*, 227.

15. Garcia, *Mexican-Americans*, 218–19; Urrutia, "Offspring of Discontent," 182. For evidence of Chicana activism during the Great Depression and World War II, see Vicki L. Ruiz, *From Out of the Shadows: Mexican Women in Twentieth-Century America* (New York: Oxford University Press, 1998), chap. 9, esp. 74–84; Adeliada R. Del Castillo, ed., *Between Borders: Essays on Mexicana/Chicana History* (Encino, Calif.: Floricanto Press, 1990), pt. 3, esp. 257–98; Barbara Kingsolver, *Holding the Line: Women in the Great Arizona Mine Strike of 1983* (Ithaca: ILR Press, 1996), 15–16. Baker also notes that in many parts of the Southwest ANMA featured women in prominent leadership roles; see Baker, "Gender Consciousness and Political Activism," 7. For discussion of the growing Chicana resistance to the sexual double standard, see Karen Anderson, *Changing Women: A History of Racial Ethnic Women in Modern America* (New York: Oxford University Press, 1996), 133–34, 136–37.

16. Interviews, Virginia Chacón and Angie Sanchez, May 21, 1976; Sonja and Edward Biberman, Feb. 1, 1976, Oral History of the American Left Collection (hereafter cited as OHAL), Series IV, Filmmakers' Tapes and Transcripts, *A Crime to Fit the Punishment*, New York, Tamiment Library, New York University, 1, 5–7. See also Henrietta Williams Interview, May 21, 1976, OHAL, 2; Author Interview, Virginia Chacón, Mar. 22, 1997, Faywood, N.M.; Hodges, "Making and Unmaking of *Salt of the Earth*," 59; Ruiz, *From Out of the Shadows*, 86.

17. Jack Cargill, "Empire and Opposition: The 'Salt of the Earth' Strike," in Robert Kern, ed., *Labor in New Mexico: Unions, Strikes, and Social History since 1881* (Albuquerque: University of New Mexico Press, 1983), 188; Margaret Meaders, "Copper Chronicle: The Story of New Mexico 'Red Gold,'" *New Mexico Business* (May–June 1958), repr., Santa Fe, New Mexico State Records Center and Archives. For discussion of the integration of the Grant County copper industry into the global economy, largely complete by the late 1940s, see Christopher J. Huggard, "Copper Mining in Grant County, 1900–1945," in Judith Boyce DeMark, ed., *Essays in Twentieth Century New Mexico History* (Albuquerque: University of New Mexico Press, 1994), chap. 3.

18. Cargill, "Empire and Opposition," 259, n. 36; Gómez-Quiñones, *Chicano Politics*, 47–48.

19. Cargill, "Empire and Opposition," 256. n. 16; Baker, "Gender Consciousness and Political Activism," 2.

20. Baker, "Gender Consciousness and Political Activism," 1–2; Cargill, "Empire and Opposition," 191–92.

21. Quoted in Monroy, "Fence-Cutters, Sedicioso, and First-Class Citizens," 30; see also Garcia, *Mexican-Americans*, 176–77; Cargill, "Empire and Opposition," 194–95; Interview, Juan Chacón, May 21, 1976, OHAL, 2–3; Gómez-Quiñones, *Mexican-American Labor*, 183; Robert Kern, "Organized Labor: Race, Radicalism

and Gender," in De Mark, *Essays in Twentieth Century New Mexico History,* 152; Foster, "Mexican Labor and the American Southwest," 161; Author Interview, Arturo and Josefina Flores, Mar. 26, 1997, Rio Rancho, N.M.; Baker, "Gender Consciousness and Political Activism," 2–3; Torres, "Juan Chacón," 6. For evidence of comparable discriminatory conditions in the neighboring mines of Arizona, see Jonathan D. Rosenblum, *Copper Crucible: How the Arizona Miners Strike of 1983 Recast Labor–Management Relations in America* (Ithaca: ILR Press, 1995), 31; Kingsolver, *Holding the Line,* 67, 68, 79.

22. Interview, Clinton Jencks, Nov. 20, 1993, OHAL, Draft 3, 1, 12. Health issues and environmental concerns are discussed in Kingsolver, *Holding the Line,* 124, 169–70. The copper industry's expropriation of human capital is discussed in Author Interview, Jencks, Oct. 3, 1997, San Diego.

23. Author Interview, Paul Jarrico, Oct. 1, 1997, Ojai, Calif.; Paul Jarrico to James J. Lorence, Apr. 19, 1996; see also Francis R. Walsh, "The Films We Never Saw: American Movies View Organized Labor, 1934–1954," *Labor History* 27 (Fall 1986), 578.

24. Author Interview with Jencks, June 6, 1996 (telephone), author transcript, 1–2. The postwar attack on the New Deal social contract is described in Elizabeth Fones-Wolf, *Selling Free Enterprise: The Business Assault on Labor and Liberalism, 1945–1960* (Urbana: University of Illinois Press, 1994); see esp. chaps. 2, 3, 4, and 285–88. While he locates the corporate attack at a later date, David L. Stebenne comments on the social contract's decline between the 1950s and the 1980s. Moreover, Stebenne finds that workers in the Southwest gained a "much smaller share of the Postwar New Deal's rewards." David L. Stebenne, "The Postwar New Deal," *International Labor and Working Class History* 50 (Fall 1996), 144, as well as 145–46.

CHAPTER 2

1. Steve Rosswurm, "Introduction: An Overview and Preliminary assessment of the CIO's Expelled Unions," in Rosswurm, ed., *The CIO's Left-Led Unions* (New Brunswick, N.J.: Rutgers University Press, 1992), 1; Garcia, *Mexican-Americans,* 198; F. S. O'Brien, "The 'Communist-Dominated' Unions in the United States since 1950," *Labor History* 9 (Spring 1968), 184–88; Bert Cochran, *Labor and Communism: The Conflict that Shaped American Unions* (Princeton, N.J.: Princeton University Press, 1977), chap. 12; Harvey A. Levenstein, *Communism, Anticommunism, and the CIO* (Westport, Conn.: Greenwood Press, 1981), chaps. 15, 16.

2. Rosswurm, "Introduction," 2–3.

3. The foregoing summary of the attack on left-led unions and the communists who worked within them is based upon Rosswurm's thoughtful introduction to a collection of revealing essays on several of the expelled organizations. See Rosswurm, "Introducton," esp. 6–13; O'Brien, "'Communist-Dominated' Unions," 185–88; Cochran, *Labor and Communism,* 297–312; Levenstein, *Communism, Anticommunism, and the CIO,* 287–94, 301–6. Judith Stepan-Norris and Maurice Zeitlin

conclude that Communist-led unions in the 1940s were more likely than their rival unions to be "highly democratic" and less likely to be "oligarchical." Judith Stepan-Norris and Maurice Zeitlin, "Insurgency, Radicalism, and Democracy in America's Industrial Unions," *Social Forces* 75 (September 1996), 26–27; see also Stepan-Norris and Zeitlin, "Union Democracy, Radical Leadership, and the Hegemony of Capital," *American Sociological Review* 60 (December 1995), 847. Commenting on the basis for the expulsions, James R. Prickett concludes that the Communist-led unions posed little threat to either the CIO or American economic and political institutions. James R. Prickett, "Some Aspects of the Communist Controversy in the CIO," *Science and Society* 33 (Summer-Fall, 1969), 320–21; see also Roger Keeran, "The Communist Influence on American Labor," Michael E. Brown et al., eds., *New Studies in the Politics and Culture of U.S. Communism* (New York: Monthly Review Press, 1993), esp. 191–92.

4. Rosswurm, "Introduction," 16; see also 13–15; Fones-Wolf, *Selling Free Enterprise*, 10, 53–54, 288.

5. O'Brien, " 'Communist-Dominated' Unions," 198; Levenstein, *Communism, Anticommunism, and the CIO*, 272–74; Cochran, *Labor and Communism*, 269–70; Rosenblum, *Copper Crucible*, 34. For what Cargill calls a "jaundiced" view that exaggerates Communist influence in Mine-Mill, see Vernon Jensen, *Nonferrous Metals Industry Unionism, 1932–1954: The Story of a Leadership Conflict* (Ithaca: Cornell University Press, 1954). Jensen's entire book is essentially an anticommunist diatribe against the IUMMSW leadership, which attempts to justify the expulsions of 1949–1950. His account assumes significance because it became the source for other equally critical accounts of the Mine-Mill leadership. Cargill, "Empire and Opposition," 265, n. 81. Interviews, Nathan Witt, 27, and Orville Larson, 40, Oral History Collection, United Steelworkers of America (hereafter cited as USWA) Papers, State College, Pennsylvania State University, Historical Collections and Labor Archives (hereafter cited as PSU, HCLA). For the Western Federation of Miners background, see Richard Lingenfelter, *The Hard Rock Miners* (Berkeley: University of California Press, 1974); Philip J. Mellinger, *Race and Labor in Western Copper: The Fight for Equality, 1896–1918* (Tucson: University of Arizona Press, 1995); and John Ervin Brinley, *The Western Federation of Miners* (Ann Arbor: University Microfilms, 1972).

6. Larson Interview, 40–41; Interview, Irving Dichter, PSU, HCLA, 34.

7. Larson Interview, 9–10; Witt Interview, 39; Interview, I. W. Abel, PSU, HCLA, II, 31; Lorenzo Torres, "Short History of Chicano Workers," *Political Affairs* 12 (November 1973), 93; Garcia, *Mexican-Americans*, 176; Dinwoodie, "Rise of the Mine-Mill Union," 51, 53–54; Foster, "Mexican Labor and the American Southwest," 160–61.

8. Interview, Vern Curtis, PSU, HCLA, 8–9; Witt Interview, 37; Dinwoodie, "Rise of the Mine-Mill Union," 54–55.

9. Quoted in Lucien K. File, "History of Labor in the Non-Ferrous Mining Industry in New Mexico" (n.d.), Lucien File Papers, New Mexico State Records Cen-

ter and Archives, Box 2. Mine-Mill's isolation and eventual expulsion from the CIO are detailed in Cargill, "Empire and Opposition," 187–89; O'Brien, "'Communist-Dominated' Unions," 198–99; Gómez-Quiñones, *Mexican American Labor,* 183–84; Levenstein, *Communism, Anticommunism, and the CIO,* 274–75, 305–6; Jensen, *Nonferrous Metals Industry Unionism,* chaps. 16, 18; Garcia, *Mexican-Americans,* 98; Torres, "Short History of Chicano Workers," 93. The left-leaning Mine-Mill policy record is detailed in Subversive Activities Control Board, Docket No. 115–56, "Robert F. Kennedy, Attorney General of the United States v the International Union of Mine, Mill, and Smelter Workers, Respondent," Report and Order of the Board, May 4, 1962, esp. 72–85, WFM and IUMMSW Papers, Ithaca, Martin P. Catherwood Library, Labor–Management Documentation Center, Cornell University, Box 15; Kennecott Copper Corporation's insistence on signature of the noncommunist affidavits as a prerequisite for bargaining is outlined in D. D. Moffat to Fellow Employee, May 15, 1948, Box 3. For further comment on the consequences of noncompliance, see Ellen W. Schrecker, "McCarthyism in the Labor Movement," in Rosswurm, *CIO's Left-Led Unions,* 148–50.

10. Cargill, "Empire and Opposition," 189–91; Gómez-Quiñones, *Mexican American Labor,* 184; Kern, "Organized Labor," 157; Rosenblum, *Copper Crucible,* 35; Foster, "Mexican Labor and the American Southwest," 161. The union's emphasis on economic equality is noted in "Portrait of a Labor Organizer," IUMMSW, ca. 1953, Michael Wilson Papers, Los Angeles, Department of Special Collections, University Research Library, UCLA, Box 40, 26–27; see also Author Interviews, Flores and Jencks.

11. Baker, "Gender Consciousness and Political Activism," 3, 4; Hodges, "Making and Unmaking of *Salt of the Earth,*" 52, 75–76; Author Interviews, Jencks and Flores; Lucianna Stermer, "'Salt of the Earth': Climax in Grant County" (April 1973), Research Paper, History 514, Western New Mexico State University, Public Library, Silver City, N.M., 8. Hodges maintains that Jencks had taken his original job at Globe Smelter "at the behest of the CPUSA." Hodges, "Making and Unmaking of *Salt of the Earth,*" 35. However, this account cannot be independently confirmed.

12. Interview, Juan Chacón, May 21, 1976, OHAL, Draft 1, 2; Jencks Interview, OHAL, 15–16; Witt Interview, p. 203; Rosenblum, *Copper Crucible,* 170; Gómez-Quiñones, *Mexican American Labor,* 184; Baker, "Gender Consciousness and Political Activism," 3; "Portrait of a Labor Organizer," 8–10; 38–39.

13. Cargill, "Empire and Opposition," 195–96; Gómez-Quiñones, *Mexican American Labor,* 184.

14. Press Release, ANMA, Dec. 1, 1951; Alfonso Sena to dear Friend, ca. January 1952, IUMMSW Papers, Box 206; Garcia, *Mexican-Americans,* 211; Cargill, "Empire and Opposition," 196–97.

15. Cargill, "Empire and Opposition," 198–200.

16. Ibid., 201–2; Gómez-Quiñones, *Mexican American Labor,* 184.

17. Italics are mine. Jencks Interview, 9; Chacón Interview, Draft 1, 2, both

OHAL. Cargill, "Empire and Opposition," 202–4; Gómez-Quiñones, *Mexican American Labor,* 184; Kern, "Organized Labor," 158; Hodges, "Making and Unmaking of *Salt of the Earth,*" 58. Although Jencks constantly told the women that they could have achieved gender cooperation and union solidarity without outside help, Angela Sanchez and Virginia Chacón continue to believe that he and his wife were instrumental in achieving this goal. Chacón-Sanchez Interview, OHAL, 3. For dramatic evidence of Jencks's personal commitment to sexual equality, see his comments in the documentary film *Memorias de Sal* (Las Cruces: KRWG-TV, 1994).

18. Chacón Interview, OHAL, Draft 1, 2–3; Cargill, "Empire and Opposition," 204; Gómez-Quiñones, *Mexican American Labor,* 185; see also Chacón-Sanchez Interview, 1–3; Hodges, "Making and Unmaking of *Salt of the Earth,*" 58–59.

19. Cargill, "Empire and Opposition," 205–7; Gómez-Quiñones, *Mexican American Labor,* 185; Baker, "Gender Consciousness and Political Activism," 9–12. Kern acknowledges the uniqueness of the women's role in the strike, but argues that its "centrality" in the story may have been overemphasized. His position stresses the long-present gender solidarity found in the mining communities of the West, which merely gained greater visibility because of the Empire strike. Kern, "Organized Labor," 158. For an account that emphasizes the breakthrough made by women as full participants in the life of the union, see Deborah Silverton Rosenfelt, "Commentary," in Rosenfelt and Michael Wilson, *Salt of the Earth* (Old Westbury, N.Y.: Feminist Press, 1978), 120–21, 124–25, 137–38, 146.

20. Quoted in Rosenfelt, "Commentary," 122; see also Cargill, "Empire and Opposition," 208–9; Gómez-Quiñones, *Mexican American Labor,* 185.

21. Quoted in Margaret Sullivan, "The Blacklisted Few Who Stood against Hollywood" (n.d.), Jenny Vincent Papers, in Possession of Jenny Vincent, San Cristóbal, N.M. For comment on the Mexican-American community's ambivalence toward women's direct involvement in the front lines in labor disputes, see Kingsolver, *Holding the Line,* 10, 178; Baker, "Gender Consciousness and Political Activism," 13.

22. Press and Radio Releases, Local 890, Aug. 3, 4, 14, 1951; International Executive Board, IUMMSW, to John L. Lewis (telegram), July 13, 1951, all in United Mine Workers of America (hereafter cited as UMWA) Papers, PSU, HCLA, Box 177734; "What Do Grant County Businessmen Want? More Business" (n.d.), Wilson Papers, Box 51; Cargill, "Empire and Opposition," 210–11; Rosenfelt, "Commentary," 123.

23. Corona, *Memories of Chicano History,* 174–76; Garcia, *Mexican-Americans,* 211; Press Release, ANMA, Dec. 1, 1951, IUMMSW Papers, Box 206; Author Interview, Montoya.

24. Torres to Lorence, Apr. 17, 1997; Author Interview, Jencks; Alfonso Sena to Dear Friend, ca. January 1952, IUMMSW Papers, Box 206; Rosenfelt, "Commentary," 123–24; "To All Organized Workers and Friends," Nov. 19, 1951, UMWA Papers, Box 177734; Rosenblum, *Copper Crucible,* 35; Garcia, *Mexican-Americans,* 211; Corona, *Memories of Chicano History,* 176; Cargill, "Empire and Opposition," 225.

25. Cargill, "Empire and Opposition," 213–15; Foster, "Mexican Labor and the American Southwest," 160–61.

26. Cargill, "Empire and Opposition," 220–23; Gómez-Quiñones, *Mexican American Labor*, 185; Rosenfelt, "Commentary," 124.

27. Witt Interview, 2–3; Flores Interview; see also Jencks Interview, OHAL, 11, 15; Cargill, "Empire and Opposition," 233–34; Rosenfelt, "Commentary," 124; Gómez-Quiñones, *Mexican American Labor*, 185. Witt's analysis of Jencks's commitment to racial equality is consistent with his own recollection. In 1975 Jencks argued that the film was not as important as the issue it focused on. To him, the significant development in the strike was "the Chicano's struggle and the women's struggle." Jencks Interview, OHAL, 11.

28. *Silver City Daily Press*, Aug. 23, 24, 1951; Cargill, "Empire and Opposition," 227–31.

29. Cargill, "Empire and Opposition," 231–32.

30. "Here They Come" (n.d.); "Aqui Vienen Los Acereros" (n.d.); "What Do Grant County Businessmen Want? More Business" (n.d.), Wilson Papers, Box 51; "Caution: Go Slow" (ca. 1951), USWA Papers, PSU, HCLA, President's Office Files, Box 167; Cargill, "Empire and Opposition," 235; Hodges, "Making and Unmaking of *Salt of the Earth*," 177.

31. Robert S. Keitel, "The Merger of the International Union of Mine, Mill, and Smelter Workers into the United Steel Workers of America," *Labor History* 15 (Winter 1974), 37; "Notice, Local 890 Meeting," ca. October 1951, Wilson Papers, Box 51; Charles J. Smith to L. T. White, Mar. 6, 1952, USWA Papers, USWA District 38 Files, Box 8; Cargill, "Empire and Opposition," 236.

32. Quoted in Rosenfelt, "Commentary," 125; Keitel, "Merger," 37; Cargill, "Empire and Opposition," 237–41.

33. Gómez-Quiñones, *Mexican American Labor*, 185; Rosenfelt, "Commentary," 124–25; Cargill, "Empire and Opposition," 242–43; Foster, "Mexican Labor and the American Southwest," 161; Radio and Press Release," Local 890, Mar. 19, 1952, Wilson Papers, Box 51; Montoya Interview, PSU, HCLA.

34. Cargill, "Empire and Opposition," 243–44; Author Interview, Jencks; Juan Chacón Interview, Draft 1, 3; Williams Interview, 4; Ruiz, *From Out of the Shadows*, 86; Rosenfelt, "Commentary," 125, 137–38, 142–43, 146; Baker, "Gender Consciousness and Political Activism," 14; Kingsolver, *Holding the Line*, 178; Gómez-Quiñones, *Mexican American Labor*, 185–86.

35. Virginia Jencks to Mike, Zelma, and Sylvia, Feb. 24, 1952, Wilson Papers, Box 51; Cargill, "Empire and Opposition," 245.

36. Virginia Jencks to Mike, June 20, 1952, Wilson Papers, Box 51.

37. The full text of the resolution is reprinted in Rosenfelt, "Commentary," 166–67; see 143–44 for discussion of Mine-Mill's stance on gender equity. See also Cargill, "Empire and Opposition," 245–46; Baker, "Gender Consciousness and Political Activism," 9–12; *Proceedings, Forty-Ninth Convention, IUMMSW*, St. Louis,

Sept. 14–19, 1953, 27–28; *Proceedings, Forty-Eighth Convention, IUMMSW,* New York, Sept. 8–12, 1952, 159–60.

38. Virginia Jencks to Mike and Zelma, Mar. 6, 1952, Wilson Papers, Box 51.

39. Cargill, "Empire and Opposition, 247; Jensen, *Nonferrous Metals Industry Unionism,* 262.

40. Cargill, "Empire and Opposition," 251. Workers often called Jencks "El Palomino," which was a reference to his striking blond hair, as well as a sign of affection, trust, and respect. "Portrait of a Labor Organizer," 17, 26; Author Interview, Virginia Chacón; Lorenzo Torres to Lorence, Apr. 17, 1997; Gómez-Quiñones, *Mexican American Labor,* 184; Kern, "Organized Labor," 157; Baker, "Gender Consciousness and Political Activism," 4. See also the excellent introduction to the strike's cultural roots in Rosenfelt, "Commentary," 109–16; Tom Miller, "Class Reunion: *Salt of the Earth* Revisited," *Cineaste* 13 (June 1984), 32, also stresses the importance of racial and sexual equality in the strike.

CHAPTER 3

1. Neve, *Film and Politics in America,* 198, 200; Ceplair and Englund, *Inquisition in Hollywood,* 142, 182–83, 233, 300, 301, 307; Dick, *Radical Innocence,* 70–71; George Lipsitz, "Herbert Biberman and the Art of Subjectivity," *Telos* 32 (Summer 1977), 174–75; Navasky, *Naming Names,* 80; Rosenfelt, "Commentary," 101.

2. Good summaries of Biberman's early life may be found in Lipsitz, "Herbert Biberman," 174–75 and Dick, *Radical Innocence,* 70–72. See also Neve, *Film and Politics in America,* 200, for comment on his view of the relationship between art and politics. Biberman's long-term radical commitment is also mentioned by Paul Jarrico, whose recollections may be found in Interview, Paul Jarrico, Mar. 13, 1990, Los Angeles, UCLA Oral History Program, Department of Special Collections (hereafter cited as UCLA, OHP), University Research Library (Regents, University of California System), 136.

3. Dick, *Radical Innocence,* 73; Thom Anderson, "Red Hollywood," in Suzanne Ferguson and Barbara Groseclose, eds., *Literature and the Visual Arts in Contemporary Society* (Columbus: Ohio State University Press, 1985), 180.

4. Lipsitz, "Herbert Biberman," 175; Dick, *Radical Innocence,* 75–76.

5. Jarrico Interview, 102–3, 113; Ceplair and Englund, *Inquisition in Hollywood,* 300–301.

6. Ceplair and Englund, *Inquisition in Hollywood,* 302–3; Neve, *Film and Politics in America,* 200; Jarrico Interview, 119–20. For discussion of Hollywood's left screenwriters in the 1930s, see Schwartz, *Hollywood Writers' Wars,* 82–95; Jarrico's later differences with Lawson are further described in Schwartz, *Hollywood Writers' Wars,* 152–53; Ceplair and Englund, *Inquisition in Hollywood,* 302–3; Jarrico Interview, 128–29.

7. Gerald Zehavi, "Passionate Commitments: Race, Sex, and Communism at Schenectady General Electric, 1932–1954," *Journal of American History* 83 (Sep-

tember 1996), 542; Rosenfelt, "Commentary," 100–102; Jarrico Interview, 51, 120. For discussion of *Salt*'s origins in the traditional Marxist view of the "woman question," see Lillian S. Robinson. "Out of the Mine and into the Canyon: Working Class Feminism Yesterday and Today," in David E. James and Rick Berg, eds., *The Hidden Foundation: Cinema and the Question of Class* (Minneapolis: University of Minnesota Press, 1996), 176–78. For comment on the CPUSA view of the "woman question," see Rosalyn Baxandall, "The Question Seldom Asked: Women and the CPUSA," in Brown et al., *New Studies in the Politics and Culture of U.S. Communism*, 151, 154–55, 159.

8. Cogley, *Report on Blacklisting*, 107–8; Rosenfelt, "Commentary," 105. In 1951 Larry Parks, under heavy pressure from HUAC, not only acknowledged his own Communist Party membership, but also provided the committee with the names of ten party associates. His capitulation was the first in a series of staged dramas, in which Hollywood leftists were to "name names" in an effort to salvage their own careers. Ceplair and Englund, *Inquisition in Hollywood*, 372–73.

9. Rosenfelt, "Commentary," 101; Interview, Michael Wilson, UCLA, OHP, 74.

10. Wilson Interview, 70; Interview, Zelma Wilson, UCLA, OHP, 102–3.

11. For the impact of Jewish radicalism on the product of the motion picture industry, see Paul Buhle, "Themes in American Jewish Radicalism," in Buhle and Geogakas, *Immigrant Left in the United States*, 102–3; see also Buhle and Thomas H. Roberts, "The Left in Hollywood," in *The Movie Book*, ed. G. Alberelli (New York, 1996). The importance of the Jewish Left in Hollywood is also well-documented in Ceplair and Englund, *Inquisition in Hollywood*; Schwartz, *Hollywood Writers' Wars*; and Neil Gabler, *An Empire of Their Own: How the Jews Invented Hollywood* (New York: Doubleday Anchor, 1988). For full discussion of the divisive impact of HUAC and the assault on the motion picture industry within the Hollywood Jewish community, see Navasky, *Naming Names*, 102–21. A review of the attack on Hollywood leftists reveals a sharp conflict between the Jewish Right and Left and indicates that anti-Semitism was one important factor in the anticommunist movement's focus on the motion picture industry and the imposition of the blacklist. Howard Suber, "Politics and Popular Culture: Hollywood at Bay, 1933–1953," *American Jewish History* 68 (March 1979), esp. 529–31.

12. Herbert Biberman, "What Kind of Company Was This? How Normal Was It? What Were the Relationships among Its Members?," 1964, Herbert Biberman–Gale Sondergaard Papers, Madison, State Historical Society of Wisconsin (hereafter cited as SHSW), Box 51; Jarrico Interview, 131; Author Interview, Jarrico.

13. Biberman and Lazarus had formed a business partnership that preceded IPC. dAuthor Interview, Jarrico; Biberman, "What Kind of Company Was This?"; U.S. Congress, House of Representatives, *Hearings Before the Committee on Un-American Activities*, 83d Cong., 1st sess., March 26, 27, 28, 1953 (Washington: Government Printing Office, 1953), 485; "Memorandum of Law in Support of Plaintiff's Motion for Production of Documents" (1963), Independent Productions Corporation and IPC Distributors, Inc., and Loew's, Inc., et al., Biberman-Sondergaard Papers, Box

32; Interview, Ben Margolis, Sept. 13, 1984, UCLA, OHP, 240; Ceplair and Englund, *Inquisition in Hollywood*, 416–17; Rosenfelt, "Commentary," 107–8. For full discussion of Lazarus, including his long-standing interest in left-wing causes, see "Research Notes—Simon Lazarus," Biberman-Sondergaard Papers, Box 53.

14. "Independent Production Corporation," Mar. 11, 1953, in Federal Bureau of Investigation, *Communist Activity in the Entertainment Industry: FBI Surveillance Files on Hollywood, 1942–1958* (microfilm ed.), ed. Daniel Leab (Bethesda, Md.: University Publications of America, 1991), Report no. LA 100–44774, Vol. 37, Reel 7; Margolis Interview, 240; *Hearings*, 481.

15. Quoted in Ceplair and Englund, *Inquisition in Hollywood*, 416–17; Biberman to Marty et al., Mar. 12, 1952, Biberman-Sondergaard Papers, Box 28; Biberman, "What Kind of Company Was This?" See also Paul Jarrico and Herbert Biberman, "Breaking Ground," in Rosenfelt and Wilson, *Salt of the Earth*, 169 (originally published in *California Quarterly* 2 (Summer 1953).

16. Jarrico and Biberman, "Breaking Ground," 169; Biberman to Marty et al., Mar. 12, 1952, Biberman-Sondergaard Papers, Box 28; Ceplair and Englund, *Inquisition in Hollywood*, 417; Neve, *Film and Politics in America*, 198; Cargill, "Empire and Opposition," 184–85; Bruce Cook, *Dalton Trumbo* (New York: Charles Scribner's Sons, 1977), 223–24.

17. Cargill, "Empire and Opposition," 185; Rosenfelt, "Commentary," 108; Interview, Sylvia Jarrico, Feb. 2, 1975, OHAL, 4–5; Author Interviews, Jencks, Paul Jarrico, and Jenny Vincent, Mar. 24, 1997, Taos, N.M.; L.K.V. to Westbrook Pegler, Westbrook Pegler Papers, Herbert Hoover Presidential Library, West Branch, Ia., Box 5, Communism File.

18. Sylvia Jarrico Interview, 5–6; Author Interviews, Jencks and Paul Jarrico; Cargill, "Empire and Opposition," 185; Rosenfelt, "Commentary," 108.

19. Paul Jarrico Interview, 132; Rosenfelt, "Commentary," 108; Ceplair and Englund, *Inquisition in Hollywood*, 417; Cargill, "Empire and Opposition," 185; Walsh, "Films We Never Saw," 578. Jencks believes that Jarrico described the story to Biberman as "part of the cover for corporate America's need to restrain union growth." Author Interview, Jencks.

20. Jencks Interview, OHAL, 7–8; Williams Interview, 4; Paul Jarrico Interview, in Patrick McGilligan and Paul Buhle, *Tender Comrades: A Backstory of the Hollywood Blacklist* (New York: St. Martin's Press, 1997), 342; Sullivan, "Blacklisted Few"; Rosenfelt, "Commentary," 108, 126–27; Cargill, "Empire and Opposition," 185; Jonathan Rosenbaum, *Placing Movies: The Practice of Film Criticism* (Berkeley: University of California Press, 1995), p. 284.

21. Biberman to Trumbo, June 6, 1952, Biberman-Sondergaard Papers, Box 1; Wilson Papers, Box 51. See also Rosenfelt, "Commentary," 127; Miller, "Class Reunion," 32; Cargill, "Empire and Opposition," 185; Paul Jarrico Interview, UCLA, OHP, 133; Author Interview, Virginia Chacón. For evidence of the seriousness with which the women of Bayard approached script review, see Trinnie to Salina, ca. 1952; Salina to Chana, ca. 1952, Wilson Papers, Box 39. Mexican-American labor

activist Bert Corona, in El Paso for an ANMA conference, was also consulted but had no changes to recommend. Corona, *Memories of Chicano History,* 174.

22. Cargill, "Empire and Opposition," 185; Neve, *Film and Politics in America,* 200–201; Robinson, "Out of the Mine and into the Canyon," 181–82. For evidence of Wilson's decision to give priority to the women's issues, see "Preliminary Notes," ca. 1952; "Salt-Story Outline," ca. 1952, Wilson Papers, Boxes 39, 48. See also Biberman to Trumbo, June 6, 1952, Biberman-Sondergaard Papers, Box 1.

23. "Memorandum" (n.d.), Wilson Papers, Box 40, 39–40; Miller, "Class Reunion," 32. For evidence that in his union work Jencks wished to deemphasize his own role as savior of the Mexican-American worker, see Jencks Interview, OHAL, 15. When Ruth Barnes criticizes her husband's previous failure to organize women and his limited commitment to equality within his own household, she seems more outspoken than the Mexican-American women; but her aggressiveness is attributable not to membership in a less *macho* culture, but rather to the weaknesses of a man who claimed to be a comrade in struggle. Lillian Robinson sees Wilson's and Biberman's approach as a device to critique the patriarchal aspects of Chicano culture in an inoffensive way. Robinson, "Out of the Mine and into the Canyon," 182; see also Biberman to Trumbo, June 6, 1952, Biberman-Sondergaard Papers, Box 1; Wilson Papers, Box 51.

24. Biberman to Trumbo, June 6, 1952, Wilson Papers Box 51; Biberman-Sondergaard Papers, Box 1; Rosenfelt, "Commentary," 128–29; Neve, *Film and Politics in America,* 201; Cargill, "Empire and Opposition," 185; Miller, "Class Reunion," 32.

25. Neve, *Film and Politics in America,* 201; Dick, *Radical Innocence,* 78–79; Cargill, "Empire and Opposition," 185; Gómez-Quiñones, *Mexican American Labor,* 186. See also Roffman and Purdy, *Hollywood Social Problem Film,* 255.

26. Neve, *Film and Politics in America,* 201; Allen L. Woll, "Hollywood Views the Mexican-American: From The Greaser's Revenge to The Milagro Beanfield War," in Robert Brent Toplin, ed., *Hollywood as Mirror: Changing Views of "Outsiders" and "Enemies" in American Movies* (Westport, Conn.: Greenwood Press, 1993), 48–49; Cordelia Candelaria, "Film Portrayals of La Mujer Hispana," in *Agenda* 3 (June 1981), 36; Gómez-Quiñones, *Mexican-American Labor,* 185. For additional favorable evaluations, see also Roffman and Purdy, *Hollywood Social Problem Film,* 295; Rosenbaum, *Placing Movies,* 284; Gary D. Keller, *Hispanics and United States Film: An Overview and Handbook* (Tempe: Bilingual Review/Press, 1994), 132–34; Linda Williams, "Type and Stereotype: Chicano Images in Film," *Frontiers* 5 (Summer 1980), 15–16.

27. Jencks Interview, OHAL, 8.

28. Italics are mine. Chacón Interview, OHAL, 3; Biberman, "Memorandum," ca. 1953, Biberman-Sondergaard Papers, Box 17; Rosaura Revueltas, "Reflections on a Journey," *California Quarterly* 2 (Summer 1953), repr. in Rosenfelt and Wilson, *Salt of the Earth,* 174. See also Esteve Riambau and Casimiro Torreiro, "This Film Is Going to Make History: An Interview with Rosaura Revueltas," *Cineaste* 19 (December 1992), 50–51; Jencks Interview, OHAL, 8.

29. Simon M. Lazarus, "Deposition," IPC Corporation v. Loew's, Inc., et al., May 23, 1957, 668–69; Roy M. Brewer, "Deposition," IPC Corporation Loew's, Inc., et al., Feb. 12–13, 1964, 148–51, 857; "Research Notes — Simon Lazarus"; Biberman, "What Kind of Company Was This?," 2; Biberman to Arthur Galligan, Mar. 11, 1965, all in Biberman-Sondergaard Papers, Boxes 39, 36, 53, 37, 29; Rosenfelt, "Commentary," 128; Ceplair and Englund, *Inquisition in Hollywood*, 417.

30. "Research Notes — Simon Lazarus"; "Memo (III) on the Making of a Motion Picture" (n.d.), Biberman-Sondergaard Papers, Box 53.

31. Cogley, *Report on Blacklisting*, 80–83; Interview, Roy Brewer (n.d.), OHAL; Miller, "Class Reunion," 32; Biberman, "What Kind of Company Was This?," 2; Tom Zaniello, *Working Stiffs, Union Maids, and Riffraff: An Organized Guide to Films about Labor* (Ithaca: ILR Press, 1996), 214; William J. Puette, *Through Jaundiced Eyes: How the Media View Organized Labor* (Ithaca: ILR Press, 1992), 21.

32. Biberman, "What Kind of Company Was This?," 3.

CHAPTER 4

1. "Report Given by Herbert Biberman at Meeting of Independent Productions Corporation," Mar. 22, 1952, Biberman-Sondergaard Papers, Box 17.

2. Biberman to Dear Ones, ca. February 1952; Salud, Bien Queridos, ca. February 1952, Biberman-Sondergaard Papers, Box 4. For discussion of IPC's commitment to social realism in the *Salt* project, see Hodges, "Making and Unmaking of *Salt of the Earth*," 113.

3. This account is based primarily on Virginia Chacón's recollection of the earliest discussions pertaining to the film project. Many observers, however, recall Local 890's unwillingness to proceed on its own. Author Interviews, Chacón, Jarrico, and Jencks.

4. Virginia Jencks to Mike and Zelma, Mar. 6, 1952, Wilson Papers, Box 51.

5. Biberman to Maurice Travis, June 16, 1952, IUMMSW Papers, Box 119; Lazarus "Deposition," 883; Biberman to Dear Ones, ca. February, 1952; Biberman, "Memorandum" (n.d.), Biberman-Sondergaard Papers, Boxes 40, 4, 17; "Union-Sponsored Radical Films," in Paul Buhle and Dan Georgakas, eds., *Encyclopedia of the American Left* (Urbana: University of Illinois Press, 1992), 799.

6. Travis to International Executive Board, June 23, 1952, IUMMSW Papers, Box 119; Jarrico to Lorence, Apr. 19, 1996; Hodges, "Making and Unmaking of *Salt of the Earth*," 119.

7. Charles J. Katz to Witt, Aug. 27, 1952; Witt to Katz, Sept. 8, 1952, Biberman-Sondergaard Papers, Box 28; *Hearings*, 486–87; IUMMSW Executive Board Minutes, June 25–27, 1952, and February 2–4, 1953, IUMMSW Papers, Box 31; Clinton Jencks Papers, Boulder, University of Colorado at Boulder Libraries, Archives, Box 2.

8. Biberman, "Memo (III) on the Making of a Motion Picture"; James L. Daugherty to Biberman, Aug. 25, 1952, James L. Daugherty Papers, Los Angeles, South-

ern California Library for Social Science and Research, Box MMSW, 1940s–1950s; Wilson to Travis, Aug. 13, 1952; Biberman to Travis, July 3, 1952, IUMMSW Papers, Box 119.

9. Author Interview, Jarrico; Biberman, "Memo (III) on the Making of a Motion Picture"; Biberman to Travis, Oct. 14, 1952, IUMMSW Papers, Box 119; Rosenfelt, "Commentary," 128; Hodges, "Making and Unmaking of *Salt of the Earth*," 130, 132.

10. Jarrico to Witt, Dec. 20, 1952, IUMMSW Papers, Box 53; Rosenfelt, "Commentary," 128–29; *Hearings*, 489; Miller, "Class Reunion," 32.

11. Quoted in Woll, "Hollywood Views the Mexican-American," 49; Rosenfelt, "Commentary," 129; Dick, *Radical Innocence*, 79; see also Hodges, "Making and Unmaking of *Salt of the Earth*" 122.

12. Rosenfelt, "Commentary," 129; Biberman to Dearests, September 1952; Biberman to Gale, Joan, Dannaman, September 1952; Biberman to Gale, Dan, July 1952; Biberman to Rodolfo Lozoya, July 23, 1952, Biberman-Sondergaard Papers, Boxes 4, 1; Corona, *Memories of Chicano History*, 176, 177; Vincent Interview.

13. Biberman to Mine, September 1952; Biberman to Dearests, September 1952; Biberman to Gale, Joan, Dannaman, September 1952, Biberman-Sondergaard Papers, Box 4.

14. Chacón Interview, 2; Sonja Dahl and Edward Biberman Interview, 17, OHAL; Lipsitz, "Herbert Biberman," 178; Rosenfelt, "Commentary," 129; Miller, "Class Reunion," 33; Woll, "Hollywood Views the Mexican-American," 49; Walsh, "Films We Never Saw," 579.

15. Author Interview, Jencks; Minutes, Special Shop Steward Meeting, Dec. 22, 1952, in Bayard District Union Minutes, November 1952–1954, IUMMSW Papers, Box 868, 24–25; Rosenfelt, "Commentary," 129; Biberman to Marianne Ramirez, July 23, 1952; Biberman to Mr. and Mrs. Clinton Jencks, July 23, 1952, Biberman-Sondergaard Papers, Box 1; Lipsitz, "Herbert Biberman," 178.

16. Minutes, Dec. 22, 1952, 25; Rosenfelt, "Commentary," 130; Juan Chacón, "Union Made," in Rosenfelt and Wilson, *Salt of the Earth*, 181–82; Author Interview, Jencks; Jencks Interview, OHAL, 8.

17. Author Interviews, Jencks and Flores; Jarrico to Lorence, Apr. 19, 1996; Rosenfelt, "Commentary," 130; Sanchez-Chacón Interview, OHAL, 5.

18. Jencks Interview, OHAL, 5; see also Baker, "Gender Consciousness and Political Activism," 12–13. Rosenfelt emphasizes the crucial role of the Ladies Auxiliary in accepting these day-to-day responsibilities. Rosenfelt, "Commentary," 129.

19. Sonja Biberman, in Edward and Sonja Biberman Interview, OHAL, 5; Sonja Biberman to Darlings, Jan. 4, 1953, Biberman-Sondergaard Papers, Box 4; see also Rosenfelt, "Commentary," 130, 138, 143, 146. Rosenfelt emphasizes the ambiguous legacy of the strike, the film, and the ongoing gender conflicts that emerged from those experiences. Her account stresses the unfinished women's struggle for equal status that persists in Grant County and elsewhere.

20. Biberman, "What Kind of Company Was This?," 3; Jencks and Ernest S.

Velásquez to Travis, Jan. 2, 1953, IUMMSW Papers, Boxes 119, 538; Rosenfelt, "Commentary," 128.

21. Lipsitz, "Herbert Biberman," 178–79; Biberman to My Loves, ca. January 1953; Jan. 10, 1953, Biberman-Sondergaard Papers, Box 4, Miller, 33.

22. Biberman to Gale, ca. January 1953; Biberman to My Loves, ca. January 1953, Biberman-Sondergaard Papers, Box 4. For comment on the impact of Biberman's "authoritarian temperament," see Rosenfelt, "Commentary," 133. Rosenfelt also notes that the casting of Rosaura Revueltas was a source of tension among the union community and IPC leaders, in that many believed a native New Mexican could have played the role of Esperanza equally well. Rosenfelt, "Commentary," 133–34; Author Interview, Jencks; Jencks Interview, OHAL, 5.

23. Biberman to My Dears, ca. February 1953, Biberman-Sondergaard Papers, Box 4; Rosenfelt, "Commentary," 133.

24. "Paul Jarrico," in Griffin Fariello, ed., *Red Scare: Memories of the American Inquisition, An Oral History* (New York: W. W. Norton, 1995), 281; Jarrico, "Salt of the Earth – Chronology," May 9, 1955; Biberman, "Report to IPC," ca. Autumn 1953, Biberman-Sondergaard Papers, Box 51, 17; Bayard District Minutes, Jan. 21, 1953, 34.

25. Victor Riesel to Buck Harris, Feb. 5, 8, 1953 (telegrams); Harris, "Memo Re Movie Being Produced by Commies at Silver City, New Mexico," Feb. 3, 1953; Harris to Riesel, Feb. 2, 1953; June Kuhlman to Harris, Jan. 28, 1953; Kuhlmann to Dear Sir, Jan. 22, 1953, Los Angeles, Screen Actors Guild Archives (hereafter cited as SAG), *Salt of the Earth* File; *Hollywood Reporter*, Feb. 9, 10, 1953; Jarrico, "Salt of the Earth – Chronology," 6–7; Rosenfelt, "Commentary," 131; Miller, "Class Reunion," 33, "Paul Jarrico," 281; Kuhlman to Johnston, Jan. 22, 1953; Michael Linden to Kuhlman, Jan. 28, 1953; Biberman, "Memorandum," 1953, Biberman-Sondergaard Papers, Boxes 46, 17; Hodges, "Making and Unmaking of *Salt of the Earth*," 157.

26. Riesel, "Inside Labor," Feb. 9, 1953, SAG Archives, *Salt of the Earth* File; Jarrico, "Salt of the Earth – Chronology," 6–7; Rosenfelt, "Commentary," 131.

27. Jarrico, "Salt of the Earth – Chronology," 6–7; "Press Release," Feb. 13, 1953, SAG Archives, Press Release Files; Rosenfelt, "Commentary," 131; Hodges, "Making and Unmaking of *Salt of the Earth*," 160–61.

28. Harris, "Memo Re Movie Being Produced by Commies at Silver City, New Mexico," Feb. 3, 1953; "Statement of Facts (and Some Conclusions) Re Motion Picture Being Made at Silver City, New Mexico," ca. Feb. 13, 1953; Harris to Riesel, Feb. 2, 1953, SAG Archives, *Salt of the Earth* File.

29. Stephen Vaughn, *Ronald Reagan in Hollywood: Movies and Politics* (Cambridge: Cambridge University Press, 1994), 217–18; for full discussion of SAG efforts under Reagan's leadership to collaborate with MPIC in developing a response to the blacklist, see 210–18; Interview, Jack Dales, UCLA, OHP, 20–21; SAG preference for cooperation with MPIC in formulating an industry-wide position is evident in

its refusal to establish an independent "clearance" procedure for blacklistees. SAG Minutes, Feb. 17, 1953, 4388; for comment on MPIC efforts to develop its response to problems "arising from Communist infiltration," see Joseph Roos to Dore Schary, Feb. 5, 1953, Community Relations Committee, Jewish Federation Council of Los Angeles Papers (hereafter cited as CRC, JFC), Northridge, Urban Archives Center, California State University-Northridge (hereafter cited as UAC, CSU-N), Box 69.

30. Biberman, "What Kind of Company Was This," 3; Jarrico Interview, UCLA, OHP, 133; Author Interviews, Jarrico and Jencks; Jencks, "Semi-Monthly Report of International Representatives," Feb. 15, 1953, IUMMSW Papers, Box 100, Clinton Jencks File; Jarrico, "Salt of the Earth — Chronology," 7; "Statement of Facts (and Some Conclusions) Re Motion Picture Being Made at Silver City, New Mexico," ca. Feb. 13, 1953; Adrian Scott to Jarrico, Feb. 19, 1953; Arthur B. Johnson to Jules Schwerin, Feb. 12, 1953, Biberman-Sondergaard Papers, Boxes 44, 46; Walsh, "Films We Never Saw," 579; Rosenfelt, "Commentary," 131–32; Zaniello, *Working Stiffs, Union Maids, and Riffraff,* 215; Ceplair and Englund, *Inquisition in Hollywood,* 417; Hodges, "Making and Unmaking of *Salt of the Earth,*" 163–64.

31. Edward and Sonja Biberman Interview, OHAL, 16; Jencks Interview, OHAL, 11; Bayard District Minutes, Feb. 18, 1953, 47; *Mine-Mill Union,* Feb. 23, 1953; Rosenfelt, "Commentary," 133; Biberman, *Salt of the Earth: The Story of a Film* (Boston: Beacon Press, 1965), 77.

32. *Congressional Record,* 83d Cong., 1st sess., Feb. 24, 1953, vol. 99, pt. 1, 1371–72; Jarrico, "Salt of the Earth — Chronology," 8; *Los Angeles Herald and Express,* Feb. 24, 1953; Biberman, "Report to IPC," ca. Autumn 1953.

33. Walter Pidgeon to Kuhlmann, Feb. 17, 1953; Harris to Riesel, Feb. 17, 1953; Harris to Jackson, ca. Feb. 25, 1953, SAG Archives, *Salt of the Earth* File; Communications Director's Files.

34. Unidentified Newspaper Article, ca. Feb. 25, 1954, Juan Chacón Papers, Silver City, Western New Mexico State University Library, Clippings File; Scott to Jarrico, Feb. 19, 1953, Biberman-Sondergaard Papers, Box 44; Elmer Rice to Jackson, Feb. 27, 1953, American Civil Liberties Union (hereafter cited as ACLU) Papers, Princeton, Seeley G. Mudd Manuscripts Library, Princeton University, Box 579.

35. Jackson to Rice, Mar. 7, 1953; "The Washington Letter," Feb. 21, 1953, ACLU Papers, Box 579.

36. Howard Hughes to Jackson, Mar. 18, 1953; Brewer to Jackson, Mar. 18, 1953, in *Congressional Record,* 83d Cong., 1st sess., Mar. 19, 1953, vol. 99, pt. 2, 2206–7; Clinton P. Anderson to Thruston B. Morton, Mar. 19, 1953; Morton to Anderson, Apr. 13, 1953; National Archives, Record Group 59, General Records of the Department of State, Box 4453, No. 811, 452/3–1953; Jarrico, "Salt of the Earth — Chronology," 11; Jarrico Interview, UCLA, OHP, 133; *Los Angeles Times,* Mar. 2, 1953. See also Rosenfelt, "Commentary," 183–87; Walsh, "Films We Never Saw,"

579; Zaniello, *Working Stiffs, Union Maids, and Riffraff,* 215; Miller, "Class Reunion," 33; "Memorandum of Law in Support of Plaintiff's Motion for Production of Documents," 1963, Biberman-Sondergaard Papers, Box 32.

37. Author Interview, Jarrico; Jarrico, "Salt of the Earth — Chronology," 11. For the full text of the Hughes letter, see Appendix 1.

38. Riambau and Torreiro, "This Film Is Going to Make History," 51; Margolis Interview, 243; "Paul Jarrico," 281–82; Biberman, "What Kind of Company Was This?," 3; Biberman, "Report to IPC," ca. Autumn 1953; Rosenfelt, "Commentary," 132; Revueltas, "Reflections on a Journey," 176; Miller, "Class Reunion," 33–34; *Silver City Daily Press,* Feb. 27, 1953; Hodges, "Making and Unmaking of *Salt of the Earth,*" 169–70.

39. Jencks Interview, OHAL, 11–12; "War against Our Union," ca. March 1953, in Jencks, "Report of International Representatives," Feb. 15, 1953, IUMMSW Papers, Box 100, Clinton Jencks File; Bayard District Minutes, Mar. 5, 1953, 57–58; *Washington News,* Mar. 4, 1953; Biberman, "What Kind of Company Was This?," 4; "Report to IPC, ca. Autumn 1953; Jarrico, "Salt of the Earth — Chronology," 9; *Silver City Daily Press,* Feb. 27 and Mar. 2, 3, 4, 7, 1953; A. B. Caldwell to Warren Olney, III, Mar. 23, 1953, U.S. Department of Justice Civil Rights Division, Case File no. 144–49–45; John Howard Lawson, *Film in the Battle of Ideas* (New York: Masses and Mainstream, 1953), 119–20; Miller, "Class Reunion," 34; Rosenfelt, "Commentary," 134–35. For a riveting personal account of the violence created by the vigilante groups, see Biberman, *Salt of the Earth,* 101–18. IUMMSW emphasized community support in the Silver City area, noting that "vigilante action" had not cut short work on the film. The International insisted that 99 percent of the population were either favorable or neutral toward the film. "Press Release," ca. March 1953, IUMMSW Papers, Box 138 (Local 890). More accurate, however, was the FBI's analysis, which confirmed the provocative behavior of the Central Protective Committee, including death threats against Jencks and other hostile actions toward the IPC group. FBI Director to Assistant Attorney General Warren Olney, III, Mar. 11, 1953, U.S. Department of Justice Civil Rights Division, Case File no. 14–49–45.

40. Boardman to FBI Director, Mar. 4, 1953, FBI File no. 100–399257; "Emergency Meeting of All Good Local 890, Mine-Mill Union Men," Mar. 4, 1953, attached to Jencks, "Report of International Representative, February 15, 1953," IUMMSW Papers, Box 100, Clinton Jencks File; *Variety,* Mar. 3, 4, 1953.

41. *Mine-Mill Union,* Mar. 9, 1953; Vincent Interview; *Peoples Daily World,* Mar 2, 1953.

42. Riambau and Torreiro, "This Film Is Going to Make History," 51; *Mine-Mill Union,* Mar. 9, 1953; *Washington Star,* Feb. 27, 1953; *Variety,* Mar. 3, 1953; *Daily Worker,* Mar. 2, 1953; Bayard District Minutes, Mar. 11, 1953, 63; Brewer Deposition, 398–99; Report on the Inter-American Conference of Mining, Metal, and Machine Workers Held in Mexico City on Feb. 27 and 28 and Mar. 1, 1953; *Progreso,* February 1953, IUMMSW Papers, Boxes 206, 178; Teletype Report,

Mar. 2, 1953, Washington City News Service, in *Communist Activity in the Entertainment Industry*, File no. 100–138754–17, Reel 10; *Hollywood Citizen News*, Mar. 2, 1953; "Statement by Juan Chacón" (n.d.), IUMMSW Papers, Box 129. INS assistant director Merrill R. Toole advised the FBI in El Paso that as of March 30, 1953, his office had received forty-eight protests urging that Revueltas be permitted to remain in the United States, forty-three of them from Hollywood and New York. FBI, "Report," Rosaura Revueltas, Apr. 13, 1953, File no. EP 100–5278; Hodges, "Making and Unmaking of *Salt of the Earth*," 171.

43. Minutes, SAG Board of Directors, Mar. 9 and May 11, 1953, SAG Archives; Lawson, *Film in the Battle of Ideas*, 120; Hodges, "Making and Unmaking of *Salt of the Earth*," 171. The end result was the SAG adoption of a loyalty oath requirement for Guild membership, after a referendum in July 1953. Press Release, July 1, 1953, SAG Archives, Press Release File; Vaughn, *Ronald Reagan in Hollywood*, 217–18.

44. "Press Release," ca. March 1953; Biberman, Report to IPC, ca. Autumn 1953; Biberman-Sondergaard Papers, Boxes 28, 17; Biberman to Travis, Mar. 26, 1953, IUMMSW Papers, Boxes 119, 538; FBI Report, Los Angeles, Mar. 13, 1953, Communist Activity in the Entertainment Industry, File no. 100–15732, Vol. 37, Reel 7; *Hearings*, 483; *Los Angeles Daily News*, Mar. 27, 1953; *New York Times*, Mar. 27, 1953; Harris to Jackson, Mar. 4, 1953, SAG Archives, Communications Director's Files.

45. Warren Olney, III, to Director, Federal Bureau of Investigation, ca. March 1953, "Subject: IPC, Registration Act," FBI File no. 100–399257–30; FBI Report, Los Angeles, July 13, 1953, FBI File no. 100–399257–44.

46. *IATSE Bulletin*, no. 395, Spring 1953; Roy Loynd, "Roy Brewer Doesn't Like His Docu 'Role,' Wants Footage Trimmed," *Variety*, Apr. 27, 1983; Brewer Interview, OHAL.

47. Brewer Deposition, 361–62, 395–96; *Hollywood Reporter*, Apr. 15, 1953; Brewer Interview, OHAL; Margolis Interview, UCLA, OHP, 245; Miller, "Class Reunion," 34; "Paul Jarrico," 283; Hodges, "Making and Unmaking of *Salt of the Earth*," 201.

48. *Variety*, July 21, 1953; *Los Angeles Times*, July 21, 1953; *Hollywood Reporter*, July 21, 1953; Jarrico, "Salt of the Earth — Chronology," 13, 14, 19; Author Interview, Jarrico; FBI Report, Los Angeles, June 16, 1953, *Communist Activity in the Entertainment Industry*, File no. 100–15732, Vol. 37, Reel 7; Hodges, "Making and Unmaking of *Salt of the Earth*," 206–7.

49. Jarrico to Brewer, July 28, 1953; Jarrico to Arthur B. Johnson, July 28, 1953; Johnson to Jarrico, Aug. 10, 1953; Sidney P. Solow to Jarrico, Aug. 13, 1953; Memo, Sound Services, Inc. (n.d.), Biberman-Sondergaard Papers, Boxes 28, 44, 53; *Peoples Daily World*, July 22, 1953; *Variety*, July 21 and 29, 1953; *Los Angeles Times*, July 21, 1953; Jarrico, "Salt of the Earth — Chronology," 13–14; Rosenfelt, "Commentary," 173.

50. *IATSE Bulletin*, Autumn 1953, 7; Lisa Kernan, " 'Keep Marching Sisters': The Second Generation Looks at *Salt of the Earth*," *Nuestro* 9 (May 1985), 25; Brewer to John Lehners, Aug. 6, 1953, Biberman-Sondergaard Papers, Box 37; Jarrico, "Salt of

the Earth — Chronology," 14; Rosenfelt, "Commentary," 173; Miller, "Class Reunion," 34; Walsh, "Films We Never Saw," 579; Biberman, *Salt of the Earth*, 131–51.

51. Brewer, "Report to the International President and the General Executive
Board, IATSE," Mar. 2, 1953, IATSE Papers, Astoria, American Museum of the
Moving Image, Box 34; Brewer Interview, UCLA Archives, 8–9; "Brewer Made
Screen Anti-Red Group Head," June 4, 1953, CRC/JFC Papers, Box 71; *Los Angeles
Times*, ca. June 4, 1953, in Biberman-Sondergaard Papers, Box 44.

52. Biberman, *Salt of the Earth*, 152; Brewer, "Report to the International Executive Board, IATSE," Mar. 2, 1953; Brewer Interview, OHAL; Cogley, *Report on
Blacklisting*, 160; Margolis Interview, 245, 160; Puette, *Through Jaundiced Eyes*, 21.
For evidence of Brewer's early reservations concerning Walsh's inability to spot
alleged Communist propaganda in films, see "Roy Brewer," in Fariello, *Red Scare*,
117–118.

CHAPTER 5

1. Jarrico Interview, UCLA, OHP, 164–65; Author Interview, Jarrico.

2. Albert Maltz, Interview, UCLA, OHP, 514, 515; Maltz is also quoted in Stephen Vaughn, "Political Censorship during the Cold War," in Francis G. Couvares,
ed., *Movie Censorship and American Culture* (Washington, D.C.: Smithsonian Institution Press, 1996), 243, and see also 238–40; Schwartz, *Hollywood Writers' Wars*, 88,
152; Ceplair and Englund, *Inquisition in Hollywood*, 60–65, 310; Navasky, *Naming
Names*, 293–95, 301–2; Dick, *Radical Innocence*, 67–69; Gabler, *Empire of Their Own*,
331–35.

3. Jarrico Interview, UCLA, OHP, 165; McGilligan and Buhle, *Tender Comrades*,
327, 337; Notes, "Salt of the Earth," John Howard Lawson Papers, Carbondale, Ill.,
Southern Illinois University, Morris Library, Special Collections, Box 40.

4. John Howard Lawson, "Memo on Film," ca. August 1953, Lawson Papers
Supplement, Carbondale, Ill., Southern Illinois University, Morris Library, Special
Collections, File Cover 34, "Salt of the Earth," 1954.

5. Ibid.

6. Ibid.

7. Ibid.

8. "Memorandum," ca. August 1953; "Comments on the Memo," ca. August
1953, Wilson Papers, Box 51; Jarrico Interview, UCLA, OHP, 165.

9. "Comments on the Memo," ca. August 1953; "Memorandum," ca. August
1953, Wilson Papers, Box 51; Hodges, "Making and Unmaking of *Salt of the Earth*,"
117.

10. Jarrico Interview, UCLA, OHP, 165; Author Interview, Jarrico; Lawson,
"Memo on Film."

11. Lawson, "Memo on Film"; Jarrico Interview, UCLA, OHP, 165.

12. Jarrico Interview, UCLA, OHP, 168; Wilson quoted in Ceplair and Englund,
Inquisition in Hollywood, 426. See also Rosenfelt, "Commentary," 108–9, for discus-

sion of the filmmakers' adherence to deeply held principles as they perfected their work.

13. FBI Report, Albuquerque, N.M., Mar. 13, 1953, 12–13, File no. 100–399257–7. For comment on the CIO's acceptance of parallel positions as evidence of Communist domination of suspect unions, see Ellen Schrecker, *Many Are the Crimes: McCarthyism in America* (Boston: Little, Brown, and Company, 1998), 339–40.

14. Wright, "Storm over Silver City," *March of Labor* (April 1953), Chacón Papers, Pamphlet File; Chacón, "Union Made," 182; *Hollywood Review*, March-April 1953, 3.

15. Albert Maltz to Biberman, Apr. 2, 1953, Biberman-Sondergaard Papers, Box 1.

16. Ceplair and Englund, *Inquisition in Hollywood*, 414–15. See also FBI Clippings File, *Salt of the Earth*, Field Office File no. LA-100–44774; Rosenfelt, "Commentary," 169–82; Hodges, "Making and Unmaking of *Salt of the Earth*," 257.

17. "Advertising Cover," *California Quarterly* (Summer 1953), in FBI Office File no. LA-100–44777; *Los Angeles Times*, July 12, 1953; Jarrico, "Salt of the Earth — Chronology," 13; Biberman to Wright, June 3, 1953, IUMMSW Papers, Box 119. See also Rosenfelt, "Commentary," 173–74; Hodges, "Making and Unmaking of *Salt of the Earth*," 257–58.

18. *Hollywood Review*, June-July 1953, in Lawson Papers, Box 13; Jarrico and Biberman, "Breaking Ground," 173–74.

19. *Los Angeles Times*, July 12, 1953; *El Universal*, Sept. 12, 1953; *Cine Mundial*, Sept. 5, 1953, copies in Wilson Papers, Box 51; Trumbo to Jarrico, July 28, 1953, Dalton Trumbo Papers, SHSW, Box 4.

20. Biberman to Travis, Mar. 26, 1953, IUMMSW Papers, Box 119.

21. Biberman to Travis, Apr. 20 and Mar. 26, 1953; Biberman to Wright, June 3, 1953, IUMMSW Papers, Box 119.

22. "To All Local Unions and Staff Members," Aug. 5, 1953; Biberman to Morris Wright, June 3, 1953; Biberman to Travis, Aug. 1, 1953, IUMMSW Papers, Boxes 119, 129, 538. See also Edward Huebsch to James Daugherty, July 21, 1953; Jarrico to Daugherty, July 2, 1953, Daugherty Papers, Box 1; Alvah Bessie to Wilson, July 1, 1953; Carl Marzani to Wilson, Sept. 8, 1953, Wilson Papers, Box 51.

23. Jencks to Wilson, July 31, 1953, Wilson Papers, Box 51.

24. Author Interview, Jarrico; Jarrico, Editing Notes, July 20, 1953, Wilson Papers, Box 40.

25. Jencks to Wilson, July 31, 1953, Wilson Papers, Box 51.

26. Jarrico to Lorence, Apr. 19, 1996; Jarrico to Travis, Aug. 1, 1953; IUMMSW Papers, Box 119; Minutes, Executive Board, IUMMSW, Aug. 12–13, 1953, Jencks Papers, Box 2; see also FBI Report, Los Angeles, Sept. 15, 1953, *Communist Activity in the Entertainment Industry*, File no. LA 100–15732, Vol. 37, Reel 7.

27. Wilson to Travis, Aug. 21, 1953, Wilson Papers, Box 51.

28. *Mine-Mill Union*, Aug. 31, 1953; Santa Fe *New Mexican*, Aug. 6, 1953; *Daily Peoples World*, Aug. 31, 1953.

29. Michael Wilson, Speech, Sept. 16, 1953, *Proceedings of the 49th Convention*,

IUMMSW, St. Louis, Mo., Sept. 14–19, 1953, 84–89. See also Wilson Papers, Box 51; Rosenfelt, "Commentary," 109, 130; FBI Report, Denver, Jan. 31, 1955, "Independent Productions Corporation," 2–3, File no. 100–399257–56; Jarrico to Lorence, Apr. 19, 1996.

30. Minutes, Executive Board, Sept. 17, 1953, IUMMSW Papers, Box 31; Jencks Papers, Box 2.

31. *Proceedings of the 49th Convention,* Sept. 14–19, 1953, 27–28, 30–31; Rosenfelt, "Commentary," 143–44.

32. Arturo Flores, "Semi-Monthly Report of International Representatives," Nov. 30, 1953, Arturo Flores File; Minutes, Regional Conference of Carlsbad, El Paso, and Bayard Locals, Oct. 17, 1953, New Mexico-Texas Mine-Mill Council File, IUMMSW Papers, Boxes 100 and 869.

33. William Gately, "Semi-Monthly Report of International Representatives," Nov. 30, Dec. 15, 1953, IUMMSW Papers, Box 100, William Gately File.

34. Vaughn, *Ronald Reagan in Hollywood,* 210–11; Cogley, *Report on Blacklisting,* 79–80; Ceplair and Englund, *Inquisition in Hollywood,* 381–82; Wilson to Travis, Nov. 5 and Oct. 22, 1953, Wilson Papers, Box 51; IUMMSW Papers, Box 119; Hodges, "Making and Unmaking of *Salt of the Earth,*" 259.

35. Gately, "Semi-Monthly Report of International Representatives," Dec. 15, 1953, William Gately File; Wilson to Travis, Oct. 22, 1953, Wilson Papers, Box 51; Author Interview (telephone), Dave Moore, Detroit, Nov. 11, 1996. For discussion of the isolation of the left wing within the UAW from mainstream unionism in Detroit and elsewhere, see Martin Halpern, *UAW Politics in the Cold War Era* (Albany: State University of New York Press, 1988), esp. chaps. 15 and 16. Local 600's independence and its Progressive caucus's struggle with Reuther is fully discussed in Judith Stepan-Norris and Maurice Zeitlin, *Talking Union* (Urbana: University of Illinois Press, 1996), 18–24, 130–74, 200–227; and William D. Andrew, "Factionalism and Anti-Communism: Ford Local 600," *Labor History* 20 (Spring 1979). See also Robert Zieger, "Showdown at the Rouge," *History Today* 40 (January 1990).

36. "To Americans It May Concern," Oct. 17, 1953; IPC and IPC Distributors, Inc., v. Loew's Incorporated et al., "Memorandum of Law in Support of Plaintiff's Motion for Production of Documents," 1963, Biberman-Sondergaard Papers, Boxes 32, 66; Hodges, "Making and Unmaking of *Salt of the Earth,*" 261–62.

37. Unidentified Correspondent to Katz, Oct. 23, 1953, Biberman-Sondergaard Papers, Box 28.

38. This description is based on the observations of an FBI agent, whose remarks are recorded in COMPIC Report, Los Angeles, Dec. 15, 1953, 14–16, *Communist Activity in the Entertainment Industry,* File no. 100–15732, Vol. 37, Reel 7.

39. Ibid., 12–13.

40. Mr. And Mrs. Craig S. Vincent to Harry Deckerhoff, Dec. 1, 1953, IUMMSW Papers, Box 302; *Silver City Daily Press,* Dec. 11, 1953; Schrecker, *Many Are the Crimes,* 310; Vincent Interview.

CHAPTER 6

1. Quoted in Ceplair and Englund, *Inquisition in Hollywood,* 418; see also Margolis Interview, 246. Biberman, *Salt of the Earth,* 151. The film was eventually to play in thirteen of the thirteen thousand theaters in the United States. "Paul Jarrico," 283; see also Miller, "Class Reunion," 34; Walsh, "Films We Never Saw," 579.

2. Author Interview, Jarrico; Interview, Sol Kaplan, OHAL, 5; Jarrico, "Salt of the Earth — Chronology," 18; Biberman, *Salt of the Earth,* 144–45, 153, 155–56; Biberman to My Loves, Jan. 27, 1954, Biberman-Sondergaard Papers, Box 4.

3. Biberman, *Salt of the Earth,* 154–55; Jarrico, "Salt of the Earth — Chronology," 20–22; Biberman to Margolis, Feb. 3 and 13, 1954; Biberman to Gale, Feb. 6, 1954, Biberman-Sondergaard Papers, Boxes 28, 4; Miller, "Class Reunion," 34; Author Interview, Lottie Gordon, New York, Aug. 4, 1997, Reference Center for Marxist Studies; Hodges, "Making and Unmaking of *Salt of the Earth,*" 263–64.

4. Biberman, *Salt of the Earth,* 154; Margolis to Biberman, Feb. 11, 1954; Biberman to Margolis, Feb. 3, 1954, Biberman-Sondergaard Papers, Box 28; *Variety,* Feb. 17, 1954; *IATSE Bulletin* (Winter 1953–1954), 7.

5. Biberman to Margolis, Feb. 3 and 13, 1954; Margolis to Biberman, Feb. 11, 1954, Biberman-Sondergaard Papers, Box 28; Hodges, "Making and Unmaking of *Salt of the Earth,*" 270–71.

6. "Memorandum," Herman M. Levy to Clifford Forster, Feb. 8, 1954, ACLU Papers, Box 579.

7. Biberman to Elmer Rice, Feb. 22, 1954, ACLU Papers, Box 579.

8. Forster to Biberman, Feb. 25, 1954; Rice to Biberman, Feb. 27, 1954, ACLU Papers, Box 579.

9. Biberman to Beloveds, Feb. 4, 1954, Biberman-Sondergaard Papers, Box 4; Biberman Diary, Feb. 4–10, 1954, Wilson Papers, Box 51; Biberman to Rice, Feb. 22, 1954, ACLU Papers, Box 579; Wilson Papers, Box 51; Biberman, *Salt of the Earth,* 153–54.

10. Diary, Feb. 18, 1954, Wilson Papers, Box 51; "Bulletin," Feb. 8, 1954, Biberman-Sondergaard Papers, Box 4; Walter White to Roy Wilkins et al., Feb. 15, 1954, National Association for the Advancement of Colored People Papers, Washington, D.C., Library of Congress, Manuscripts Division, Group 2, Box 276; Biberman, *Salt of the Earth,* 151.

11. *Mine-Mill Union,* Jan. 4, Mar. 1, 1954; Biberman to Dear, Dear and Dearests, Jan. 30, 1954; Biberman to Margolis, Feb. 13, 1954, Biberman-Sondergaard Papers, Boxes 4 and 28; Hodges, "Making and Unmaking of *Salt of the Earth,*" 271–72.

12. Biberman to My Dears, Feb. 17, 1954, Biberman-Sondergaard Papers, Box 4; Biberman, *Diary,* Feb. 10, 17, 1954, Wilson Papers, Box 51; *Variety,* Feb. 17, 1954. Eventually, thirty New York unions participated in the promotion of *Salt of the Earth.* Dear Fred, May 4, 1954, Biberman-Sondergaard Papers, Box 53.

13. Memo, Feb. 28, 1954; Hazel Plate to Jack Vizzard, July 11, 1956, Production

Code Administration Files, Beverly Hills, Margaret Herrick Library, Academy of Motion Picture Arts and Sciences Library, *Salt of the Earth* File; *Variety*, Mar. 11, 1954; New York *Daily Mirror*, Feb. 22, 1954; Jarrico, "Salt of the Earth — Chronology," 21; Brewer Interview, OHAL; Biberman to My Beloveds, Feb. 10, 1954, Biberman to My Dears, Feb. 17, 1954, Biberman-Sondergaard Papers, Box 4. Reisel's report coincided with the ACLU inquiry into IATSE intentions. For comment on IPC's reluctance to sue at this time, see Biberman, *Salt of the Earth*, 154.

14. Jarrico, "Salt of the Earth — Chronology," 21–22; Author Interview, Jarrico; Biberman to Margolis, Feb. 13, 1954; "Notes, Michael Rose" (n.d.), Biberman-Sondergaard Papers, Boxes 28 and 42.

15. Jarrico, "Salt of the Earth — A Chronology," 22; Biberman, *Salt of the Earth*, 157–58; "Research Notes — Richard F. Walsh" (n.d.), Biberman-Sondergaard Papers, Box 53.

16. Author Interview, Steven D'Inzillo, New York, July 2, 1996 (transcript in author's hands). For evidence of D'Inzillo's later differences with Walsh, see "Fact or Fiction: A Historical Analysis from the Mouth of Steve D'Inzillo," ca. 1970; John Horohan to Sir and Brother, n.d., IATSE Papers, AMMI, Box 34.

17. Biberman to Dear . . . Dears, Mar. 8, 1954, Biberman-Sondergaard Papers, Box 4; D'Inzillo Interview; Biberman, *Salt of the Earth*, 160, 162–64.

18. "At Last," ca. March 1954, IUMMSW Papers, Box 129; Biberman *Salt of the Earth*, 165, 169–70; Biberman to My Dear Beloved Ones, Mar. 13, 1954; "Vea, Admire — Comente: La Sal de la Tierra," ca. April 1954, Biberman-Sondergaard Papers, Boxes 4 and 52.

19. Biberman, *Salt of the Earth*, 171; Jarrico, "Salt of the Earth — Chronology," 24; Jarrico Interview, UCLA, OHP, 166; Hodges, "Making and Unmaking of *Salt of the Earth*," 271.

20. Trumbo to Mr. and Mrs. Hugo Butler and Mr. and Mrs. George Pepper, ca. February 1954, in Dalton Trumbo, *Additional Dialogue: Letters of Dalton Trumbo, 1942–1962*, ed. Helen Manfull, (New York: M. Evans and Co., 1970), 293; *Masses and Mainstream* 7 (April 1954), 1, 4; *Daily Worker*, Mar. 15, 1954; *Variety*, Mar. 11, 15, 16, 1954; *New York Herald Tribune*, Mar. 15, 1954; *New York Times*, Mar. 15, 1954; Biberman, *Salt of the Earth*, 171–73; Ceplair and Englund, *Inquisition in Hollywood*, 418.

21. Biberman to Dears, Mar. 24, 1954, Biberman-Sondergaard Papers, Box 4; Biberman, *Salt of the Earth*, 173–74; "Paul Jarrico," 282.

22. Biberman, *Salt of the Earth*, 174; Biberman to Dears, Mar. 24, 1954, Biberman-Sondergaard Papers, Box 4.

23. "Paul Jarrico," 282; Jarrico Interview, UCLA, OHP, 166; Author Interview, Jarrico; Jarrico, "Salt of the Earth — A Chronology," 24.

24. Steve D'Inzillo, "Deposition," Jan. 2, 1964, IPC and IPC Distributors, Inc., v. Loew's, Incorporated, et al., Biberman-Sondergaard Papers, Box 37; "Research Notes — Richard F. Walsh"; Biberman, *Salt of the Earth*, 175.

25. *Hollywood Reporter* Apr. 26, 1954; *Variety*, Mar. 29, 1954; Jarrico, "Salt of the

Earth — Chronology," 26; Biberman, *Salt of the Earth*, 175–76; Biberman to Travis, Apr. 25, 1954, IUMMSW Papers, Box 119 (letter misdated — March 25 correct date); D'Inzillo Deposition, 66, 93–95, 115; "Memorandum for Files: Independent v. Loew's (D'Inzillo-Walsh)," Biberman-Sondergaard Papers, Box 53. While D'Inzillo's deposition stresses discussions about *Salt* within Local 306, including the agreement that individual prerogative would prevail, he later emphasized the primacy of the International's "directive." D'Inzillo Interview; Hodges, "Making and Unmaking of *Salt of the Earth*," 278–79.

26. Jarrico, "Salt of the Earth — Chronology," 26; Biberman, *Salt of the Earth*, 176.

27. Margolis to Biberman, Mar. 24, 1954, Wilson Papers, Box 51; *Daily Worker*, Mar. 9, 1954; Witt to Travis, Mar. 15, 1954; Biberman to Travis, Apr. 25, 1954 (date incorrectly typed; March correct), IUMMSW Papers, Boxes 119, 129.

28. Biberman to Travis, Apr. 25, 1954 (date incorrectly typed; correct date March), IUMMSW Papers, Boxes 119, 129.

29. Biberman, *Salt of the Earth*, 176; Hodges, "Making and Unmaking of *Salt of the Earth*," 282–83.

30. Wilson to Clark, Jan. 15, 1954; Travis to Wilson, Jan. 22, 1954, IUMMSW Papers, Boxes 119, 129, 538.

31. *Ford Facts*, Jan. 16, 1954; *Michigan CIO News*, Aug. 9, 1962; *UAW Solidarity*, September 1973; Interview, Horace Sheffield, Blacks in the Labor Movement Oral History Collection, and James Watts Biographical File, Detroit, Archives of Labor History and Urban Affairs, Wayne State University (hereafter cited as ALHUA). Moore Interview.

32. Moore interview; Riesel, "Union Fete for Red Lady" (n.d.), in SAG Archives, Communications Department File; *Ford Facts*, Jan. 16, 1954.

33. Harold Sanderson to Gately, Feb. 15, 1954; Gately to Sanderson, Feb. 2, 1954, IUMMSW Papers, Box 51.

34. Biberman to Travis, Apr. 24, 1954 (date incorrectly typed; correct date March), IUMMSW Papers, Box 119; Biberman to My Loves, Mar. 25, 1954, Biberman-Sondergaard Papers, Box 4.

35. Biberman to My Loves, Mar. 24, 1954, Biberman-Sondergaard Papers, Box 4.

36. Biberman to My Loves, May 2, 1954, Biberman-Sondergaard Papers, Box 4; Jarrico, "Salt of the Earth — Chronology," 31; Biberman, *Salt of the Earth*, 178–79.

37. Biberman to My Loves, May 2, 1954, Biberman-Sondergaard Papers, Box 4; Biberman, *Salt of the Earth*, 179.

38. Moore Interview; *Ford Facts*, Apr. 10, 1954; "Detroit Unionists Thrilled by Salt of the Earth Film," Federated Press, Apr. 24, 1954, Jencks Papers, Box 23; *Potash Dust*, May 22, 1954, in Chacón Papers, *Salt of the Earth* Clippings File.

39. Biberman, *Salt of the Earth*, 179; "Detroit Unionists Thrilled by Salt of the Earth Film, Jencks Papers, Box 23."

40. Biberman to My Loves, May 2, 1954, Biberman-Sondergaard Papers, Box 4; Biberman, *Salt of the Earth*, 180.

41. Biberman, *Salt of the Earth*, 182.

42. Biberman to My Dears, May 12, 1954, Biberman-Sondergaard Papers, Box 4; Jarrico, "Salt of the Earth — Chronology," 35–36.

43. "Fact Sheet on the Attempted Private Censorship of 'Salt of the Earth,'" Oct. 9, 1964; Kermit Russell, "Deposition," Feb. 17, 1956, IPCD, Inc., v. H. Schoenstadt and Sons, Inc.; Biberman to Dear Ones, May 1, 1954; Jarrico, "Salt of the Earth — Chronology," 36, all in Biberman-Sondergaard Papers, Boxes 49, 54, 4, 51; *Chicago Maroon*, May 14, 1954, ACLU (Illinois Division) Papers, Chicago, Special Collections, University of Chicago Library (hereafter cited as ACLUI) Papers, Box 36; James Durkin to Rod Holmgren, Nov. 12, 1953, IUMMSW Papers, Box 538; Biberman, *Salt of the Earth*, 185; Hodges, "Making and Unmaking of *Salt of the Earth*," 295.

44. "Research Notes — Patrick E. Gorman" (n.d.), Biberman-Sondergaard Papers, Box 53; Patrick Gorman to H. Schoenstadt and Sons, May 17, 1954; Gorman to Gene Atkinson, May 17, 1954, United Packinghouse Workers of America Papers, SHSW, Box 359 (hereafter cited as UPWA Papers); Biberman to Gorman, May 17, 1954, Amalgamated Meat Cutters and Butcher Workmen of America Papers, SHSW, Reel 205; James Durkin, "Semi-Monthly Report of International Representatives," Apr. 15 and 30, 1954; May 31, 1954, IUMMSW Papers, James Durkin File, Box 100.

45. Biberman to Richard Durham, July 30, 1954; Dick Bruner to Durham, July 29, 1954; Durham to Bruner, July 30, 1954; Cathy Bronan to Durham, July 12, 1954; Cathy to Martha and Dick, July 29, 1954, UPWA Papers, Box 359; Leon Beverly and George Kovacevich to Biberman and Mandel Terman (telegram), May 28, 1954, Biberman-Sondergaard Papers, Box 44.

46. "Fact Sheet on the Attempted Private Censorship of 'Salt of the Earth,'" Oct. 9, 1964; Biberman to Clarence Jallas (*sic*), May 9, 1954, Biberman-Sondergaard Papers, Boxes 49, 44; ACLUI Papers, Box 36.

47. Hodges, "Making and Unmaking of *Salt of the Earth*," 295; *Chicago Southtown Economist*, May 12, 1954; *The Firing Line* 3(May 10, 1954 — Special Edition), in J. B. Matthews Papers, Durham, Perkins Library, Special Collections, Duke University, Box 487. See also Biberman-Sondergaard Papers, Boxes 53, 58; "Americanism: 'Salt of the Earth,'" *American Legion Magazine*, July 1954, 35–36. *The Firing Line* was intended to keep American Legion officers, its Americanism Division, and the interested public up to date on "developments in the area of subversion." James O'Neill, "Deposition," Dec. 12, 1963, 159, Biberman-Sondergaard Papers, Box 42.

48. *The Firing Line*, ca. June 1954; M. A. Terman to Edward Clamage, May 14, 1954; Clamage to Terman, May 12, 1954, Biberman-Sondergaard Papers, Boxes 28, 44; ACLUI Papers, Box 36; Biberman, *Salt of the Earth*, 185–86; Hodges, "Making and Unmaking of *Salt of the Earth*," 295, 298.

49. IPC Distributors, Inc. to Friends, May 11, 1954; Edward H. Meyerding to Arthur Schoenstadt, May 18, 1954; Meyerding to Jalas, May 18, 1954; Meyerding

to Daniel D. Carmell, May 18, 1954, Leon M. Despres Papers, Chicago, Archives, Chicago Historical Society, Box 243; ACLUI Papers, Box 36.

50. Biberman, *Salt of the Earth*, 187–91; *Daily Worker*, June 6, 1954; *Chicago American*, June 3 and 5, 1954.

51. *Variety*, May 17, 1954; *The Brief*, June 1954; Biberman to Beloveds, June 9, 1954; Press Release, ca. June 1, 1954, Biberman-Sondergaard Papers, Boxes 66, 4, 46; Jarrico, "Salt of the Earth — Chronology," 36; ACLUI Papers, Box 36; *Chicago Sun-Times*, June 3, 1954; Author Interview, Jarrico; Biberman to Despres, ca. May, 1954, Despres Papers, Box 243.

52. Biberman to Sir and Brother, June 7, 1954; "An Open Letter to All Members of Local 110, Moving Picture Operators, AFL," June 7, 1954, Biberman-Sondergaard Papers, Box 46.

53. Herbert Biberman, *Salt of the Earth*, 191; Biberman to My Beloveds, May 21, 1954; "Memorandum for Files: Independent v. Loew's (D'Inzillo-Walsh)," Dec. 11, 1956, Biberman-Sondergaard Papers, Boxes 4, 53.

54. Biberman, "What Kind of Company Was This?," 5; Abraham Lipkin to Travis, June 17, 1954, IUMMSW Papers, Box 119; Biberman to My Beloveds, May 21, 1954, Biberman-Sondergaard Papers, Box 4; Hodges, "Making and Unmaking of *Salt of the Earth*," 305.

55. Biberman to Travis, Apr. 25, 1954 (date incorrectly typed; correct date March); Travis to All Local Unions, Apr. 20, 1954, IUMMSW Papers, Box 119, 129; Wright to Herb and Paul, Apr. 6, 1954; Clark to Biberman, Apr. 6, 1954 (telegram), Biberman-Sondergaard Papers, Box 28; *Mine-Mill Union*, Apr. 12, 1954; Hodges, "Making and Unmaking of *Salt of the Earth*," 337–38.

56. Travis to All Local Unions, Apr. 20, 1954; Travis to Wilson, Apr. 15, 1954, IUMMSW Papers, Box 129; "An Account of Unsuccessful Efforts to Arrange for Commercial Showing of 'Salt of the Earth' in Denver in 1954," Oct. 12, 1956, Biberman-Sondergaard Papers, Box 28.

57. Travis to All Local Unions, Apr. 20, 1954, IUMMSW Papers, Box 129.

58. "An Account of Unsuccessful Efforts to Arrange for Commercial Showing of 'Salt of the Earth' in Denver in 1954," Oct. 12, 1956; Jarrico to Wright, Mar. 31, 1954; Wright to Biberman and Jarrico, Apr. 6, 1954, in Biberman-Sondergaard Papers, Box 28.

59. "An Account of Unsuccessful Efforts to Arrange for Commercial Showing of 'Salt of the Earth' in Denver in 1954," Oct. 12, 1956; Wright to Sonja Dahl, Apr. 26 and May 12, 1954, Biberman-Sondergaard Papers, Boxes 28, 52.

60. Wright to Biberman and Jarrico, Apr. 6, 1954; "An Account of Unsuccessful Efforts to Arrange for Commercial Showing of 'Salt of the Earth' in Denver in 1954," Oct. 12, 1956, Biberman-Sondergaard Papers, Box 28; Hodges, "Making and Unmaking of *Salt of the Earth*," 341–42.

61. "An Account of Unsuccessful Efforts to Arrange for Commercial Showing of 'Salt of the Earth' in Denver in 1954," Oct. 12, 1956, Biberman-Sondergaard Papers, Box 28.

62. *Colorado Labor Advocate*, Apr. 8, 1954.

63. "Statement," ACLU, Colorado Branch, ca. May 1954, IUMMSW Papers, Box 129; "Dear Member of the Arvada Community," ca. May 1954, Biberman-Sondergaard Papers, Box 28.

64. "An Account of Unsuccessful Efforts to Arrange for Commercial Showing of 'Salt of the Earth' in Denver in 1954," Oct. 12, 1956; "Dear Member of the Arvada Community," Biberman-Sondergaard Papers, Box 28.

65. "Notes on Meeting with Herbert Biberman," Apr. 18, 1954, IUMMSW Papers, Box 129; Author Interview, Jencks.

66. Virginia Jencks to Wilson, ca. May, 1954; Travis to Wilson, June 11, 1954, Wilson Papers, Box 50, 51; Chacón, "The Miners Make a Film" (n.d.), IUMMSW Papers, Box 129.

67. Unidentified Clipping, Apr. 1, 1954, Chacón Papers, *Salt of the Earth* Clippings File; Author Interview, Virginia Chacón; *Silver City Press and Daily Independent*, Feb. 6, 11, and 13, 1954; Flores Interview.

68. Virginia Jencks to Wilson, ca. May 1954; Wilson Papers, Box 50; "A Report on 'Salt of the Earth,'" July 16, 1954, IUMMSW Papers, Box 129; *Daily Worker*, June 6, 1954.

69. Biberman, *Salt of the Earth*, 178; Miller, "Class Reunion," 34; *Daily Worker*, May 20, 1954; Author Interview, Jencks; *El Paso Herald Post*, May 17, 1954; "Reporte a la Gente," May 19, 1954, IUMMSW Papers, Box 874; Jarrico, "Salt of the Earth — Chronology," 27.

70. Vincent Interview; Chacón to Independent Productions Company, July 26, 1954, Biberman-Sondergaard Papers, Box 39; Dahl to Gately, June 11, 1954; Wilson, Jarrico, Dahl, and Biberman to Chacón and Executive Board, Local 890, July 16, 1954, IUMMSW Papers, Boxes 324, 129. The plan for the Vincents' supervision of southwestern distribution was never implemented. Vincent Interview; Hodges, "Making and Unmaking of *Salt of the Earth*," 346–47.

71. Torres to Lorence, Nov. 9, 1997; Flores Interview; Author Interview, Montoya; Howard Mooney to Travis, Apr. 28, 1954; Montoya and Gately, "Semi-Monthly Report of International Representatives," May 15 and Sept. 30, 1954; Sept. 15, 1954, Alfredo C. Montoya and William Gately Files; "You Can't Eat Red Herring" (leaflet), July 19, 1954; Montoya to IPC Distributors, Inc., Apr. 29, 1954; Maclovio R. Barraza to Chacón, July 13, 1954, IUMMSW Papers, Boxes 119, 101, 129; Rosenblum, *Copper Crucible*, 34–35; Wright to Dahl, Apr. 26, 1954, Biberman-Sondergaard Papers, Box 28.

72. Seattle *Argus*, Aug. 14, 1954; Gately to Dahl, June 8, 1954; Gately to Biberman, Aug. 4, 1955; Jarrico to Biberman, June 12, 1964; "Memorandum of Law in Support of Plaintiff's Motion for Production of Documents," Mar. 8, 1963, Independent Productions Company and IPC Distributors, Inc. v Loews, Inc., et al., Biberman-Sondergaard Papers, Boxes 28, 44, 29, 32; Dahl to Gately, June 11, 1954; Gately, "Semi-Monthly Report of International Representatives," July 31,

1954, William Gately File, IUMMSW Papers, Boxes 324, 101; Jarrico, "*Salt of the Earth* — Chronology," 36; Author Interviews, Jencks and Jarrico.

73. *San Francisco Chronicle*, May 7, 1954; Jarrico, "Salt of the Earth — Chronology," 27; *Peoples Daily World*, May 17 and 24, 1954; R. L. de Cordova, "La Sal de la Tierra," ca. May 1954, in Biberman-Sondergaard Papers, Box 52; *The Dispatcher*, Apr. 30 and May 14, 1954; *San Francisco Labor*, May 14, 1954, in Dorothy Healey Papers, Long Beach, Special Collections Library, California State University — Long Beach, Box 39; Hodges, "Making and Unmaking of *Salt of the Earth*," 306–7.

74. Leonard R. Titelman, "Salt of the Earth Audience Organization," ca. May 1954; Titelman to Robert Slater, May 3, 1954; Dear Sir and Brother, ca. May 1, 1954; Titelman to Amalgamated Clothing Workers, June 22, 1954; Titelman to Durkin, Apr. 22, 1954; "The Voice of 770" (Retail Clerks Union), June 1954; "We Are the Salt of the Earth," ca. July 1954, Biberman-Sondergaard Papers, Boxes 53, 28, 52; *The Dispatcher*, July 9, 1954; Dear Sir and Brother, ca. May 1954, California CIO Council, Research and Information Services Papers, Los Angeles, Southern California Library for Social Studies and Research, Box 4.

75. "For Immediate Release," May 12, 1954; IPC Distributors, Inc., to W. J. Bassett and Albert T. Lunceford, May 13, 1954, Biberman-Sondergaard Papers, Boxes 53, 28; Titleman to Lunceford, ca. May 1954, Jencks Papers, Box 23; *Los Angeles Daily News*, May 20, 1954; *Los Angeles Times*, May 8, 1954; *Hollywood Reporter*, May 12, 1954; *Variety*, May 15, 1954; Press Release, May 20, 1954; Dales to Lunceford, June 4, 1954, SAG Archives, Press Releases File and Communications Director's Correspondence; Minutes, Executive Board, Los Angeles CIO Council, May 25, 1954, Los Angeles County Federation of Labor, AFL-CIO Papers, UAC, CSUN, Box 30; Author Interview (telephone), James Daugherty, Oct. 2, 1997, Los Angeles; Hodges, "Making and Unmaking of *Salt of the Earth*," 309–11.

76. *Variety*, May 25, 21, 10, 1954; *Hollywood Reporter*, May 25, 1954; FBI Report, Los Angeles, June 15, 1954, File no. 100–15732, *Communist Activity in the Entertainment Industry*, Vol. 37, Reel 7; Jarrico, "Salt of the Earth — Chronology," 32; Hodges, "Making and Unmaking of *Salt of the Earth*" 310–311.

77. Jarrico to Dore Schary, May 19, 1954, Dore Schary Papers, SHSW, Box 16; Author Interview, Jarrico; Dahl, "To Chicago, New York, Silver City, Denver, and San Francisco," May 14, 1954, Jencks Papers, Box 23; "Memorandum," Herman Waldman to Margolis, July 22, 1954; "Report on Negotiations with KABC Concerning Purchase of Radio Spots for Salt of the Earth," ca. June 1954; Biberman, "Memorandum (I) on the Attitude of Los Angeles Newspapers to 'Salt of the Earth' Showing at the Marcal Theater, May, 1954," Sept. 28, 1956, Biberman-Sondergaard Papers, Boxes 42, 52, 53; Jarrico, "Salt of the Earth — Chronology," 33. It was not unusual for the press to deny advertising space to events or activities suspected of Communist ties or support. Schrecker, *Many Are the Crimes*, 523, n. 62; Michael R. Belknap, *Cold War Political Justice: The Smith Act, the Communist Party, and*

American Civil Liberties (Westport, Conn.: Greenwood Press, 1977), 136; Hodges, "Making and Unmaking of *Salt of the Earth*," 314–15.

78. FBI Reports, Los Angeles, Mar. 19, 1954, June 15, 1954, "COMPIC," File no. 100–15732, *Communist Activity in the Entertainment Industry*, Vol. 37, Reel 7; Lawson, *Film in the Battle of Ideas*, 119–20; FBI, Los Angeles to Director, FBI, Mar. 15, 1954, Teletype Message, File no. 100–399257.

79. "A Message from Rosaura," ca. May 1954; Rose Chernin to Friend, July 15, 1954, Biberman-Sondergaard Papers, Box 52; Press Release, May 3, 1954, Los Angeles Committee for the Protection of the Foreign Born, CRC-JFC Papers, Box 93; "The Torch," April 1954, American Committee for Protection of the Foreign Born Papers, Area Ethnic Committees (California—Los Angeles) File, 1954; "Come to the Gala 'Cinco de Mayo' Celebration," ca. May 1, 1954, Healey Papers, Box 64; *Daily Worker*, May 27, 1954; *Daily People's World*, May 24, 1954; FBI Report, Los Angeles, Oct. 21, 1954, "Independent Productions Corporation," File no. 100–399257–143; FBI Report, Los Angeles, June 7, 1954, "Salt of the Earth, Independent Productions Corporation," File no. 100–44774.

80. Interview, Helen Slote Leavitt, UCLA, OHP, 199, 200, 201; Ceplair and Englund, *Inquisition in Hollywood*, 413.

81. Biberman to Salt of the Earth Audience, Marcal Theater, Hollywood (telegram), May 20, 1954, Biberman-Sondergaard Papers, Box 5; *Daily Worker*, May 27, 1954; *Los Angeles Daily News*, June 4, 1954; *California Jewish Voice*, May 21, 1954; *Daily People's World*, May 24, 1954; Jarrico, "Salt of the Earth—Chronology," 34.

82. "Memorandum of Law in Support of Plaintiff's Motion for Production of Documents," Mar. 8, 1963, Independent Productions Corporation and IPC Distributors, Inc., v. Loew's Incorporated, et al., 1963; "Results of Conferences with Unionists and Organizations," Aug. 6, 1954; Dave Servis to Paul Jarrico, June 6, 1954, Biberman-Sondergaard Papers, Boxes 32, 52, 53; *Daily Worker*, Aug. 12, 1954; Jarrico, "Salt of the Earth—Chronology," 34–35; Author Interview, Jarrico.

CHAPTER 7

1. *Variety*, Mar. 17, 1954.

2. Biberman, *Salt of the Earth*, 196; Jarrico, "Salt of the Earth—Chronology," 29; "Excerpts of Speech Made by Nathan Cohen" (n.d.), M. Solski to Dahl, Aug. 26 and May 14, 1954; William Longridge to Dahl, July 22, 1954, Biberman-Sondergaard Papers, Boxes 44, 28, 52; Longridge to Dahl, June 30, 1954, IUMMSW Papers, Box 119; FBI Report, Los Angeles, COMINFIL-IUMMSW, Sept. 20, 1954, File no. 100–44774–326; *Variety*, July 7, 1954. For full discussion of *Salt's* modest successes in Canada, see Hodges, "Making and Unmaking of *Salt of the Earth*," 343–46.

3. Biberman, *Salt of the Earth*, 200–201; Biberman, "What Kind of Company Was This?," 5, Biberman-Sondergaard Papers, Box 51.

4. *El Nacional*, Oct. 10, 1954; *La Aficion*, Oct. 24, 1954; *El Universal*, Oct. 12, 1954; *Novedades*, Oct. 31, 1954; *Tiempo*, Oct. 18, 1954, attached to "Memorandum . . .

Mexico City Press on 'Salt of the Earth,'" ca. October 1954, Wilson Papers, Box 51; "Notes on Meeting with Herbert Biberman," Apr. 18, 1954, IUMMSW Papers, Box 129; Biberman to Sweetheart and Sweethearts, Oct. 10, 1954; "Second Report on 'Salt of the Earth,'" Oct. 23, 1954, Biberman-Sondergaard Papers, Box 52; Biberman, *Salt of the Earth*, 201–2; *Hollywood Reporter* 1 (November-December 1954); Miller, "Class Reunion," 34.

5. Jarrico Interview, UCLA, OHP, 166–68; Author Interview, Jarrico. For evidence of *Salt*'s favorable reception in China, see Chacón Papers, China File.

6. *New York Times*, ca. June 1959; Jarrico Interview, UCLA, OHP, 169; Author Interview, Jarrico; Biberman to Juan, Virginia, and Hijos, Oct. 16, 1961, Chacón Papers, Correspondence File; FBI Report, Los Angeles, COMPIC, Nov. 11, 1955, File no. 100–15732, *Communist Activity in the Entertainment Industry*, Vol. 37, Reel 7; Margolis to Revueltas, Sept. 19, 1958; Margolis to George Brussel, Jr.; "Report on 'Salt of the Earth,'" Apr. 25, 1955, Biberman-Sondergaard Papers, Boxes 52, 53; FBI Report, Los Angeles, COMINFIL, IUMMSW, Sept. 20, 1954, File no. 100–44774–326. From its inception in 1954, USIA had been keenly aware of the impact of American motion pictures overseas. In March 1954, USIA director Theodore Streibert told MPIC that the industry's cooperation was vital to the task of combating communism. Theodore Streibert, Address, MPIC (press release), Mar. 15, 1954, MPIC Papers, "Ambassadors Abroad" File.

7. Norbert Fayd, "Czechs Debate 'Porgy and Bess' — and Compare it with 'Salt,'" *Daily Peoples World*, n.d.; see also Aug. 2, 1954, Biberman-Sondergaard Papers, Box 53; Biberman, *Salt of the Earth*, 205; *Hollywood Reporter*, Aug. 4, 1954.

8. Jarrico, "Salt of the Earth — Chronology," 29; *Hollywood Reporter*, Aug. 6, 1954; *Variety*, Aug. 6, 1954; *Washington Star*, Aug. 6, 1954; Legislative Excerpts, "Donald L. Jackson," n.d., California CIO Council Union Research and Information Services Papers, Box. 6. For full text of Jackson's speech, see *Congressional Record*, 83d Cong. 2d sess., Aug. 5, 1954, vol. 100, pt. 10, 13483–84.

9. Biberman, *Salt of the Earth*, 206–7, 217–18; "Paul Jarrico," 283; "Report on 'Salt of the Earth,'" Apr. 25, 1955, Biberman-Sondergaard Papers, Box 53; Ceplair and Englund, *Inquisition in Hollywood*, 418; Vaughn, "Political Censorship during the Cold War," 246.

10. Author Interview, Jarrico; Biberman, "What Kind of Company Was This?," 5, Biberman-Sondergaard Papers, Box 51; *Catholic Herald*, Sept. 24, 1954; *London Tribune*, Sept. 17, 1954; *Punch*, Sept. 29, 1954; *Western Evening Herald*, Sept. 18, 1954; *Glasgow Herald*, Sept. 21, 1954, all in "Reviews of 'Salt of the Earth' from the London Press," IUMMSW Papers, Boxes 119, 129; Biberman, *Salt of the Earth*, 196.

11. "Paul Jarrico," 283; Jarrico, "Salt of the Earth — Chronology," 36; *New York Times*, ca. June 1959; FBI Report, Los Angeles, COMPIC, ca. December 1954, File no. 100–15732, *Communist Activity in the Entertainment Industry*, Vol. 37, Reel 7; FBI Report, SA to SAC, "Independent Productions Corp., IS-C; Registration Act," Aug. 2, 1954, File no. 100–44774–28; Hodges, "Making and Unmaking of *Salt of the Earth*," 378, 384.

12. "Report on 'Salt of the Earth,'" Apr. 25, 1955, Biberman-Sondergaard Papers, Box 53.

13. Biberman, *Salt of the Earth*, 184–85; Biberman to My dears, Apr. 30, 1954, Biberman-Sondergaard Papers, Box 4; Jarrico to Travis, Sept. 4, 1954, IUMMSW Papers, Box 119, and see also Box 867.

14. Biberman to My Dears, Apr. 30, 1954; Biberman to IPC Distributors, May 4, 1954, Biberman-Sondergaard Papers, Boxes 4, 41; Biberman, *Salt of the Earth*, 185–86.

15. Jarrico to Travis, Sept. 4, 1954, IUMMSW Papers, Box 119; see also Box 867; Seymour Baskind, Deposition, Nov. 21, 1963, Independent Productions Corporation Distributors, Inc. v Loew's, Incorporated, et al., 11–13, Biberman-Sondergaard Papers, Box 35; Hodges, 349.

16. Biberman to Boys and Girls, May 28, 1954, Biberman-Sondergaard Papers, Box 4.

17. Biberman to My Friends, June 23, 1954; Biberman to My World of Loves, June 15, 1954; Biberman to Gale, June 21, 1954, Biberman-Sondergaard Papers, Boxes 45, 79, 4. By June 22, AFL was sufficiently interested in *Salt* to order a preview copy. Caroline Hodges to IUMMSW, June 22, 1954, IUMMSW Papers, Box 119.

18. Biberman to My Friends, June 23, 1954, Biberman-Sondergaard Papers, Box 45.

19. Biberman to My World of Loves, June 15, 1954, Biberman-Sondergaard Papers, Box 4.

20. Biberman, "What Kind of Company Was This?"; Biberman to My Loves, July 4, 1954; Levin to Biberman, June 21, 1954; Baskind Deposition, 39–40, Biberman-Sondergaard Papers, Boxes 51, 4, 49, 35; Hodges, "Making and Unmaking of *Salt of the Earth*, 351.

21. Levin to Biberman, July 6, 27, 1954; Biberman to My Loves, July 4, 1954; Biberman, "What Kind of Company Was This?," Biberman-Sondergaard Papers, Boxes 41, 49, 4, 51.

22. Sam Pollock to James McDevitt, July 29, 1954; Pollock to Biberman, July 3, 1954, Biberman to My Loves, July 4, 1954, Biberman-Sondergaard Papers, Boxes 54, 4.

23. *Variety*, May 3, 11, 12, 19, 25, 1954; Brewer Interview, OHAL; Biberman, *Salt of the Earth*, 193; Brewer Deposition, 134–36; "Roy Brewer," 117–18; Brewer Interview, UCLA Archives, 17, 209, 210; Hodges, "Making and Unmaking of *Salt of the Earth*," 353. For contemporary comment on Brewer's anticommunist activities, see George Sokolsky, "Hollywood Purges Reds, But Is It Permanent?," *Milwaukee Sentinel*, June 3, 1954.

24. *Silver City Press and Daily Independent*, July 1 and June 30, 1954; Brewer Deposition, 129–31; Charles R. Gilmour to Unidentified correspondent (copy), Mar. 2, 1953; Robert Corkery to Ken Clark, Mar. 9, 1953; Sidney Schreiber to Mr. Hetzel, Mar. 10, 1953, Biberman-Sondergaard Papers, Box 46; Brewer Interview, OHAL.

25. *Silver City Press and Daily Independent*, July 2, 1954; Harris to Edward Costigan, June 29, 1954; Pidgeon and George Murphy to Pat O'Brien, Pedro

Gonzalez-Gonzalez, Ann Doran, Marian Carr, and Ann Robinson (telegram), July 1, 1954, SAG Archives, *Salt of the Earth* File. See also Pidgeon and Murphy to Gonzalez-Gonzalez, July 1, 1954, Silver City, N.M., Silver City Museum, Pedro Gonzalez-Gonzalez File.

26. *Washington Post and Times Herald*, July 29, 1954; *Los Angeles Times*, Nov. 5, 1954; *Silver City Enterprise*, July 8, 1954; Brewer Deposition, 129–31; Brewer Interview, OHAL.

27. Minutes, SAG Board of Directors, July 12, 1954, SAG Archives; Virginia Chacón and Flores Interviews. In November, the Silver City Chamber of Commerce presented Brewer, Doran, and Gonzalez-Gonzalez with special awards for their role in "combating the possible propaganda effects" of *Salt of the Earth*. *Los Angeles Times*, Nov. 5, 1954; *Silver City Press and Daily Independent*, Nov. 4, 1954.

28. *Proceedings, IATSE*, 1954, 1035, 1038–39; see also *Proceedings and Officers' Reports*, California State Federation of Labor, 52d Convention, Santa Barbara, Aug. 23–27, 1954, 230, 389, for the California Federation's decision to boycott theatrical showings of *Salt of the Earth*. Levin to Biberman, Aug. 13, 1954, Biberman-Sondergaard Papers, Box 53.

29. Biberman, *Salt of the Earth*, 193; Author Interview, Jarrico; Jarrico to Travis, Sept. 4, 1954, IUMMSW Papers, Boxes 119, 867; Biberman to Baskind, Aug. 17, 1954, Biberman-Sondergaard Papers, Box 49; Hodges, "Making and Unmaking of *Salt of the Earth*," 353.

30. Biberman to Baskind, Aug. 17, 1954; Biberman to Levin, Aug. 17, 1954, Biberman-Sondergaard Papers, Box 49.

31. Baskind to Biberman, Aug. 18, 1954, Biberman-Sondergaard Papers, Box 49.

32. Biberman to Baskind, Aug. 20, 1954; Baskind Deposition, 56, Biberman-Sondergaard Papers, Boxes 49, 35; Jarrico to Travis, Sept. 4, 1954, IUMMSW Papers, Box 119.

33. Jarrico to Travis, IUMMSW, Sept. 4, 1954, IUMMSW Papers, Box 119.

34. Biberman to Mine All, All Mine, Sept. 1, 1954; Biberman, "What Kind of Company Was This?," 7, Biberman-Sondergaard Papers, Boxes 4,51; Jarrico to Travis, Sept. 4, 1954, IUMMSW Papers, Box 119.

35. IPC to Membership and Ladies Auxiliary at Local 890, Oct. 23, 1954; Biberman, "What Kind of Company Was This?," 8; Biberman to Baskind, Sept. 16, 1954, Biberman-Sondergaard Papers, Boxes 65, 51, 16; Biberman to Travis, Sept. 19, 1954, IUMMSW Papers, Box 119; Author Interview, Jencks.

36. Jarrico to Lorence, Apr. 19, 1996; Author Interview, Jarrico; "Research Notes — Richard F. Walsh" (n.d.); "Desperate Situation of IPC," Oct. 26, 1956; Baskind Deposition, 56, 68–69, Biberman-Sondergaard Papers, Boxes 53, 41, 35. For evidence of McDevitt's stand in favor of *Salt*, see Jarrico to Travis, Sept. 4, 1954, IUMMSW Papers, Box 119.

37. "Desperate Situation of IPC," Oct. 26, 1956; Richard F. Walsh, Deposition, Mar. 10, 1962, Independent Productions Corporation and IPC Distributors, Inc. v. Loew's, Incorporated, et al., 125–31, Biberman-Sondergaard Papers, Boxes 41, 44.

38. Biberman to George Brussel, Mar. 28, 1957; "Notes re: Biberman Testimony" (n.d.), 43; "Desperate Situation of IPC," Oct. 26, 1956; Walsh Deposition, 134–35; Baskind Deposition, 76–77, Biberman-Sondergaard Papers, Boxes 53, 54, 41, 44, 35; Hodges, "Making and Unmaking of *Salt of the Earth*," 357. In 1957, IPC legal counsel George Brussel supported Biberman's analysis of Walsh's role in undermining the LLPE plan. After a personal conference with Walsh, Brussel concluded, Baskind had "toned down" his account of the Walsh-Baskind meeting to "accommodate" the situation in 1957. Brussel sensed that Baskind was "less than candid." Brussel, "Memorandum for the File," Mar. 25, 1957, Biberman-Sondergaard Papers, Box 53.

39. Biberman to Baskind, Nov. 3, 1954, Biberman-Sondergaard Papers, Box 41.

40. "Desperate Situation of IPC," Oct. 26, 1956; "Research Notes-Richard F. Walsh" (n.d.), Biberman-Sondergaard Papers, Boxes 41, 53; Gómez-Quiñones, *Mexican American Labor*, 186; Biberman to Travis, Nov. 26, 1954, IUMMSW Papers, Box 119.

41. Biberman to Travis, Nov. 26, 1954, IUMMSW Papers, Box 119.

42. Travis to Biberman, Nov. 30, 1954, IUMMSW Papers, Box 119.

43. Jarrico to Travis, Dec. 3, 1954; Biberman to Travis, Dec. 1, 1954, IUMMSW Papers, Box 119; Minutes, IUMMSW Executive Board, Aug. 13, 1954, Jencks Papers, Box 2.

44. Author Interview, Jencks; Jarrico to Lorence, Apr. 19, 1996; Biberman, "What Kind of Company Was This?," 8, Biberman-Sondergaard Papers, Box 51.

45. Jencks, "Semi-monthly Report of International Representatives," June 30, 1954, IUMMSW Papers, Box 101, Clinton Jencks File.

46. Biberman to Baskind, Jan. 17, 1954; "A Report on 'Salt of the Earth'" Jan. 17, 1954; Jarrico, "Salt of the Earth — Chronology," 30, Biberman-Sondergaard Papers, Boxes 41, 53, 51.

47. Quoted in Biberman, *Salt of the Earth*, 195; Sondergaard to Biberman, July 12, 1954; Maltz to Biberman, Dec. 3, 1953, Biberman-Sondergaard Papers, Boxes 4, 1.

48. Biberman, *Salt of the Earth*, 203–4; Biberman to Travis, Dec. 28, 1954, IUMMSW Papers, Box 129; Biberman, "What Kind of Company Was This?," Biberman-Sondergaard Papers, Box 51.

CHAPTER 8

1. "Brief *Amicus Curiae* in Support of Complaint," IPC Distributors, Inc. vs. Chicago Moving Picture Machine Operators Union, Local 110, Civil Action No. 55 C 147, n.d.; Illinois Division, ACLU, Press Release, Mar. 22, 1955, ACLUI Papers, Box 36; Biberman, *Salt of the Earth*, 203–4; Biberman to Travis, Dec. 28, 1954, IUMMSW Papers, Box 119.

2. *Variety*, June 17, 1955; *Mine-Mill Union*, June 30, 1955; *Daily Worker*, June 17, 1955; FBI Report, Los Angeles, "Independent Productions Corporation," Sept. 7, 1955, File no. 100–399257–170; ACLU, "Weekly Bulletin," no. 1708, July 25,

1955, IUMMSW Papers, Box 129; IPC Distributors, Inc., "Press Release," June 13, 1955, Biberman-Sondergaard Papers, Box 53; Biberman, *Salt of the Earth*, 204–6.

3. Biberman, *Salt of the Earth*, 207; ACLU, "Weekly Bulletin," no 1708, July 25, 1955; *Mine-Mill Union*, June 30, 1955; IPC Distributors, Inc., "Press Release," June 13, 1955, Biberman-Sondergaard Papers, Box 53.

4. Biberman, *Salt of the Earth*, 207; F. Raymond Marks, Jr., to Max R. Kargman, Dec. 2, 1955, ACLUI Papers, Box 36; Independent Productions Corporation to Those it May Concern, Nov. 15, 1955, Biberman-Sondergaard Papers, Box 53.

5. Biberman, *Salt of the Earth*, 212, and see also 206–7, 211; Schrecker, *Many Are the Crimes*, 335.

6. Morton to Biberman, Feb. 1, 1956; Independent Productions Corporation to Those it May Concern," Nov. 15, 1955, Biberman-Sondergaard Papers, Boxes 1, 53; Margolis Interview, 247–48; Jarrico to Lorence, Apr. 19, 1996.

7. Author Interviews, Jarrico and Jencks; Biberman, *Salt of the Earth*, 215; *Variety*, June 22, 1956; *New York Times*, June 22, 1956; *Daily Worker*, June 22, 1956; "Press Release," June 21, 1956; Biberman to Sonja Dahl and Edward Biberman (contains press statement), May 9, 1956, Biberman-Sondergaard Papers, Boxes 52, 4; Teletype Message, June 21, 1956, Washington City News Service, in FBI Report, Washington, D.C., File no. 100–399257; FBI Report, New York, "Independent Productions Corporation," Aug. 15, 1956, File no. 100–399257–179; Ceplair and Englund, *Inquisition in Hollywood*, 417–18.

8. Lazarus to Those it May Concern, June 28, 1956; "Press Release," June 21, 1956, Biberman-Sondergaard Papers, Boxes 53, 52; *Daily Worker*, June 22, 1956.

9. Maurice Benjamin, "Memo," Mar. 20, 1953; Jack Baker to Mayer Lavenstein, Mar. 21, 1953; REC/MHL to RSC, Mar. 23, 1953; Charles E. Oberle to Baker, Aug. 14, 1953, Biberman-Sondergaard Papers, Box 61; "Paul Jarrico," 283; Author Interview, Jencks, 7.

10. Brewer Interview, OHAL.

11. Author Interviews, Jarrico and Jencks.

12. Wilson to Biberman, Nov. 11, 1955; Biberman to George Brussel, Jr., June 3, 1959, Biberman-Sondergaard Papers, Box 28; Biberman, *Salt of the Earth*, 216, 218.

13. Biberman to Alvah Bessie, ca. 1962, Alvah Bessie Papers, SHSW, Box 26; Herbert Biberman, "Deposition," June 17, 1959, Independent Productions Corporation and IPC Distributors, Inc. v. Loew's, Incorporated, et al., 104, 113–15, 132, 155; Biberman to Brussel, June 3, 1959, Biberman-Sondergaard Papers, Boxes 36, 28; Jarrico to Lorence, Apr. 19, 1996; Schrecker, *Many Are the Crimes*, 335.

14. Jarrico Interview, OHAL, 134–35; "Paul Jarrico," 283; Author Interview, Jencks; Biberman, "What Kind of Company Was This?"; "Summation," Biberman-Sondergaard Papers, Box 51; Ceplair and Englund, *Inquisition in Hollywood*, 418; Kanfer, *Journal of the Plague Years*, 278–79; Schrecker, *Many Are the Crimes*, 335; Larry Wertheim, "Nedrick Young, et al. v. MPAA, et al.: The Fight against the Hollywood Blacklist" (May 14, 1973), Research Paper, History 902, 21, Healy Papers, Box 21.

15. "Statement by the CIO," ca. 1954; David J. McDonald to Al C. Gordon, Dec. 17, 1953; McDonald to Charles J. Smith, Dec. 28, 1953, all USWA Papers, Box 8, District 38 File; Interview, Alfredo C. Montoya, PSU, HCLA; O'Brien, "'Communist-Dominated' Unions," 184–85; Keitel, "Merger," 37–38; Jensen, *Nonferrous Metals Industry Unionism*, 304–5.

16. Is it 'Red-Baiting' to Call a Communist a Communist?," ca. 1955; "Statement by CIO," ca. 1954, USWA Papers, Box 167, President's Office Files; Box 8, District 38 File; Keitel, "Merger," 37; "Red Invasion," ca. January 1954, Gene Saari Papers, ALHUA, Box 10; "Mine-Mill is Going . . . and it Won't Be Back," February 1962, Jencks Papers, Box 22.

17. Keitel, "Merger," 37; N. A. Zonarich, "Analysis of the Campaign Conducted by the USA against the MMSW in Butte, Montana," USWA Papers, Box 8, District 38 File, April 1954; Zonarich to McDonald, Dec. 4, 7, 1953, USWA Papers, Box 8, District 38 File; Box 167, President's Office File. For further analysis of the USWA's organizing tactics, see Jensen, *Nonferrous Metals Industry Unionism*, 270, 304–5; O'Brien, "'Communist-Dominated' Unions," 199; Cochran, *Labor and Communism*, 331.

18. Foster, "Mexican Labor and the American Southwest," 161; Cochran, *Labor and Communism*, 331; Adolfo Barela to Brothers and Sisters, Mar. 10, 1952 (correct date is 1953), IUMMSW Papers, Box 538; Author Interview, Montoya.

19. Charles J. Smith to Friend, Sept. 20, 1953, USWA Papers, Box 8, District 38 File; Barela to Brothers and Sisters, Mar. 10, 1952 (correct date 1953), IUMMSW Papers, Box 538.

20. Keitel, "Merger," 36; O'Brien, "'Communist-Dominated' Unions," 199–200; Foster, "Mexican Labor and the American Southwest," 151; Angelo Verdu to Howard Hague, Jan. 18, 1956; "Mine-Mill Mutual Aid Pact with Teamsters," ca. 1956, USWA Papers, Box 8, District 38 File; *The Southwest Miner*, May and September 1955.

21. "Clinton Jencks," in Fariello, *Red Scare*, 387–88; Montoya Interview; Author Interview, Montoya; Cochran, *Labor and Communism*, 331; Kern, "Organized Labor," 158; Gómez-Quiñones, *Mexican American Labor*, 186; Keitel, "Merger," 41, 43.

22. "Mine-Mill Brought Rich and Militant Tradition," USWA Fiftieth Anniversary Commemorative Brochure (Pittsburgh: USWA, 1986).

23. Al Skinner to Executive Board and International Staff, May 1, 1961, USWA Papers, Box 28, Howard Hague File.

24. For a judicious summary of the Empire strike's significance as an important incident in American labor history, see Cargill, "Empire and Opposition," 252–53. See also Gómez-Quiñones, *Mexican American Labor*, 186; Zaniello, *Working Stiffs, Union Maids, and Riffraff*, 214–15; Walsh, "Films We Never Saw," 579–80.

25. Clinton Jencks never wavered in denying CP membership, and no definitive evidence exists to contradict his assertions. However, Schrecker concludes that he "belonged to the communist movement," and that his experiences "reveal the dense

web of personal and institutional relationships that constituted the interconnected worlds of American communism and anticommunism." Finally, Jencks's experience reveals the devious means employed to destroy the left-led labor movement of the late 1940s. Schrecker, *Many Are the Crimes*, 310, 311; see also David M. Oshinsky, *Senator Joseph McCarthy and the American Labor Movement* (Columbia: University of Missouri Press, 1976), 176; "Clinton Jencks," 383; Author Interview, Jencks. For an alternative analysis that goes further to identify Clinton Jencks as an active communist, see Hodges, "Making and Unmaking of *Salt of the Earth*," 35, 52–53, 394. For Matusow's unsubstantiated charges, see "Harvey Job Matusow," in Fariello, *Red Scare*, 103–4. On the Taft-Hartley Act, see Schrecker, *Many Are the Crimes*, 336–39; Alton Lee, *Truman and Taft-Hartley: A Question of Mandate* (Lexington: University of Kentucky Press, (1966); Susan M. Hartmann, *Truman and the Eightieth Congress* (Columbia: University of Missouri Press, 1971).

26. *Daily People's World*, Apr. 27, 1953; "Press Release," Apr. 23, 1953, Local 890, IUMMSW, IUMMSW Papers, Box 150; "Clinton Jencks," 386.

27. The best description of Matusow's role in the Jencks case may be found in Schrecker, *Many Are the Crimes*, 311–13; for a discussion of Matusow's false charges against Jencks, see ibid., 346, 347.

28. Ibid., 347.

29. Minutes, Executive Board Meeting, Local 890, June 1, 1953, Minute Book, 134–35; *Daily People's World*, Apr. 27, 1953; "Press Release," Apr. 23, 1953, Local 890, IUMMSW, IUMMSW Papers, Box 150. For evidence of Local 890's continuing fundraising and moral support for the Jencks defense, see Chacón et al. to All Southwest Locals, December 1955; Chacón to William Sanderson, Dec. 2, 1955; Virginia Chacón to All Ladies Auxiliaries, December 1955, IUMMSW Papers, Box 153, Local 890 File. See also Dennis Chavez Papers, Albuquerque, University of New Mexico Library, Center for Southwest Research, Clinton Jencks File.

30. *Proceedings, Forty-ninth Annual Convention, IUMMSW*, 1953, 104; see also 92–104.

31. Schrecker, *Many Are the Crimes*, 350–52.

32. "Clinton Jencks," 386–87; "Harvey Job Matusow," 103–4; Witt Interview, USWA Papers, 7; Jencks Interview, OHAL, 17; "Statement Adopted by International Executive Board," June 8, 1957, IUMMSW Papers, Box 317;.Schrecker, *Many Are the Crimes*, 352–53. For evidence of Local 890's ongoing effort to defend Jencks, see its scathing analysis of the Matusow revelations in "The Truth, the Whole Truth, and Nothing but the Truth," ACLU of Southern California Papers, Los Angeles, UCLA, Special Collections, Box 22.

33. Sonja Dahl Biberman to Sam Feldman, Apr. 24, 1954; Feldman to Wilson, May 20, 1954; Wilson to Travis, May 14, 1954, IUMMSW Papers, Box 129; Travis to Wilson, June 11, 1954, Wilson Papers, Box 51.

34. Jarrico to Travis, Aug. 31, 1954; Minutes, Executive Board, IUMMSW, Aug. 12–13, 1954; "Resolution on the Defense of Clinton Jencks," IUMMSW Wage and Policy Conference, Apr. 3–5, 1954; Travis to Executive Board, ca. April 1954,

IUMMSW Papers, Boxes 867, 63; Travis to Wilson, June 11, 1954, Wilson Papers, Box 51; Author Interview, Jarrico.

35. Minutes, Executive Board, IUMMSW, Oct. 15–21, 1954, Jencks Papers, Box 2; "Report of the Committee in Defense of the Union of the Mine-Mill Area Conference," Nov. 13–14, 1954; Jencks, "Semi-Monthly Report of International Representatives," Nov. 30, 1954, Clinton Jencks File, IUMMSW Papers, Boxes 880, 101.

36. Miller, "Class Reunion," 35; "Clinton Jencks," 387–89; Jencks Interview, OHAL; Author Interview, Jencks. For comment on Jencks's persecution, see "Clinton Jencks: The Times and the Man," *Albuquerque Journal Magazine,* Apr. 28, 1981; see also Schrecker, *Many Are the Crimes,* 354–55.

37. Betty Millard, "Salt of the Earth: A Postscript," *Latin America Today* 5 (March 1955), 5–6.

38. For an excellent summary of the strike and the film as influences on gender relations among the women and men of Local 890 and Grant County, see Rosenfelt, "Commentary," 140–46. For Virginia Chacón's analysis of *Salt's* limited impact on women's consciousness, see Miller, "Class Reunion," 36; Kingsolver, *Holding the Line,* 178; Author Interview, Jencks. On women's roles in the union and the Ladies Auxiliary, see Chacón Interview, OHAL, 3; Millard, "Salt of the Earth," 7.

39. Chacón to Sisters and Brothers, Jan. 10, 1975, Wilson Papers, Box 48; Chacón, "Why I Want to Be President" (1973); "The Rank and File Must Challenge the Weak Leadership," ca. September 1971, Chacón Papers, Pamphlet File; Gómez-Quiñones, *Mexican American Labor,* 188; Cargill, "Empire and Opposition," 253; Miller, "Class Reunion," 36. For comment on Chacón's defiant attitude toward management, see Rosenblum, *Copper Crucible,* 170.

40. Quoted in Miller, "Class Reunion," 36; "Press Release and Fact Sheet," ca. January 1975; Chacón to Brothers and Sisters, Jan. 10, 1975, Wilson Papers, Box 48; Chacón Interview, OHAL, 4.

41. "Press Release," ca. January 1975; Chacón to Sisters and Brothers, Jan. 10, 1975, Wilson Papers, Box 48; Chacón Interview, OHAL, 4.

42. "Reportero," October 1975; Press Release, January 1975; Muriel and Clint Jencks to Mike and Zelma Wilson, Jan. 19, 1975; Chacon to Brothers and Sisters, Jan. 10, 1975; Chacón Papers, Pamphlet File; Wilson Papers, Box 48; "Walton Arrives," Dec. 27, 1974; Communist Labor Party, "We Defend Local 890," 1974, Chacón Papers, Clippings File and Pamphlet File.

43. Quoted in Miller, "Class Reunion," 36; Chacón Interview, OHAL, 5; Author Interview, Virginia Chacón.

44. Riambau and Torreiro, "This Film Is Going to Make History," 50–51; Millard, "Salt of the Earth," 8; Miller, "Class Reunion," 35–36; Rosaura Revueltas to Margolis, Nov. 19, 1960, Biberman-Sondergaard Papers, Box 28; Author Interview, Jencks; Interview, Rosaura Revueltas, Aug. 1, 1975, Cuernavaca, Mexico, in possession of Tony Grutman, Los Angeles.

45. Brewer Interview, OHAL; Roy Loynd, "Roy Brewer Doesn't Like his Docu

'Role': Wants Footage Trim," *Variety*, Apr. 27, 1983; see also "Roy Brewer"; Brewer Interview, UCLA Archives, 7.

46. Dick, *Radical Innocence*, 81. The Biberman Papers, housed at the State Historical Society of Wisconsin, afford historians a dramatic and extensive glimpse of the making and suppression of *Salt of the Earth*. Furthermore, the records of the Independent Productions Corporation, also a part of the Biberman-Sondergaard collection, document the history of the company in extensive detail, including material relating to the antitrust suit filed and litigated between 1956 and 1964.

47. Jarrico to Lorence, Apr. 19, 1996; Miller, "Class Reunion," 35; Wilson Interview, OHAL; "Paul Jarrico," 283; Jarrico Interview, UCLA, OHP, 135, 161–62. Jarrico also argued that in a sense the film had not been suppressed, since millions of people may have viewed it in China and the former Soviet Union. Author Interview, Jarrico.

48. Jarrico Interview, UCLA, OHP, 134, 168; Margolis Interview, 246, 248; "Paul Jarrico." If the value of the *Salt* group's personal time is included, the film's cost soars well beyond 400,000 dollars. Author Interview, Jarrico.

49. IPC and IPCD to Those it May Concern, Nov. 15, 1955; IPC and IPCD, "Consolidated Financial Summary, November 1,1955," Biberman-Sondergaard Papers, Box 53; IUMMSW Papers, Box 129. See also FBI Report, Los Angeles, COMPIC, ca. November 1955, File no. 100–15732, *Communist Activity in the Entertainment Industry*, Vol. 37, Reel 7.

50. Biberman to Lazarus, Sept. 6, Nov. 3, 1959, Biberman-Sondergaard Papers, Box 28; FBI Report, Los Angeles, COMPIC, May 20, 1958, File no. 100–15732, *Communist Activity in the Entertainment Industry*, Vol. 37, Reel 7.

51. Author Interview, Jarrico; also quoted in Miller, "Class Reunion," 34; "Paul Jarrico," 283; Jarrico Interview, UCLA, OHP, 135; Gómez-Quiñones, *Mexican American Labor*, 186; Ceplair and Englund, *Inquisition in Hollywood*, 418; "Union-Sponsored Radical Films," 799.

52. As Steven J. Ross has recently shown, a vibrant working-class film movement had thrived prior to the 1920s. However, as modern Hollywood took shape, liberal and radical films declined in importance. The product of the studio system emphasized the alleged absence of class differences in American society. Steven J. Ross, *Working Class Hollywood: Silent Film and the Shaping of Class in America* (Princeton, N.J.: Princeton University Press, 1998).

EPILOGUE

1. Nora Sayre, *Running against Time: Films of the Cold War* (New York: Dial, 1982), 174–75; Charles Ramirez Berg, "Bordertown, the Assimilation Narrative, and the Chicana Social Problem Film," in Chon A. Noriega, ed., *Chicanos and Film: Essays on Chicano Representation and Resistance* (New York: Garland Publishing Co., 1992), 42–47; Molly Haskell, *From Reverence to Rape* (New York: Holt Rinehart, and Winston, 1973), 233; Casey St. Chamez, *Shoot in New Mexico: Hollywood at Work in*

the Land of Enchantment, 1898–1993 (Santa Fe: New Mexico Film Commission, 1993), 27; Rosenfelt, "Commentary," 94; Neve, *Film and Politics in America,* 201; Roffman and Purdy, *Hollywood Social Problem Film,* 254–55, 264–65, 295; Keller, *Hispanics and United States Film,* 133; Woll, "Hollywood Views the Mexican-American," 49; Walsh, "Films We Never Saw," 478–79; Gómez-Quiñones, *Mexican American Labor,* 186; "Union-Sponsored Radical Films," 799–800; Anderson, "Red Hollywood," 180; Robinson, "Out of the Mine and into the Canyon," 189–90; Christensen, *Reel Politics,* 94–95; Lipsitz, "Herbert Biberman," 180, 182; Puette, *Through Jaundiced Eyes,* 20–21. See also James M. Skinner, *"Salt of the Earth* (1953): The Morning Star of the American Feminist Cinema?," unpublished paper in author's files.

2. Pauline Kael, "Morality Plays Right and Left," in *I Lost It at the Movies* (Boston: Little, Brown, and Company, 1954), 331–32; see also Neve, *Film and Politics in America,* 201. Jonathan Rosenbaum accurately labels Kael's review a "hatchet job" that is both negative and "unreliable." Rosenbaum, *Placing Movies,* 284.

3. Interview, July 2, 1975, Paul Jarrico (conducted by Deborah Silverton Rosenfelt), in possession of Tony Grutman, Los Angeles.

4. Report, AC of S, G-2, Hq. Fifth Army, Chicago, "Review of the Film: *Salt of the Earth,"* FBI File no. 100–399257–145. Sponsors reported a more positive response from the audience of four hundred "socially-minded men and women" who had a "wonderful experience in the life of [their] church." Edwin T. Buehrer to ACLU, Sept. 16, 1994; June N. Sark to ACLU, Sept. 18, 1954, ACLUI Papers, Box 36.

5. Hodges, "Making and Unmaking of *Salt of the Earth,"* 391–93.

6. Lawson, "Toward a People's Culture" (draft manuscript), n.d., Lawson Papers Supplement, File no. AI3, 4, 39–40.

7. For judicious discussion of the Communist role in Local 890, see Cargill, "Empire and Opposition," 250–52. See also Schrecker, *Many Are the Crimes,* chap. 9; Hodges, "Making and Unmaking of *Salt of the Earth,* 45–46, 74–76; and Baker, "Gender Consciousness and Political Activism."

8. Biberman to Albert Pezzati, Mar. 28, 1955, IUMMSW Papers, Boxes 119, 129; Jencks Interview, OHAL, 4–5, 8; Author Interviews, Jencks and Flores; Miller, "Class Reunion," 35, 36; Chacón Interview, OHAL, 3; Millard, "Salt of the Earth," 6–7; see also Rosenblum, *Copper Crucible,* 35; Riambau and Torriero, "This Film Is Going to Make History," 51. For comment on *Salt's* importance as a film that portrayed Chicanos and Chicanas redefining success in "personal and local terms," see Berg, "Bordertown," 47; see also Keller, *Hispanics and United States Film,* 132, 133; and Gomez-Quiñones, *Mexican American Labor,* 186.

9. Ruth McCormick, *"Salt of the Earth," Cineaste* 5 (Fall 1972), 54–55; Berg, "Bordertown," 42, 44; Rosenfelt, "Commentary," 144–46; Wilson Interview, OHAL; Author Interviews, Flores, Jarrico, Jencks, and Vincent; Skinner, *"Salt of the Earth* (1953)," esp. 10–11; Neve, *Film and Politics in America,* 201; Sayre, *Running Time,* 175; "Union-Sponsored Radical Films," 800; Kern, "Organized Labor," 158; Dick, *Radical Innocence,* 79. A favorable, yet ambivalent, analysis of *Salt's* feminist

implications may be found in Robinson, "Out of the Mine and into the Canyon," esp. 173–82, 189–90.

10. Biberman to All, Sept. 21 and Oct. 15, 1965; Biberman to Wilson, July 26, 1965, Wilson Papers, Box 48; Biberman to Yale Law School Cinema Club, March 1955, Biberman-Sondergaard Papers, Box 46; *New York Times*, Oct. 31, 1965, in Billy Rose Archives, New York, Lincoln Center for the Performing Arts, Clippings File. For comment on the film's distribution on college campuses and the reaction, see Gómez-Quinones, *Mexican American Labor*, 186; "Union-Sponsored Radical Films," 799–800.

11. *Frontier*, ca. August 1965, Lawson Papers, Box 32; Gorman to Biberman, June 21, 1965, AMCBW Papers, Reel 205.

12. *National Guardian*, June 5, 1965, Lawson Papers, Box 32.

13. Lawson, "Review for *Science and Society*" (draft), ca. August 1965, Lawson Papers, Box 89.

14. Biberman, "Questions Respecting Protest," in Biberman to Arthur Galligan, May 15, 1964; Lazarus to Note-Holder, Feb. 15, 1965; Biberman to Margolis, Nov. 27, 1964, all in Biberman-Sondergaard Papers, Box 29; Biberman to Round Robins, Nov. 14, 1964, Wilson Papers, Box 48.

15. Wilson Interview, OHAL; Author Interview, Jarrico; Neve, *Film and Politics in America*, 200; Navasky, *Naming Names*, 337.

16. Roffman and Purdy, *Hollywood Social Problem Film*, 295; Ceplair and Englund, *Inquisition in Hollywood*, 418; Neve, *Film and Politics in America*, 198.

17. Puette, *Through Jaundiced Eyes*, 21; Walsh, "Films We Never Saw," 580; see also Zaniello, *Working Stiffs, Union Maids, and Riffraff*, 214; Vaughn, "Political Censorship during the Cold War," 246; Gómez-Quiñones, *Mexican American Labor*, 186. See also Ross, *Working Class Hollywood*, 251–52.

18. Quoted in Gordon Hitchens, "Notes on a Blacklisted Film: *Salt of the Earth*," *Film Culture* 50–51 (Fall–Winter 1970), 81; Lazarus to Note-Holder, Feb. 15, 1965, Wilson Papers, Box 48.

Bibliography

ARCHIVES AND MANUSCRIPTS

California

Academy of Motion Picture Arts and Sciences Library, Margaret Herrick Library, Beverly Hills
    Biographical Files: Ann Doran, Will Geer, Pedro Gonzalez-Gonzalez, Ann Revere
    Motion Picture Industry Council Papers
    Production Code Administration Papers
California State University — Long Beach Library, Special Collections
    Dorothy Healey Papers
California State University — Northridge, Urban Archives Center
    Gilbert Benjamin Papers
    Community Relations Committee, Jewish Federation Council of Los Angeles Papers
    Los Angeles County Federation of Labor Papers
Ann Rand Memorial Library, San Francisco
    International Longshoremen and Warehousemen Union Archives
Screen Actors Guild
    SAG Archives
    SAG Minutes, Executive Board
Southern California Library for Social Studies and Research
    California CIO Council, Union Research and Information Services Papers
    James Daugherty Papers
    Ben Margolis Papers
University of California, Los Angeles, Department of Special Collections, University Research Library
    American Civil Liberties Union of Southern California Papers
    Ken Englund Papers
    Dorothy Healey Papers

Carey McWilliams Papers
Edward Roybal Papers
Dalton Trumbo Papers
U.S. Government Materials Regarding Ben Margolis, 1941–1973
University of California, Los Angeles, Arts Library, Special Collections
Michael Wilson Papers

Colorado

University of Colorado, Boulder, Libraries
Archives of the Western Federation of Miners and International Union of
Mine, Mill, and Smelter Workers
Clinton Jencks Papers

Illinois

Chicago Historical Society
Chicago Federation of Labor Papers
Ernest DeMaio Papers
Leon Despres Papers
Sidney Lens Papers
Southern Illinois University, Carbondale, Special Collections, Morris Library
John Howard Lawson Papers
University of Chicago Library, Special Collections
American Civil Liberties Union, Illinois Division Papers

Iowa

Herbert Hoover Presidential Library, West Branch
Westbrook Pegler Papers

Michigan

Archives of Labor and Urban Affairs, Walter P. Reuther Library, Wayne State University, Detroit
CIO Secretary Treasurer's Office Papers
CIO Washington Office Papers
Nat Ganley Papers
Nat Ganley/Saul Wellman Papers
Carl Haessler Papers
Metropolitan Detroit AFL-CIO Papers
Walter P. Reuther Papers
Gene Saari Papers

UAW Ford Department Papers
UAW Local 600 Papers
Michigan State University, Library, Special Collections
    Radicalism Collection
    Saul Wellman Papers
University of Michigan, Ann Arbor, Harlan Hatcher Research Library, Joseph La-
    badie Collection
    American Committee for the Protection of the Foreign Born Papers
    American Committee for the Protection of the Foreign Born, Los Angeles
        Chapter, Papers

New Jersey

Princeton University, Princeton, Seeley G. Mudd Manuscript Library
    American Civil Liberties Union Papers

New Mexico

University of New Mexico, Zimmerman Library, Center for Southwest
    Research
    Dennis Chavez Papers
New Mexico Archives and Records Center, Santa Fe
    Lucien A. File Papers
San Cristóbal
    Jenny Vincent Papers, Privately Held
    Silver City Museum
    Pedro Gonzalez-Gonzalez File
Western New Mexico State University, Silver City, Miller Library
    Juan Chacón Papers

New York

American Museum of the Moving Image, Astoria
    International Alliance of Theatrical Stage Employees Papers
International Alliance of Theatrical Stage Employees, International Office, New
    York
    Archives
Lincoln Center for the Performing Arts, New York
    New York Public Library for the Performing Arts Research Collection (Billy
        Rose Theater Collection)
Martin P. Catherwood Library, Cornell University, Ithaca
    Western Federation of Miners and International Union of Mine, Mill, and
        Smelter Workers Papers

Tamiment Library, New York University, New York
    International Alliance of Theatrical Stage Employees, Local 1644, Papers

North Carolina

Duke University, Durham, Special Collections, Perkins Library
    J. B. Matthews Papers

Pennsylvania

Pennsylvania State University, State College, Pattee Library Historical Collections
    and Labor Archives
    International Union of Mine, Mill, and Smelter Workers Papers
    United Mine Workers of America Papers
    United Steel Workers of America Archives

Washington, D.C.

Catholic University of America, Archives
    John Brophy Papers
    Congress of Industrial Organizations Papers
    Philip Murray Papers
Library of Congress, Manuscripts Division
    Clinton P. Anderson Papers
    National Association for the Advancement of Colored People Papers
    Joseph Rauh Papers
George Meany Memorial Archives, Silver Spring
    COPE Research Division Files
    Office of the President, George Meany Papers
    George Meany Papers
    Minutes of Executive Council, AFL-CIO

Wisconsin

State Historical Society of Wisconsin, Madison
    Amalgamated Meatcutters and Butcher Workmen of North America
        Papers
    American Legion Papers, Wisconsin Division
    Herbert Biberman-Gail Sondergaard Papers
    Adolph Germer Papers
    Albert Maltz Papers
    Philip Stevenson Papers

Dalton Trumbo Papers
Nedrick Young Papers
United Packinghouse, Food, and Allied Workers Papers

INTERVIEWS

California

Author
James Daugherty (telephone), Los Angeles
Paul Jarrico, Ojai
Clinton Jencks, San Diego
—— (telephone)
Tony Grutman Collection
Paul Jarrico
Rosaura Revueltas
Maurice Travis
Frances Williams
University of California, Los Angeles, Oral History Program, Department of Special Collections, University Research Library (Regents of the University of California System)
Edward Biberman
Jack Dales
Ben Dobbs
Dorothy Healey
Paul Jarrico
Helen Slote Levitt
Ben Margolis
Herbert Sorrell
Michael Wilson
Zelma Wilson

Michigan

Archives of Labor and Urban Affairs, Wayne State University, Detroit
Nat Ganley
Carl Haessler
Horace Sheffield
Author
Dave Moore (telephone)
Robert Repas (telephone)

New Mexico

Author
  Virginia Chacón
  Arturo and Josefina Flores
  Jenny Vincent

New York

Author
  Steve D'Inzillo
  Lottie Gordon
Tamiment Library, New York University, New York, Oral History of the American Left Collection, Series IV, Filmmakers Tapes and Transcripts, *A Crime to Fit the Punishment*
  Sonja and Edward Biberman
  Roy Brewer
  Juan Chacón
  Virginia Chacón and Angie Sanchez
  Sylvia Jarrico
  Clinton Jencks
  Clinton Jencks and Juan Chacón
  Henrietta Williams
  Michael Wilson

Pennsylvania

Pennsylvania State University, State College, Pattee Library Historical Collections and Labor Archives, United Steel Workers of America Oral History Project
  I. W. Abel
  Vern Curtis
  Irving Dichter
  Asbury Howard
  Orville Larson
  Alfredo Montoya
  Chase Powers
  Reid Robinson
  William Sanderson
  Al Skinner
  Nathan Witt
  Nicholas Zonarich

Texas

Author
Alfredo Montoya, El Paso

Wisconsin

State Historical Society of Wisconsin, Madison
· Eugene Mailes
Stephen Vaughn Collection, Privately Held
Roy Brewer

GOVERNMENT RECORDS

Published Documents

California, Senate
Seventh Report of the Senate Fact Finding Committee on Un-American Activities,
1953
Eighth Report of the Senate Fact-Finding Committee on Un-American Activities,
1955
Federal Bureau of Investigation, Confidential Files
Communist Activity in the Entertainment Industry: FBI Surveillance Files in Holly-
wood, 1942–1958 (microfilm ed.), ed. Daniel Leab. Bethesda, Md.: Uni-
versity Publications of America, 1991.
U.S. Congress.
Congressional Record, 1952–1955. Washington, D.C.
Annual Report of the Committee on Un-American Activities for the Year 1953. 83d
Cong., 2d sess., 1954. House Rept. 1192.
House. Committee on Un-American Activities. *Hearings.* 83d Cong., 1st sess.,
1953.

Unpublished Records

FBI Records Obtained under the Freedom of Information Act, 1952–1956.
Herbert Biberman
Independent Productions Corporation
Salt of the Earth
New Mexico State Records Center and Archives (Santa Fe)
Governor's Archives (Edwin Mecham)
New Mexico Bureau of Mines and Mineral Resources Collection

Report of State Inspector of Mines to the Governor of New Mexico, 1952–
    1954
National Archives (Archives II)
    Record Group 59. General Records of the Department of State
    Record Group 174. Records of the Department of Labor
    Record Group 280. Records of the Federal Mediation and Conciliation Ser-
    vice

MINUTES AND PROCEEDINGS

American Federation of Labor, Executive Council.
    Minutes of Meetings, 1953–1954.
Motion Picture Projectionists, Video Technicians, and Allied Crafts, IATSE, Local
    306. New York.
    Minutes of Executive Board, 1953–1955.
California State Federation of Labor.
    Proceedings and Officers Reports, 1953–1956.
International Alliance of Theatrical Stage Employees and Motion Picture Opera-
    tors of the United States and Canada.
    Proceedings, 1952–1956.
International Union of Mine, Mill, and Smelter Workers.
    Proceedings, 1950–1954.
American Legion.
    Proceedings, 1953–1955.

JOURNALS, NEWSPAPERS, MAGAZINES

The American Federationist. 1952–1955
Daily Worker, 1950–1956
The Dispatcher, 1953–1955
Ford Facts, 1953–1955
Hollywood Reporter, 1950–1956
The Labor Leader, 1953–1955
Los Angeles Herald and Express, 1953–54
Los Angeles Times, 1950–1965
Mine-Mill Union, 1950–1960
*Official Bulletin, International Alliance of Theatrical Stage Employees and Moving Pic-
    ture Operators of the United States and Canada,* 1951–1955
New York Times, 1950–1965
Party Voice, 1953–1955
Peoples' Daily World, 1953–55

Political Affairs, 1952–1955
RKO Radio Flash, 1953–1954
Silver City Daily Press, 1950–1956
The Southwest Miner, 1955
Variety, 1950–1965
Washington News, 1953

MISCELLANEOUS PUBLISHED PRIMARY SOURCES

Bernstein, Walter. *Inside Out: A Memoir of the Blacklist*. New York: Alfred A. Knopf, 1966.

Bessie, Alvah. *Inquisition in Eden*. New York: Macmillan, 1965.

Biberman, Herbert. *Salt of the Earth: The Story of a Film*. Boston: Beacon Press, 1965.

Burnhill, James. "The Mexican-American Question." *Political Affairs* 32 (December 1953): 50–63.

———. "The Mexican People in the Southwest." *Political Affairs* 32 (September 1953): 43–53.

California Quarterly 2. Summer, 1953.

Cogley, John. *Report on Blacklisting*. Vol. 1: *The Movies*. Santa Barbara: Fund for the Republic, 1956.

Cole, Lester. *Hollywood Red: The Autobiography of Lester Cole*. Palo Alto: Pamphlet Press, 1981.

Corona, Bert. *Memories of Chicano History: The Life and Narrative of Bert Corona*. Edited by Mario T. Garcia. Berkeley: University of California Press, 1994.

Fariello, Griffin, ed. *Red Scare: Memories of the American Inquisition, an Oral History*. New York: W. W. Norton and Co., 1995.

Flynn, Elizabeth Gurley. "What 'Salt of the Earth' Means to Me." *Political Affairs* 33 (June 1954): 63–65.

Healey, Dorothy, and Maurice Isserman. *Dorothy Healey Remembers: A Life in the Communist Party*. New York: Oxford University Press, 1990.

Jarrico, Paul. "Some Remarks by Paul Jarrico at a WGAW Forum on the Blacklist." Writers Guild Conference, Jan. 19, 1989.

Kael, Pauline. *I Lost It at the Movies*. Boston: Little, Brown and Co., 1954.

Lawson, John Howard. *Film in the Battle of Ideas*. New York: Masses and Mainstream, 1953.

McGilligan, Patrick, and Paul Buhle. *Tender Comrades: A Backstory of the Hollywood Blacklist*. New York: St. Martin's Press, 1997.

Millard, Betty. "Salt of the Earth: A Postscript." *Latin America Today* 5 (March 1955): 4–8.

Reisz, Karl. "Hollywood's Anti-Red Boomerang." *Sight and Sound* 22 (January-March 1953): 132–48.

Sillen, Samuel. "Our Time." *Masses and Mainstream* 7 (April 1954): 1–5.

Tenayuca, Emma, and Homer Brooks. "The Mexican Question in the Southwest." *The Communist* 18 (March 1939): 257–68.

Trumbo, Dalton. *Additional Dialogue: Letters of Dalton Trumbo, 1942–1962.* Edited by Helen Manfull. New York: M. Evans and Co., 1970.

——. *The Time of the Toad: A Study of the Inquisition in America.* New York: Harper and Row, 1949 (repr., 1972).

SECONDARY SOURCES

Books

Acuña, Rodolfo. *Occupied America: The Chicano's Struggle toward Liberation.* San Francisco: Canfield Press, 1972.

Anderson, Karen. *Changing Women: A History of Racial Ethnic Women in Modern America.* New York: Oxford University Press, 1996.

Aronowitz, Stanley. *False Promises: The Shaping of American Working Class Consciousness.* New York: McGraw-Hill, 1973.

Belknap, Michael R. *Cold War Political Justice: The Smith Act, The Communist Party, and American Civil Liberties.* Westport, Conn.: Greenwood Press, 1977.

Bloom, Jonathan, and Paul Buhle. *Guide to the Oral History of the American Left.* New York: New York University Libraries, 1984.

Brinley, John Ervin, Jr. *The Western Federation of Miners.* Ann Arbor: University Microfilms, 1972.

Brown, Michael E., et al., eds. *New Studies in the Politics and Culture of U.S. Communism.* New York: Monthly Review Press, 1993.

Buhle, Paul, and Dan Georgakas, eds. *The Immigrant Left in the United States.* Albany: State University of New York Press, 1996.

Carr, Barry. *Marxism and Communism in Twentieth Century Mexico.* Lincoln: University of Nebraska Press, 1992.

Caute, David. *The Great Fear: The Anti-Communist Purge under Truman and Eisenhower.* New York: Simon and Schuster, 1978.

Ceplair, Larry, and Steven Englund. *The Inquisition in Hollywood: Politics in the Film Community, 1930–1960.* Berkeley: University of California Press, 1979.

Christensen, Terry. *Reel Politics: American Political Movies from "Birth of a Nation" to "Platoon".* Cambridge and New York: Basil Blackwell, 1987.

Cochran, Bert. *Labor and Communism: The Conflict that Shaped American Unions.* Princeton, N.J.: Princeton University Press, 1977.

Cook, Bruce. *Dalton Trumbo.* New York: Charles Scribner's Sons, 1977.

Couvares, Francis G., ed. *Movie Censorship and American Culture.* Washington, D.C.: Smithsonian Institution Press, 1996.

Davis, Ronald L. *Celluloid Mirrors: Hollywood and American Society since 1945*. Fort Worth: Harcourt Brace College Publishers, 1997.

De Mark, Judith Boyce, ed. *Essays in Twentieth Century New Mexico History*. Albuquerque: University of New Mexico Press, 1994.

Del Castillo, Adelaida R., ed. *Between Borders: Essays on Mexicana/Chicana History*. Encino, Calif.: Floricanto Press, 1990.

Dick, Bernard F. *Radical Innocence: A Critical Study of the Hollywood Ten*. Lexington: University of Kentucky Press, 1989.

Ferguson, Suzanne, and Barbara Groseclose, eds. *Literature and the Visual Arts in Contemporary Society*. Columbus: Ohio State University Press, 1985.

Fincher, E. B. *Spanish-Americans as a Political Factor in New Mexico, 1912–1950*. New York: Arno Press, repr., 1970.

Fones-Wolf, Elizabeth. *Selling Free Enterprise: The Business Assault on Labor and Liberalism, 1945–1960*. Urbana: University of Illinois Press, 1994.

Foster, James C., ed. *American Labor in the Southwest: The First One Hundred Years*. Tucson: University of Arizona Press, 1982.

Fried, Richard M. *Nightmare in Red: The McCarthy Era in Perspective*. New York: Oxford University Press, 1990.

Gabler, Neil. *An Empire of Their Own: How the Jews Invented Hollywood*. New York: Doubleday-Anchor, 1988.

Galarza, Ernesto, et al. *Mexican-Americans in the Southwest*. Santa Barbara: McNally and Lofton, 1969.

Galenson, Walter. *Communists and Trade Union Democracy*. Cambridge: Basil Blackwell, 1974.

Garcia, John R., et al., eds. *The Chicano Struggle: Analysis of Past and Present Efforts*. Binghamton, N.Y.: Bilingual Press, 1984.

Garcia, Mario T. *Mexican-Americans: Leadership, Ideology, and Identity, 1930–1960*. New Haven: Yale University Press, 1989.

Gomery, Douglas. *Shared Pleasures: A History of Movie Presentation in America*. Madison: University of Wisconsin Press, 1992.

Gómez-Quiñones, Juan. *Chicano Politics: Reality and Promise, 1940–1990*. Albuquerque: University of New Mexico Press, 1990.

———.*Mexican American Labor, 1790–1990*. Albuquerque: University of New Mexico Press, 1994.

Goodman, Walter. *The Committee: The Extraordinary Career of the House Committee on Un-American Activities*. New York: Farrar, Straus, and Giroux, 1968.

Griffith, Robert, and Athan Theoharis. *The Specter: Original Essays on the Cold War and the Origins of McCarthyism*. New York: New Viewpoints/Franklin Watts, 1974.

Gutiérrez, David G. *Walls and Mirrors: Mexican-Americans, Mexican Immigrants, and the Politics of Ethnicity*. Berkeley: University of California Press, 1995.

Hadley-Garcia, George. *Hispanic Hollywood: The Latins in Motion Pictures*. New York: Citadel Press, 1990.

Halpern, Martin. *UAW Politics in the Cold War Era*. Albany: State University of New York Press, 1988.

Haskell, Molly. *From Reverence to Rape: The Treatment of Women in the Movies*. New York: Holt, Rinehart and Winston, 1973.

IATSE, 1893–1993: One Hundred Years of Solidarity. New York: IATSE, 1993.

Isserman, Maurice. *If I Had A Hammer: The Death of the Old Left and the Birth of the New Left*. New York: Basic Books, 1987.

James, David E., and Rick Berg, eds. *The Hidden Foundation: Cinema and the Question of Class*. Minneapolis: University of Minnesota Press, 1996.

Jensen, Vernon H. *Nonferrous Metals Industry Unionism, 1932–1954: The Story of a Leadership Conflict*. Ithaca: Cornell University Press, 1954.

Kahn, Gordon. *Hollywood on Trial*. New York: Arno Press and *The New York Times*, 1972.

Kanfer, Stefan. *A Journal of the Plague Years*. New York: Atheneum, 1973.

Keller, Gary D., ed. *Chicano Cinema: Research, Reviews, and Resources*. Tempe: Bilingual Review/Press, 1984.

——.*Hispanics and United States Film: An Overview and Handbook*. Tempe: Bilingual Review/Press, 1994.

Kern, Robert, ed. *Labor in New Mexico: Unions, Strikes, and Social History since 1881*. Albuquerque: University of New Mexico Press, 1983.

Kindem, Gorham, ed. *The American Motion Picture Industry: The Business of Motion Pictures*. Carbondale: Southern Illinois University Press, 1982.

Kingsolver, Barbara. *Holding the Line: Women in the Great Arizona Mine Strike of 1983*. Ithaca: ILR Press, 1996.

Klehr, Harvey, John Earl Haynes, and Fridrith Igorevich Firsov. *The Secret World of American Communism*. New Haven: Yale University Press, 1995.

Larralde, Carlos. *Mexican-American Movements and Leaders*. Los Alamitos, Calif.: Hwong Publishing, 1976.

Levenstein, Harvey A. *Communism, Anticommunism, and the CIO*. Westport, Conn.: Greenwood Press, 1981.

Lingenfelter, Richard. *The Hard Rock Miners*. Berkeley: University of California Press, 1974.

Lovell, Hugh, and Tasile Carter. *Collective Bargaining in the Motion Picture Industry: A Struggle for Stability*. Berkeley: Institute for Industrial Relations, 1955.

McAuliffe, Mary Sperling. *Crisis on the Left: Cold War Politics and American Liberals, 1947–1954*. Amherst: University of Massachusetts Press, 1978.

Mehr, Linda Harris. *Motion Pictures, TV, and Radio: A Union Catalog of Manuscript and Special Collections in the Western U.S.* Boston: G. K. Hall, 1977.

Mellinger, Philip J. *Race and Labor in Western Copper: The Fight for Equality, 1896–1918*. Tucson: University of Arizona Press, 1995.

Navasky, Victor S. *Naming Names*. New York: Viking Press, 1980.

Neve, Brian. *Film and Politics in America: A Social Tradition.* London: Routledge, 1992.

Nielsen, Mike, and Gene Mailes. *Hollywood's Other Blacklist: Union Struggles in the Studio System.* London: British Film Institute, 1995.

Noriega, Chon A., ed. *Chicanos and Film: Essays on Chicano Representation and Resistance.* New York: Garland Publishing Co., 1992.

Oshinsky, David M. *Senator Joseph McCarthy and the American Labor Movement.* Columbia: University of Missouri Press, 1976.

Pencak, William. *For God and Country: The American Legion, 1919–1941.* Boston: Northeastern University Press, 1989.

Pettit, Arthur G. *Images of Mexican-Americans in Fiction and Film.* College Station: Texas A and M Press, 1980.

Powers, Stephen, et al. *Hollywood's America: Social and Political Themes in Motion Pictures.* Boulder: Westview Press, 1996.

Prindle, David F. *The Politics of Glamour: Ideology and Democracy in the Screen Actors Guild.* Madison: University of Wisconsin Press, 1988.

Puette, William J. *Through Jaundiced Eyes: How the Media Viewed Organized Labor.* Ithaca: ILR Press, 1996.

Roffman, Peter, and Jim Purdy. *The Hollywood Social Problem Film: Madness, Despair and Politics from the Depression to the Fifties.* Bloomington: Indiana University Press, 1981.

Rosen, David M. *Off-Hollywood: The Making and Marketing of Independent Films.* New York: Grove Weidenfeld, 1990.

Rosenbaum, Jonathan. *Placing Movies: The Practice of Film Criticism.* Berkeley: University of California Press, 1995.

Rosenblum, Jonathan D. *Copper Crucible: How the Arizona Miners' Strike of 1983 Recast Labor–Management Relations in America.* Ithaca: ILR Press, 1995.

Rosenfelt, Deborah Silverton, and Michael Wilson. *Salt of the Earth.* Old Westbury, N.Y.: Feminist Press, 1978.

Ross, Steven J. *Working-Class Hollywood: Silent Film and the Shaping of Class in America.* Princeton, N.J.: Princeton University Press, 1998.

Rosswurm, Steve, ed. *The CIO's Left-Led Unions.* New Brunswick, N.J.: Rutgers University Press, 1992.

Ruiz, Vicki L. *From Out of the Shadows: Mexican Women in Twentieth-Century America.* New York: Oxford University Press, 1998.

St. Chamez, Casey. *Shoot in New Mexico: Hollywood at work in the Land of Enchantment, 1898–1993.* Santa Fe: New Mexico Film Commission, 1993.

Sayre, Nora. *Running Time: Films of the Cold War.* New York: Dial Press, 1982.

Schrecker, Ellen. *Many Are the Crimes: McCarthyism in America.* Boston: Little, Brown,and Company, 1998.

Schwartz, Nancy Lynn. *The Hollywood Writers' Wars.* New York: Alfred A. Knopf, 1982.

Sklar, Robert. *Movie-Made America: A Cultural History of American Movies.* 2d ed. New York: Vintage, 1994.

Solski, Michael, and John Smaller. *Mine-Mill: The History of the IUMMSW since 1895.* Ottawa: IUMMSW, 1985.

Starobin, Joseph R. *American Communism in Crisis, 1943–1957.* Cambridge: Harvard University Press, 1972.

Stepan-Norris, Judith, and Maurice Zeitlin. *Talking Union.* Urbana: University of Illinois Press, 1996.

Taft, Philip. *Labor Relations American Style: The California State Federation of Labor.* Cambridge: Harvard University Press, 1968.

Toplin, Robert Brent, ed. *Hollywood as Mirror: Changing Views of "Outsiders" and "Enemies" in American Movies.* Westport, Conn.: Greenwood Press, 1993.

USWA Fiftieth Anniversary Commemorative Brochure. Pittsburgh: USWA, 1986.

Valdes, Dennis. *El Pueblo Mexicano en Detroit y Michigan: A Social History.* Detroit: Wayne State University Press, 1982.

Vaughn, Stephen. *Ronald Reagan in Hollywood: Movies and Politics.* Cambridge: Cambridge University Press, 1994.

Vélez-Ibáñez, Carlos G. *Border Visions: Mexican Cultures of the Southwest United States.* Tucson: University of Arizona Press, 1996.

Whitfield, Stephen J. *The Culture of the Cold War.* 2d ed. Baltimore: Johns Hopkins Press, 1997.

Zaniello, Tom. *Working Stiffs, Union Maids, and Riffraff: An Organized Guide to Films about Labor.* Ithaca: ILR Press, 1996.

Articles

Abrams, Brett. "The First Hollywood Blacklist." *Southern California Quarterly* 77 (Fall 1995): 215–53.

Andrew, William. "Factionalism and Anticommunism: Ford Local 600." *Labor History* 20 (Spring 1979): 227–55.

Arnold, Frank. "Humberto Silex: CIO Organizer from Nicaragua." *Southwest Economy and Society* 4 (Fall 1978): 3–20.

Arroyo, Luis Leobardo. "Chicano Participation in Organized Labor: The CIO in Los Angeles, 1938–1950." *Aztlán* 6 (Summer 1975): 277–303.

———."Notes on Past, Present, and Future Directions of Chicano Labor Studies." *Aztlán* 6 (Summer 1975): 137–50.

Candelaria, Cordelia. "Film Portrayals of La Mujer Hispana." *Agenda* 3 (June 1981): 32–36.

Cargill, Jack. "Empire and Opposition: The 'Salt of the Earth' Strike." In Robert Kern, ed., *Labor in New Mexico: Unions, Strikes, and Social History since 1881,* 183–267. Albuquerque: University of New Mexico Press, 1983.

Cooper, Sarah. "On the Trail of the CIO and Hollywood's Labor Wars." *California History* 75 (Spring 1996): 34–40.

Foote, Cheryl J. "The History of Women in New Mexico: A Selective Guide to Published Sources." *New Mexico Historical Review* 57 (July 1982): 387–94.

Garcia, Mario T. "Working for the Union." *Mexican Studies: Estudianos Mexicanos* 9 (Summer 1993): 241–58.

Gutiérrez, David G. "Significant to Whom?: Mexican-Americans and the History of the American West." *Western Historical Quarterly* 24 (November 1993): 519–39.

Haley, Lindsey. "Hearts on Fire." *Americas 2001* 1 (June 1988): 18–21.

Hartsough, Denise. "Film Union Meets Television: IA Organizing Efforts, 1947–1952." *Labor History* 33 (Summer 1992): 357–71.

Heale, M. J. "Red Scare Politics: California's Campaign against Un-American Activities, 1940–1970." *Journal of American Studies* 20 (April 1986): 5–32.

Hitchens, Gordon. "Notes on a Blacklisted Film: *Salt of the Earth.*" *Film Culture* 50–51 (Fall-Winter 1970): 79–81.

Horowitz, Roger. "Aftermath: The Transition to Peace in America after World War II." *International Labor and Working Class History* 50 (Fall 1996): 162–64.

Huggard, Christopher J. "Copper Mining in Grant County, 1900–1945." In Judith Boyce De Mark, ed., *Essays in Twentieth Century New Mexico History*, 43–62. Albuquerque: University of New Mexico Press, 1994.

Keitel, Robert S. "The Merger of the International Union of Mine, Mill, and Smelter Workers into the United Steel Workers of America." *Labor History* 15 (Winter 1974): 36–43.

Kern, Robert. "Organized Labor: Race, Radicalism, and Gender." In Judith Boyce De Mark, ed., *Essays in Twentieth Century New Mexico History*, 149–68. Albuquerque: University of New Mexico Press, 1994.

Kernen, Lisa. " 'Keep Marching Sisters': The Second Generation Looks at *Salt of the Earth.*" *Nuestro* 9 (May 1985): 23–25.

Leab, Daniel J. " 'The Iron Curtain' (1948): Hollywood's First Cold War Movie." *Historical Journal of Film, Radio, and Television* 8 (1988): 153–88.

——. "How Red Was My Valley: Hollywood, the Cold War Films, and *I Married a Communist.*" *Journal of Contemporary History* 19 (1984): 59–88.

Lipsitz, George. "Herbert Biberman and the Art of Subjectivity." *Telos* 32 (Summer 1977): 174–82.

Loynd, Roy. "Roy Brewer Doesn't Like His Docu 'Role': Wants Footage Trim." *Variety* 318 (April 27, 1983): 1.

May, Lary. "Movie Star Politics: The Screen Actors Guild, Cultural Conversion, and the Hollywood Red Scare." In Lary May, ed., *Recasting America: Culture and Politics in the Age of the Cold War*, 125–53. Chicago: University of Chicago Press, 1989.

McCarthy, Patrick. "*Salt of the Earth*: Convention and Invention in the Domestic Melodrama." *Rendezvous: Journal of Arts and Letters* 19 (Fall 1983): 22–32.

McCormick, Ruth. "*Salt of the Earth.*" *Cineaste* 5 (Fall 1973): 53–55.

Miller, Tom. "Class Reunion: *Salt of the Earth* Revisited." *Cineaste* 13 (June 1984): 31–36.

Monroy, Douglas. "Anarquismo y Communismo: Mexican Radicalism and the Communist Party in Los Angeles during the 1930s." *Labor History* 24 (Winter 1983): 34–59.

O'Brien, F. S. "The 'Communist-Dominated' Unions in the United States since 1950." *Labor History* 9 (Spring 1968): 184–209.

Pintar, Laurie Caroline. "Herbert K. Sorrell as the Grade B Hero: Militancy and Masculinity in the Studios." *Labor History* 37 (Summer 1996): 392–416.

Prickett, James R. "Some Aspects of the Communist Controversy in the CIO." *Science and Society* 33 (Summer-Fall 1969): 299–321.

Pritchard, Robert. "California Un-American Activities Investigations: Subversion on the Right." *California Historical Quarterly* 49 (June 1970): 309–27.

Riambau, Esteve, and Casimiro Torreiro. "This Film Is Going to Make History: An Interview with Rosaura Revueltas." *Cineaste* 19 (December 1992): 50–51.

Robinson, Lillian S. "Out of the Mine and into the Canyon: Working Class Feminism Yesterday and Today." In James, David E., and Rick Berg, eds., *The Hidden Foundation: Cinema and the Question of Class* (Minneapolis: University of Minnesota Press, 1996), 172–92.

Schickel, Richard. "Return of the Hollywood Ten." *Film Comment* 17 (March-April 1981): 11–17.

Sigal, Clancy. "Hollywood during the Great Fear." *Present Tense* 9 (Winter 1982): 45–48.

Stebenne, David. "The Postwar New Deal." *International Labor and Working Class History* 50 (Fall 1996): 1401–47.

Stepan-Norris, Judith. "The Integration of Workplace and Community Relations at the Ford Rouge Plant, 1930s–1940s." *Political Power and Social Theory* 11 (1997): 3–44.

Stepan-Norris, Judith, and Maurice Zeitlin. "Insurgency, Radicalism, and Democracy in America's Industrial Unions." *Social Forces* 75 (September 1996): 1–32.

———. "Union Democracy, Radical Leadership, and the Hegemony of Capital." *American Sociological Review* 60 (December 1995): 829–50.

Suber, Howard. "Politics and Popular Culture: Hollywood at Bay, 1933–1953." *American Jewish History* 68 (March 1979): 517–34.

Torres, Lorenzo. "Juan Chacón." Tucson: Salt of the Earth Labor College, n.d.

———. Short History of Chicano Workers." *Political Affairs* 12 (November 1973): 88–99.

Urrutia, Liliana. "An Offspring of Discontent: The Asociación Nacional México-Americana, 1949–1954." *Aztlán* 15 (Spring 1984): 177–84.

Walsh, Francis R. "The Films We Never Saw: American Movies View Organized Labor, 1934–1954." *Labor History* 27 (Fall 1986): 564–80.

Williams, Linda. "Type and Stereotype: Chicano Images on Film." *Frontiers* 5 (Summer 1980): 14–17.

Zehavi, Gerald. "Passionate Commitments: Race, Sex, and Communism at Schenectady General Electric, 1932–1954." *Journal of American History* 83 (September 1996): 514–48.

Zieger, Robert. "Showdown at the Rouge." *History Today* 40 (January 1990): 1–8.

Unpublished Materials

Baker, Ellen. "Gender Consciousness and Political Activism in New Mexico's Working Classes." Paper Presented at North American Labor History Conference, Detroit, Oct. 25, 1997.

Cauble, John Russell. "A Study of the IATSE of the United States and Canada." Master's thesis, University of California at Los Angeles, 1964.

Hodges, Robert C. "The Making and Unmaking of *Salt of the Earth:* A Cautionary Tale." Ph.D. diss., University of Kentucky, 1997.

McLaughlin, Mary L. "A Study of the National Catholic Office for Motion Pictures." Ph.D. diss., University of Wisconsin, 1974.

Nielsen, Michael Charles. "Motion Picture Craft Workers and Craft Unions in Hollywood: The Studio Era, 1912–1945." Ph.D. diss., University of Illinois, 1985.

Scobie, Ingrid Winther. "Jack B. Tenney: Molder of Anticommunist Legislation in California, 1940–1949." Ph.D. diss., University of Wisconsin, 1970.

Skinner, James M. "*Salt of the Earth* (1953): The Morning Star of American Feminist Cinema?" Unpublished paper in author's files.

Stermer, Lucianna. " 'Salt of the Earth': Climax in Grant County." April 1973. Research Paper, History 514. Western New Mexico State University, Silver City Public Library.

Wertheim, Larry. "Nedrick Young, et al. v. MPAA, et al.: The Fight against the Hollywood Blacklist." May 14, 1973. Research Paper, History 902. Dorothy Healey Papers. Long Beach, California State University-Long Beach.

Film Resources

A Crime to Fit the Punishment. New York: Voyager, 1984.

Memorias de Sal. Las Cruces: KRWG-TV, 1994.

Salt of the Earth. Los Angeles: Independent Productions Corporation, 1954.

Index